CONTENTS

Community Languages in Primary Education

Paula Tansley

with case studies by
David Houlton
Hasina Nowaz
and
Maria Roussou

NFER-NELSON

Published by The NFER-NELSON Publishing Company Ltd.,
Darville House, 2 Oxford Road East,
Windsor, Berkshire SL4 1DF

and in the United States of America by

NFER-NELSON, 242 Cherry Street, Philadelphia, PA 19106 – 1906.
Tel: (215) 238 0939. Telex: 244489.

First Published 1986
©SCDC Publications 1986

Library of Congress Cataloging in Publication data

Tansley, Paula.
  Community languages in primary education.

  Bibliography: p.
  1. Education, Bilingual – Great Britain.   2. Mother Tongue Project
(Great Britain).   3. Native language and education – Great Britain.
4. Minorities – Education (Primary) – Great Britain.   5. Children –
Language.   6. Great Britain – Languages.   I. Title.
LC3736.G6T36   1986   371.97'00941   85–29031
ISBN 0–7005–0689–6 (pbk.)

Photoset by David John (Services) Ltd., Maidenhead

Printed in Great Britain by A. Wheaton & Co. Ltd, Exeter

ISBN 0 7005 0689 6
Code 8191 02 1

Foreword

The Mother Tongue Project (MTP) owed its existence to a European Commission (EC) initiative. In 1980 the Schools Council (SC) was invited by the EC to set up a curriculum development project which would reflect the spirit of the Community Directive of 1977 with its call to Member States to 'promote, in co-ordination with normal education, teaching of mother tongue and culture of the country of origin' for children of EC nationals.

The remit of the MTP was, however, far wider than the terms of the Directive since it was the aim of the Project, as formulated by the SC and approved by the EC, to help teachers, both mainstream and community, of all pupils whose home language was not English.

The MTP was established in May 1981 and completed its programme by August 1985. During this period the Project was largely financed by the EC, with some funding from the SC and, since the closure of the Schools Council in 1984, the School Curriculum Development Committee (SCDC), and support from two LEAs which were particularly closely involved in the project. The Project Office was based at the Inner London Education Authority Centre for Urban Educational Studies (CUES), with an outpost in the London Borough of Haringey.

The Project Team, in years 1 to 3, comprised the director, David Houlton, formerly headmaster of a multilingual primary school in Leicester, the evaluator, Paula Tansley, an experienced researcher in the multicultural field, and two bilingual team members, Hasina Nowaz and Maria Roussou, both experienced bilingual teachers. The Project's secretary, Lyn Keen, was also a teacher.

In the autumn of 1984 David Houlton joined the School of Education at the University of Nottingham and Paula Tansley became the director of the Project. It was at that time that Hasina Nowaz and Maria Roussou, who had undertaken a range of responsibilities in connection with the development, evaluation and dissemination of teaching materials in Bengali and Greek, moved to a broader advisory and supportive role, working with groups of bilingual teachers of many languages.

The Project's task was linguistically, politically and pedagogically complex and no single strategy could have developed resources to help the enormous potential audience of teachers in mainstream and community schools. So the Project was organized as three complementary mini programmes, working to a different, intersecting time-scale.

The first of these programmes within a programme involved developing teaching materials in two languages, Bengali and Greek. Although it was characteristic of the team's style that they worked collaboratively, the curriculum development was, inevitably, the particular responsibility of the two bilingual team members, Hasina Nowaz and Maria Roussou.

In 1984 substantial packs of curricular resources were published by SCDC Publications and the influence of these pioneering materials is steadily spreading.

The potential audience for resources designed for Bengali- and Greek-speaking teachers was, inevitably, small but the potential audience for guidelines developed for teachers, not themselves bilingual, but interested in supporting their pupils' bilingualism was enormous. It was for that large audience of primary school teachers that the team published *All Our Languages* (Edward Arnold), which draws on the experience of teachers in 27 LEAs who worked with David Houlton and his colleagues.

From the Project's first day the team had been aware of their third teacher-audience: bilingual teachers of over a hundred languages for whom the experimental Bengali and Greek materials would, it was hoped, provide useful guidance and a starting point for their own development work. In 1985 the team worked with eight groups of teachers covering 12 languages. These groups, and others like them, will continue to develop resources for bilingual children using the experience and the materials of the Mother Tongue Project as their springboard.

Successful curriculum development is a coral reef of countless individual thoughts and actions. That this particular coral reef emerged from the choppy waters of the eighties is largely due to the skill and determination of David Houlton, Paula Tansley, Hasina Nowaz and Maria Roussou.

Helen Carter
School Curriculum Development Committee

Preface

It is becoming widely recognized in educational circles that Britain today is both a multicultural and a multilingual society. Although the variety of cultures represented by pupils in our schools has been acknowledged for some years, the range of languages spoken by these same pupils has only recently received attention. Stimulated by a number of developments including the EC Directive and growing demand from the ethnic minority communities, interest in the 'mother tongue debate', as it has come to be known, has burgeoned. A recent government-sponsored report, *Education for All* (1985), acknowledged this as follows:

> of all the various issues relating to language which have been raised with us, the one which has undoubtedly aroused the strongest feeling is the role of the education system in relation to the maintenance and support of languages of ethnic minority communities, through what is generally referred to as 'mother tongue provision'; we have indeed received more evidence on this issue than on any other encompassed by our overall remit.

This book reports on the work of the Mother Tongue Project, a major curriculum development initiative, focusing on primary age children, which was set up in 1981 in the midst of this growing interest. It charts the Project's progress in developing strategies and materials for bilingual and non-bilingual teachers and children and sets its experience within the context of the current debate about provision for the languages of ethnic minority pupils.

Chapter 1 sets out the background to the Project's work. It describes the linguistic diversity found in Britain today and analyses the response of the education system to the mother tongue debate that has arisen. The place of the Project within this debate is pin-pointed and its contribution to curriculum developments in the field assessed.

Chapter 2 draws on the experiences of the Project to analyse ways in which community languages can be supported by local education authorities, schools and teachers.

Chapter 3 focuses on the development of materials for supporting children's mother tongues and describes the Project's contributions in this respect.

Chapter 4 describes the processes of working with schools in this new and often controversial area and discusses some of the main issues which arise.

x Chapter 5 looks at the impact of the Project on children and parents.

Chapter 6 focuses on working with ethnic minority communities in an educational context, and, with the help of two case studies, illuminates some of the issues that arise.

Chapter 7 assesses the impact of the Project nationally and locally.

Chapter 8 considers some of the main issues arising from the Project's work and attempts to identify future trends in the field of mother tongue.

Acknowledgements

This book reports on the outcomes of the Mother Tongue Project's four years of work. During that time the Project Team worked with nearly 30 LEAs, over a hundred schools, and hundreds of teachers. Each contributed to the success of the Project and our sincere thanks are due to them all.

The Project worked particularly closely with two LEAs – the Inner London Education Authority and the London Borough of Haringey. We should like to thank the chief education officers of those authorities, William Stubbs and Tony Lenney, who co-chaired an EC colloquium on the Project's work, and also the two advisers concerned with multicultural education, Jim Wight and Chris Power, for the sustained help and encouragement which they gave.

We should also like to express our gratitude to the staff at the Centre for Urban Educational Studies (CUES), where the Project was based, for their support and co-operation, and especially to Silvaine Wiles, Director of the Language Division, for her generous help and valuable advice. Our special thanks go to the staff at the SCDC, particularly Helen Carter and Alma Craft, both professional officers, and Gail Ford and Gillian Baderman, administrative officers, for their constant unstinting support and their careful guidance and prudent advice. Similarly the Project's Advisory Group, whose members are listed in Appendix A, read every draft publication and advised the team on a host of complex issues.

We are grateful for the co-operation and support given by the Cyprus High Commission, the Greek Embassy, the Greek Parents Association and the Bangladesh High Commission, who provided critical advice and, in some cases, teachers to help with the trials of the Project's materials. We should also like to thank our secretary Lyn Keen who provided important behind-the-scenes backup throughout the Project's lifetime and who typed this report.

Warm gratitude must be expressed to the EC and, in particular, Lucien Jacoby of the Directorate-General of the EC, whose support never wavered.

Community Languages in Primary Education x   *Community Languages in Primary Education*

But most of all we would like to express our sincere gratitude to all the children and teachers in both mainstream and community mother tongue schools who made the Project possible and must take credit for its successful outcomes. We hope that the Project's work and its published materials will be of benefit to the many bilingual children who are struggling to maintain the language and culture of their homes.

Project Team

The Mother Tongue Project was based at the Inner London Education Authority Centre for Urban Educational Studies (CUES) from May 1981 to August 1985.

Project Team
David Houlton   Director (to August 1984)
Paula Tansley   Evaluator (to August 1984)
                         Director (from September 1984)
Hasina Nowaz   Bengali Co-ordinator
Maria Roussou   Greek Co-ordinator
Lyn Keen   Administrative Assistant

The Project was supported by the Commission of the European Communities.

Chapter 1
The Context

Many children growing up in Britain today regularly use two or more languages as part of their everyday lives at home, in the community and, to some extent, at school too. Whereas previously the teaching and learning of English was considered the major priority for these pupils, educationalists are now beginning to accept that support for community languages in the classroom not only benefits the speakers themselves but enriches the educational experience of all pupils and indeed provides an important resource for the nation as a whole.

Accompanying this shift in attitude, there have been a number of initiatives in schools and other educational institutions aimed at exploring the ideological and practical implications of acknowledging the languages children bring with them to school. Yet this is still a controversial area of the curriculum and many of the issues remain unresolved.

This chapter sets out some of the main areas of debate and development and locates the work of the Mother Tongue Project within this broader framework.

Linguistic diversity

Bilingualism is not of course a new phenomenon in Britain. In fact, Britain has never been a linguistically homogeneous society.

The history of the British Isles shows a succession of linguistic influences beginning with the first Celtic arrivals about the third century BC where we see the roots of Welsh, Irish, Gaelic, Cornish and Manx. These survived the 500 years of Latin domination resulting from the Roman invasion and today are the focus for concerted revival and maintenance movements. For almost 1000 years following the Viking invasion of about 800 AD Norse was a very significant language in many parts of Britain, becoming extinct only in 1800 on the Isles of Orkney and Shetland. French flourished, especially in official circles, for approximately 400 years and records show that Flemish was still spoken in parts of England as late as 1600. English itself is a comparatively recent development, its origins lying with the arrivals of the Angles, Saxons and Jutes in the fifth century, and the English we know today is a hybrid of many influences (G. Price, 1984).

In present day Britain there are still many speakers of indigenous British languages. Although the number of monoglot speakers is now very small (for example, monoglot speakers of Gaelic were reported as 974 in 1961, as quoted in Perren, 1976), bilingual speakers of Welsh and Gaelic form a sizable minority and may even be increasing. The 1971 Census gave an overall figure of 20.8 per cent Welsh speakers (covering a range in the counties as they were then from 75.1 to 2.1 per cent (Sharp, 1976)), whilst Gaelic speakers numbered 80,000 in 1961 (Perren, 1976).

Since the Second World War, and particularly in the last 15 years, there has been an influx of minority language groups from many overseas countries and it is these 'newer' minorities, sometimes constituting large percentages of school intakes in particular areas, that generally form the focus of discussion when current questions about linguistic diversity are raised.

A distinction must be made, however, between language and ethnicity. A number of ethnic groups make up British society: the indigenous English, Welsh and Scots, as well as, for example, Bengali, Greek, Portuguese, Urdu and Italian speakers. Some of these groups are in a subordinate position and are generally referred to as 'minority/ies' whilst others are in a dominant, 'majority' position. Language is a vital part of both an ethnic group's identity and an outsider's perception of that group. To a large extent linguistic diversity may overlap with ethnic diversity but there may be cases where a person might, for example, speak Greek but not be part of the Greek speaking ethnic minority in Britain (they may have learned Greek at school) or belong to an ethnic minority group such as the Gujaratis but not speak Gujarati (possibly because they were born here and English is spoken at home). Another significant minority which has a long historical tradition of settlement in Britain is the Jews. Campbell Platt (1976) quotes the Board of Deputies of British Jews as estimating an approximate figure of 410,000 Jews in Britain, the majority of whom were born here. Yiddish is spoken by a very small proportion but understanding of modern Hebrew may be more widespread due to its necessity for practising Jews.

These complexities make a description of the present pattern of linguistic diversity a difficult task. Many of the statistics, such as those derived from the 1971 Census, include no information on language as such but provide figures on the country of birth, which give only a crude approximation of possible numbers of different language speakers. These statistics show that out of a total population of nearly 54 million, just over three million residents were born overseas, although not all of these would fall into the category of ethnic minorities; some would be from indigenous British families temporarily overseas. Of this three million, rather more than half a million were born in South Asia. Approximately one-third of a million came from Africa, the Mediterranean and Far East and half a million from Europe (Runnymede Trust, 1980; CRE, 1979). The 1981 Census did not include a question on either language or country of origin but a recent estimate (Children's Language Project, 1984) suggests that there existed in Britain as a whole in 1981 a population of well over a million people of South Asian origin plus in addition significant numbers of speakers of Arabic (100,000), Chinese[1] (140,000), Vietnamese (no figures given), Greek Cypriots[2] (120,000), Turkish Cypriots (30,000), Italians (180,000), Polish and Ukrainians (160,000), Portuguese (30,000) and Spanish (50,000). The 1981 Labour survey showed that of the 12,088,000 heads of household covered by the survey, 11.4 per cent traced their ethnic origin to a country other than the UK, the majority originating in the Caribbean or Indian sub-continent, although this does not, of course, mean that the people thus identified necessarily speak the languages of their countries of origin.

A government survey of all local education authorities carried out in 1982 as part of investigating the response to the EC[3] Directive *On the Education of the Children of Migrant Workers* referred more specifically to linguistic statistics (DES, 1982). It indicated that of the total school population in the UK aged between five and 16, approximately four per cent (375,000) of children come from homes where English is not the first language and that more than half of these children live in just 12 English LEAs. The report further pointed out that comparison with data from the 1981 Census suggests that this may be a conservative estimate, with a truer figure of over 500,000. The proportion of such children ranges from less than one in 1,000 in Northern Ireland to one in seven in Greater London. These figures should, however, be treated with caution as no distinction was made between ethnic and linguistic statistics on the questionnaire used to elicit the information.

The Project's own survey carried out in 1983 (Tansley and Craft, 1984) was also concerned with the number of pupils in schools rather than with the population as a whole, and sought information specifically on languages spoken by pupils rather than their national or ethnic origin.

In particular the survey focused on primary schools with significant numbers (over ten per cent) of bilingual pupils on the assumption LEAs would be more likely to make provision for such pupils if they formed a viable percentage of a school population. Almost two-thirds (56) of the 92 LEAs returning questionnaires had at least one school which fell into this category. Just over one-third of these LEAs had between one and ten multilingual schools[4] and just under two-thirds had between 11 and 85 multilingual schools. One LEA (Inner London) reported 502 primary schools in this category. Altogether the 92 LEAs answering the questionnaire reported a total of 1,892 schools where at least ten per cent of the pupils have a mother tongue other than English (details are shown in Figure 1.1). Sixty-three LEAs gave details of the languages most frequently occurring in their areas. The number of languages mentioned ranged from one to 11, with an average of four languages for each LEA. Over 30 languages were named, with Urdu mentioned most frequently (by 46 LEAs), followed by Panjabi (43), Bengali (36) and Gujarati (35).

Besides these national surveys, several local studies provide more in-depth information about patterns of linguistic diversity. A study of 4,600 pupils in 28 secondary schools in London (Rosen and Burgess, 1980) showed that 14 per cent of the pupils surveyed were bilingual, speaking between them 55 different languages whilst the ILEA's 1983 Language Census (ILEA, 1983) recorded 147 languages spoken by school age children, representing 16 per cent of the school population. It is not unusual to find that in some London schools 75 per cent or more of pupils speak a particular community language in addition to English, whilst in others there is a wider range of linguistic diversity, with the Authority's 12 main languages (in order of numbers of speakers) – Bengali, Turkish, Gujarati, Spanish, Greek, Urdu, Panjabi, Chinese, Italian, Arabic, French and Portuguese – all being well represented among pupils.

But the most important study of linguistic diversity in schools was carried out in 1980–81 in five LEAs by the Linguistic Minorities Project (LMP, 1985). Their Schools Language Survey (SLS) documented the range of pupils reporting spoken skills in a minority language in schools in Bradford, Coventry, Haringey, Peterborough and Waltham Forest, ranging from about seven per cent in Peterborough to over 30 per cent in Haringey. A consistent 40 per cent to 50 per cent of these pupils in each LEA reported some literacy skill in a minority language (for details see LMP, 1983, 1985). There was variation in the combinations of languages found in the school population of different areas but normally the most frequent three or four languages accounted for at least two-thirds of the bilingual pupils in an Authority with the ten or 12 most frequently occurring languages accounting for 85–90 per cent of children concerned.

Taking the national and local figures together, a picture emerges of a wide diversity of languages spoken in Britain today with a few languages (largely South Asian) being predominant. Roughly four to five per cent of the school population come from homes where English is not the first language and these are concentrated mainly in conurbations, with the biggest single majority in London. Increasingly, the children are British-born although this does not necessarily indicate loss of facility in the home language. Although there is obviously a tendency for the dominance of English to increase, almost half of the children studied in some of the surveys reported above (Rosen and Burgess, 1980; LMP, 1985) had some literacy in their community languages. Furthermore, there has been a steady, if not dramatic, increase in the number of children attending community run classes in order to develop their oracy and literacy skills and present trends seem to indicate that this is likely to grow rather than diminish in the future. In the light of these and other findings education authorities have been reassessing their response to the needs of bilingual children.

Terminology

Before research findings and curriculum developments in the field can be discussed, it is necessary to consider various problems associated with terminology and to clarify the approach taken in this book.

There is considerable confusion about the different types of possible provision for bilingual children which focuses on their 'mother tongue' as opposed to their 'English' language needs. Generally speaking, there are four main types of response which have received consideration in Britain. In the first of these, 'bilingual education', the school's work is structured to allow the use of a pupil's mother tongue as a medium of instruction alongside English for a significant part of the day. In such a programme both the first and second languages are used as 'necessary vehicles for the general education of the child' and the mother tongue is treated as 'the medium through which a substantial and overlapping part of the topics and activities constituting the whole curriculum are covered' (MOTET, 1981). There has been only one example of such a programme in England: the Mother Tongue and English Project (MOTET) which is described in more detail in the next section, although bilingual education in Wales has flourished for many years in some schools (Evans, 1976).

Attention in Britain has generally focused on three other types of provision. The Swann Committee Report (*Education for All*, 1985) distinguished between 'mother tongue maintenance', where the development of a pupil's fluency in his or her mother tongue is aided by timetabling a set number of hours each week for the teaching of the mother tongue, and 'mother tongue teaching', where languages of ethnic minority communities are taught as part of the modern languages curriculum of secondary schools.

'Mother tongue support' is an important addition to the list, encompassing help given to minority language speakers, usually by bilingual teachers, to aid transition to English or to provide encouragement for children to maintain their mother tongues, as part of

Figure 1.1 LEAs in England and Wales with multilingual[4] primary schools

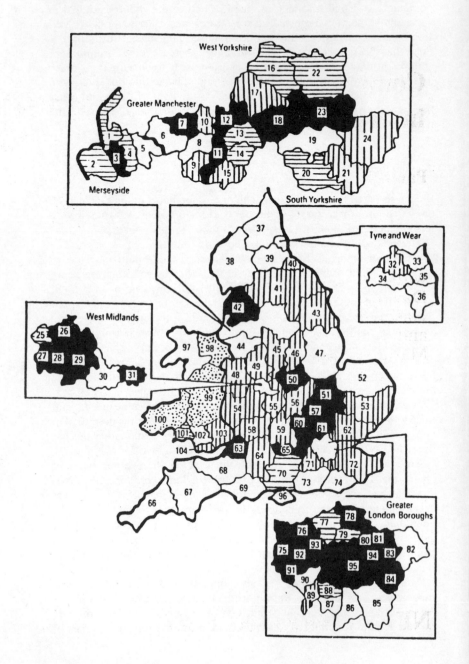

Key

■ LEAs with over ten per cent multilingual[4] schools
▥ LEAs with up to ten per cent multilingual[4] schools
▦ Welsh LEAs where Welsh is the mother tongue
▢ LEAs with no multilingual[4] schools
☰ LEAs which did not return a questionnaire

LEAs

1. Sefton	36. Sunderland	71. Surrey
2. Wirral	37. Northumberland	72. Kent
3. Liverpool	38. Cumbria	73. West Sussex
4. Knowsley	39. Durham	74. East Sussex
5. St Helens	40. Cleveland	75. Hillingdon
6. Wigan	41. North Yorkshire	76. Harrow
7. Bolton	42. Lancashire	77. Barnet
8. Salford	43. Humberside	78. Enfield
9. Trafford	44. Cheshire	79. Haringey
10. Bury	45. Derbyshire	80. Waltham Forest
11. Manchester	46. Nottinghamshire	81. Redbridge
12. Rochdale	47. Lincolnshire	82. Havering
13. Oldham	48. Shropshire	83. Barking
14. Tameside	49. Staffordshire	84. Bexley
15. Stockport	50. Leicestershire	85. Bromley
16. Bradford	51. Cambridgeshire	86. Croydon
17. Calderdale	52. Norfolk	87. Sutton
18. Kirklees	53. Suffolk	88. Merton
19. Barnsley	54. Hereford &	89. Kingston upon
20. Sheffield	Worcester	Thames
21. Rotherham	55. Warwickshire	90. Richmond upon
22. Leeds	56. Northamptonshire	Thames
23. Wakefield	57. Bedfordshire	91. Hounslow
24. Doncaster	58. Gloucestershire	92. Ealing
25. Wolverhampton	59. Oxfordshire	93. Brent
26. Walsall	60. Buckinghamshire	94. Newham
27. Dudley	61. Hertfordshire	95. ILEA
28. Sandwell	62. Essex	96. Isle of Wight
29. Birmingham	63. Avon	97. Gwynedd
30. Solihull	64. Wiltshire	98. Clwyd
31. Coventry	65. Berkshire	99. Powys
32. Newcastle	66. Cornwall	100. Dyfed
33. North Tyneside	67. Devon	101. W. Glamorgan
34. Gateshead	68. Somerset	102. Mid Glamorgan
35. South Tyneside	69. Dorset	103. Gwent
	70. Hampshire	104. S. Glamorgan

the normal curriculum rather than through set hours of tuition. Furthermore, increasing attempts have been made recently to ensure that an awareness of linguistic diversity is conveyed to *all* pupils.

In addition to the confusion surrounding the different types of 'mother tongue' provision, there are also difficulties of terminology when using terms to refer to children who speak minority languages. Although in popular parlance bilingualism is generally taken to mean equal competence in two languages, academics and linguists concerned with children from linguistic minorities tend to view bilingualism as existing along a continuum, varying from minimal competence to complete mastery of more than one language.

For the purposes of this book, 'bilingual' is used to describe all children whose first language is not English and who are at some stage along the English language learning continuum. It is important to remember, of course, that some of these children may in fact be multilingual and speak more than two languages during the course of their daily lives, although for ease of description they are generally included under the 'bilingual' label.

But a more intractable problem remains with the term 'mother tongue'. Gorman (1977) refers to a UNESCO report in 1950 which defined 'mother tongue' as the language in which a person 'first learns to formulate and express ideas about himself' but not necessarily 'the language he first learns to speak'. It is 'the language acquired in early years' but not necessarily 'the language his parents use'. Gorman finds this definition vague and liable to misinterpretation, preferring the term 'first language' i.e. the language or languages a person first learns to speak. Brook (1980) also favours 'first language', adding a further disclaimer; that the use of the term *mother* tongue perpetuates the notion that only the mother has responsibility for the child's language development. She raises a number of other difficulties with the term, including whether or not it is the language of origin, whether it is in some sense a 'natural' language and whether dialects should be considered to be mother tongues.

Although many of these points are valid, it still remains the case that the term 'mother tongue' has a certain lingua franca amongst teachers and parents, even if not among linguists and academics. A recent HMI inquiry, for instance, is unequivocally entitled *Mother Tongue Teaching in School and Community* (DES, 1984) and the Project which provides much of the substance of this book is called the SCDC Mother Tongue Project. More recently the Swann Report (op. cit.) likewise acknowledged the range of terms in current use, together with the difficulties arising from the use of the term 'mother tongue', but decided nevertheless to use the term 'because it remains most widely used and understood'.

Nevertheless the expression has certain important shortcomings which need to be brought out. The major problems with the term 'mother tongue' in British education today is that for many pupils the language other than English that is the subject of our attention may not be their 'mother tongue' or even their 'first language'. Most children of immigrant origin have actually been born here and many speak English as their first or dominant language, although there may be a strong desire to maintain the language of the country of origin. For some language groups, such as the Italians, the 'mother tongue' may be a dialect but the preferred language of literacy will almost always be the standard language. Other groups, such as Moslem Panjabi speakers, may opt for learning Urdu instead of Panjabi, because for them this is considered the traditional language of learning. Lastly, parents may prefer children to learn a language which has religious significance for them, rather than, or in addition to, the language spoken at home.

Many writers and teachers in the field therefore prefer to use the terms 'community language', 'home language', and 'minority language'. Consultations held by the CRE with local ethnic minority communities (CRE, 1981) showed dissatisfaction with the term 'mother tongue' which was seen to have low status. The term 'community language' was preferred as it includes 'mother tongue' and in addition provides access to speech communities and cultures across the world. For these reasons, and for the sake of variety, all these terms as well as the term 'mother tongue' are used in this book, usually interchangeably but occasionally a particular term is used for purposes of greater accuracy.

Research evidence

Most of the available research evidence comes from overseas sources. A considerable number of studies have now been carried out, ranging from Canada and the United States to Israel and the Philippines, looking variously at bilingual pupils and their involvement in bilingual programmes.

Several of the early studies in the 1950s and 1960s seemed to show that bilingual pupils compared unfavourably with their monolingual peers in various respects. They scored less well on tests of verbal ability, they seemed to learn neither language and they were even considered to have a higher incidence of maladjustment (as later reported in Wright, 1982). Subsequent research, however, revealed that no attempt had been made to control for intervening factors such as socio-economic status; once bilingual and monolingual groups of the same socio-economic status were compared, the negative effects disappeared (Peal and Lambert, 1962). Furthermore, the bilinguals' degree of knowledge of their second language seemed to have been ignored so that their scores on verbal intelligence tests were often obtained by testing them in their second, weaker language and then comparing these with scores from children tested in their first and only language.

Other writers have, in contrast, drawn attention to the specific advantages of bilingualism. Titone (1978) refers to the open-mindedness, effective thinking, intellectual enrichment and linguistic creativity that come from bilingualism. The CRE Report (1982) points to research in Singapore, Switzerland, South Africa, Israel and New York, all yielding positive results on bilingualism and, in addition, quotes Cummins (1979–80) on the beneficial effects of bilingualism in five areas: the ability to analyse and become aware of language, overall academic language skills, general conceptual thinking and sensitivity to the communication needs of the listener. Wright (op. cit.) adds enhanced status for minority children, increased reflectivity about language as a symbolic system and greater sensitivity to semantic relationships between words to the list of advantages of bilingualism.

A different but related line of research concerns the impact of different education programmes on bilingual children, particularly where the status of their first language varies. Skutnabb-Kangas and Toukomaa (1976) showed that Finnish children in Sweden who had the best opportunity to develop their mother tongue were also the best learners of Swedish. They recommended intensive mother tongue teaching for young children due to the lack of linguistic support in the environment. Swain and Cummins (1979), reporting on the St. Lambert experiment, where English speakers were immersed[5] in a high status language programme (French), concluded that in programmes where bilingualism was additive, i.e. another socially relevant language was added at no cost to the first language, then positive results were achieved, but where bilingualism was subtractive, i.e. the first language was replaced by a more prestigious second language, negative outcomes ensued. They proposed, in similar vein to Skutnabb-Kangas and Toukomaa, that where the home language was different from the school language and subject to denigration, instruction should begin in the first language and switch to the majority language at a later stage, but where the home language was the majority language then initial instruction should be started in this majority language.

Mitchell (1978), in a wide ranging review of research evidence on bilingual education, analysed the achievement of minority language individuals in three different educational situations: monolingual English medium education, monolingual minority language education, and bilingual minority language education. She found that in the first situation, monolingual English medium education, where all the children are educated entirely through English, minority language children did not generally do so well as English speakers, largely due to socio-economic status effects (Peal and Lambert, op. cit.), except in situations where the second language was of equal status, such as French in Canada and Hebrew in Israel (Lambert, 1977).

In the second situation, monolingual minority language education, where children are educated entirely through the medium of a minority language, found only in Quebec and Ireland, the situation was again compounded by socio-economic complexities. Evidence on Irish medium education (MacNamara, 1966) showed it to have been ineffective in overcoming the under-achievement shown by Irish-speaking children in comparison with their English-speaking peers.

The third option, bilingual minority language education, is of two kinds: for English speakers and for minority language community children. Where English speakers were involved in bilingual minority language programmes such as the immersion programme in Quebec[6] the effect was mainly additive but evidence from similar programmes for minority language speakers is more equivocal.

Much depends on whether the objectives of the teaching are assimilationist or pluralist. Where they are assimilationist, then the main criterion of success is achievement in English. Few studies have been conducted which are relevant to this question, none of which was carried out in a majority English speaking country. Two studies done in the Philippines (one summarized by MacNamara, 1968; one reported by Davis, 1967) showed that children taught in their home language first before being transferred to English medium education did no better, and in some cases worse, than children getting English medium education from the start, although the situation and education system in the Philippines cannot be directly compared with that pertaining to other countries. However, where pluralist objectives are accepted, the criteria for measuring success are different and attainment in the minority language, as well as English, is relevant. In this situation, Mitchell concludes, on the basis of American data, that:

> bilingual education of a pluralist character does not appear either to enhance or to depress the bilingual child's performanace in the majority language, English, or in non-language subjects. It may promote his achievement in the minority first language, particularly in relation to reading and writing skills.

Britain has lagged behind her overseas counterparts in both research studies and bilingual education programmes. The report of the Linguistic Minorities Project (LMP, 1983) commented:

> The lack of research and information on multilingualism in England is a clear reflection of the official invisibility of multilingualism in

England – at least until the 1970s. The lack of interest shown by educationalists in England in the research findings and evaluations of bilingual schemes in Wales, Scotland or Ireland suggests that the experience of bilingualism among indigenous British populations was not perceived to be relevant either to the bilingualism of non-indigenous British populations in England, or to the debate about modern language teaching.

LMP attribute this lack of research information to the international role of English, the inferior status of minority languages and their speakers, the dominant view of minorities as problems, and the historical development of policies on immigration which viewed the acquisition of English by non-native speakers to be hindered rather than helped by supporting the first language.

In a research review commissioned by the Swann Committee (op. cit.) Taylor (1985) could find only three research projects concerned with Asian pupils carried out in the UK, all involving Panjabi speakers.

The first project, set up in 1976 in Birmingham and funded by the Council of Europe, aimed to develop literacy for secondary age, newly arrived Panjabi-speaking pupils in their first language at the same time as they were learning English. Panjabi lessons for four periods per week gave pupils the opportunity to discuss their new environment in Panjabi and as a result the status of Panjabi was improved, interest in Panjabi culture encouraged and an awareness of other language speakers developed.

The second project, the EC/Bedfordshire Mother Tongue and Culture Project (1976–80) was one of several EC funded projects mounted throughout Europe to allow Member States to explore the practical implications of introducing mother tongue teaching, particularly in the light of the EC Directive. The Bedfordshire project focused largely on socio-psychological aspects of mother tongue teaching, such as enhancing the self-image of the pupil, facilitating integration and promoting esteem for the minority groups concerned. Two language groups were involved; Panjabis and Italians, who were each taught for approximately one hour per day in their mother tongue over the four-year period. During the latter stages of the project there was more emphasis on assessment of progress and it was generally found that pupil progress in English was not unduly hindered, although not particularly helped, and children's confidence, self-identity and esteem was considerably enhanced by the experience. An especially striking outcome of the project was a notable improvement in home-school relationships, stimulated by the regular weekly home visiting initiated by project teachers.

The third project, the Mother Tongue and English Teaching Project (MOTET, 1978–80), funded by the DES, was based in two settings, an infant centre in Bradford and a first school in Keighley. A bilingual programme for children (aged 4½ to 5½) speaking Mirpuri, a variety of Panjabi, was set up and pupils spent fortnightly periods being taught through Panjabi, or English. Tests and observations showed that pupils in the bilingual programme were more confident and articulate in their language use and social adjustment and there was some evidence that they actually acquired English more effectively than controls.[7]

It is difficult to draw conclusions from three diverse projects but Taylor (op. cit.) points to increased self-confidence, improved competence in pupils' first languages and no adverse effect on the acquisition of English. She suggests that the studies have shown the importance of the attitudes of *all* associated with such projects, the necessity to clarify aims and objectives at the start, adequate preparation of teachers, materials and assessment methods, and evaluation of cognitive and affective development which takes account of language status and vitality in the wider socio-economic and cultural context.

The Swann Report (op. cit.) quotes selectively from the NFER review (Taylor, op. cit.) to draw the following conclusions: there is as yet very little research evidence in the field; much of the work was undertaken abroad and might not be relevant in Britain; and what evidence there is does not provide conclusive evidence of the value of bilingual education. However, a number of critical points can be added to the discussion. The lack of research evidence highlighted by the review does not in itself provide grounds for inaction or rejection of bilingual education. Indeed, it could be used to support demands for more research, especially in the British context, so that the relevance of research findings for British pupils can be assessed. Particular research priorities may be the study of mother tongue maintenance and mother tongue teaching which have been the main focus of attention in Britain, rather than bilingual education which has never been regarded as a serious option in this country.

Of the 'three major research projects' concerned with bilingual pupils on which the Swann Report relies heavily, only one, the MOTET Project, can actually be considered to be a research project, at least in so far as the merits of providing tuition in the mother tongue for non-English speakers were assessed using accepted research procedures. Again, only the MOTET Project was concerned with 'bilingual education' *per se* as opposed to a limited amount (four periods per week in the Birmingham project, five hours weekly in the Bedford project) of mother tongue provision. Obviously, while mother tongue provision remains piecemeal and frequently tokenistic, little success can realistically be expected.

But perhaps the most serious shortcoming of the Swann Report in considering the research evidence for bilingual education is the assumption that mother tongue provision can be justified only on educational grounds, and more particularly on the basis of its contribution to pupil achievement in English. On these grounds it might be equally difficult to justify the inclusion of subjects such as art, sport and cookery on the curriculum. A number of other arguments for supporting home languages, some of which, such as the importance of increasing children's self-esteem and the status of their languages, are in fact supported by the projects quoted above, can, however, also be advanced. And beyond the justifications for individual bilingual children are of course the wider social issues relating to social, economic and political rights of minority groups, many of which impinge directly on the education system.

In conclusion, it would seem that research evidence for bilingual education, particularly that emanating from British sources, is scanty and subject to interpretation. Much depends on the majority group's attitudes and the aims and underlying values embodied in different programmes, rather than the research findings as such. Indeed as Mitchell (op. cit.) points out, decisions to promote minority languages are not generally taken on the basis of research evidence; wider social and political factors may be more important. These are considered later in the chapter.

The changing climate of opinion

Emergence of the multicultural curriculum

As immigration to Britain gathered momentum during the 1960s and 70s, those responsible for education had to take account of the large numbers of non-English-speaking children appearing in British schools. Generally speaking three major trends in the approach to the education of children from immigrant backgrounds can be identified. These tend to follow a chronological order, although the ideas are not of course mutually exclusive and many people continue to subscribe to one or other view.

During the early sixties the idea of assimilation was predominant. Immigrants were expected to adopt the English language and submerge their differences into the mainstream British culture. The cultures and home languages of non-English-speaking children were frequently thought to be irrelevant and even inferior and emphasis was placed on children adopting the English way of life, including the language, as quickly as possible.

In the late sixties and seventies this rather extreme position was modified as it became obvious that ethnic minority children would not simply disappear into the crowd upon acquisition of English. At this time Roy Jenkins, in a now famous speech, spoke of the 'flattening process of assimilation' which would be replaced by equal opportunity, accompanied by 'cultural diversity' in 'an atmosphere of mutual tolerance' (quoted in

Rose *et al.*, 1969). This new philosophy of integration recognized that the majority society needed to be more aware of the cultures, religions and social factors affecting the various minorities, but the eventual aim was still for these communities to change and adapt themselves to the host society which, on its part, saw little need to modify its prevailing attitudes or practices.

In the late seventies a new conception of society emerged, known as pluralism, which envisaged the co-existence of many different, sometimes conflicting, cultural and ethnic groups, each of which contributed to the society as a whole.

During this period of time, accompanying these changes, the idea of a multicultural curriculum was gradually developing. At first, in the fifties and sixties, ethnic minority pupils were expected to adapt to the dominant culture and little account was taken of their different backgrounds, except through provision of English as a Second Language (ESL) tuition. Then in the late sixties and seventies, as teachers became aware of the need to become informed about the background of the children they taught, courses were provided which dealt with these issues. Lastly, in the late seventies, the values, traditions and experiences of ethnic minorities came to be seen as equally valid as those of the majority and a culturally diversified value system became widely accepted, involving the teaching of aspects of minority cultures alongside the British culture to *all* pupils. Recently, this has been taken a step further by curriculum developers in some areas who have pointed to structural racism present in British educational institutions and adopted an anti-racist approach.

Multicultural education is not simply a descriptive term, marking out the field of educational topics, issues and problems relating to Britain as a multicultural society. It is also a normative term referring to a variety of policies and strategies and can be characterized by two competing ideologies. The first of these, which may be referred to as the 'liberal' view, underpins most versions of multicultural education and is concerned primarily with two aims: the self-realization of ethnic minority pupils, and the education of *all* pupils for adulthood in a multicultural society. Critics of this traditional view of multicultural education, generally associated with broadly Marxist ideologies, claim that by ignoring the function of schooling in a capitalist society (i.e. to reproduce the class structure and social divisions inherent in the economic organization of capitalism), and by concentrating on diversionary issues such as 'culture', 'identity' and self-concept', multicultural education in effect (if not in intention) serves the interests of the state as a form of social control, appeasing progressive white opinion and defusing black resistance.[8]

Recently there have been signs that the two approaches may be coming together in their practical recommendations for teachers. There have been renewed calls for a total response across the curriculum rather than occasional multicultural or multiracial inputs, and attention has been focused on the inherent racism in many apparently multi-ethnic curricula. Critics point out that such curricula are generally defined by, and reflect the interests of, the majority white society and do not fundamentally deal with the problems of racism. A number of LEAs, such as the ILEA and Berkshire, have taken up this challenge and it has also received limited support from the Swann Committee Report.

Although significant developments in approaches have taken place, progress has been slow in translating these into actual curricular responses to the changing nature of British society.

Little and Willey's report (Little and Willey, 1981) on progress made by LEAs and schools in multi-ethnic education since an earlier report (1973) found a considerable gap between views and policies about what should be happening and actual practice. In some areas little advance had been made, whilst in others significant developments had taken place. There was widespread acceptance of the need to make arrangements to meet perceived 'special' needs of minority ethnic groups (although this did not include West Indians or second phase learners) and there was more reappraisal of the whole curriculum rather than 'adding on' special subjects to meet these needs. However, there was little action or curriculum development in schools with few or no ethnic minority pupils despite the 1977 Green Paper spelling out the implications of the presence of ethnic minority groups for the education of *all* children.

Other developments in the field have included efforts to evaluate children's books (Dixon, 1977; Schools Council, 1981; Verma, 1981) and examinations from a multicultural perspective (Schools Council, 1983–4), attempts to describe a multicultural curriculum (Jeffcoate, 1981) and the development of some LEA policies on multicultural education. But on the whole the response of schools, teachers and even the DES has been modest and piecemeal.

Arguments for mother tongue teaching in Britain

Earlier it was pointed out that research evidence alone does not normally form the basis for decisions about educational provision. As the debate about the place of community languages in education has gained momentum, a variety of arguments for mother tongue support have been advanced, some deriving from research findings, others based on educational principles or deeply held beliefs. Although there is no shared body of opinion and little agreement about the aims of mother tongue teaching, a number of reasons are commonly put forward.

An edition of *Issues in Race and Education* (Spring 1982), for example, devoted entirely to the question of mother tongue, listed four educational arguments for supporting children's mother tongues in the mainstream classroom: to support continuity of learning and avoid a 'learning freeze'; to provide confidence as an essential prerequisite to any learning; to develop skills in a second language; and to validate the pupil's home culture. Similarly, the National Congress on Languages in Education Report (Reid, 1984) contains two papers addressed to the question of rationale for minority group languages. One sets down goals of three different types when considering provision in schools: socio-political goals, educational goals and linguistic goals (Fitzpatrick, 1984) whilst the other discusses the linguistic and educational benefits for both bilinguals and monolinguals in a pluralist society of promoting a bi/multilingual environment for learning (Polling, 1984).

More recently, the Swann Report (op. cit.) listed three broad arguments on which the case for mother tongue teaching has been made: in order to accord ethnic minority pupils 'equality of opportunity'; as a form of 'natural justice'; and as sound educational practice (for pupils to have the opportunity to study for and obtain a qualification in a language in which they already have some facility). It goes on to quote a range of more specific aims advanced in favour of mother tongue provision as summarized by the authors of the specially commissioned NFER review of research (Taylor, 1985):

1. To promote the cognitive and social growth of the young child whose first language is not English, as these are closely associated with language development.

2. To increase a pupil's confidence so that psychological and social benefits may improve learning ability and increase motivation towards other curriculum subjects.

3. To develop the full potential of a pupil whose first language is not English which in accordance with broad educational objectives includes development of mother tongue skills.

4. To enhance the value of a minority pupil's culture and language as part of that culture, thereby increasing the language's status, encouraging its maintenance, and reducing social and cultural barriers between English and minority speakers.

5. To encourage linguistic minorities' pride in their language and hence to enhance their sense of identity through their language.

6. To facilitate communication between parents, children and relatives by maintaining linguistic competence in the first language and to preserve cultural and religious traditions.

7.   To enrich the cultural life of the country as a whole by means of diverse linguistic resources utilised in the participation of minority language speakers in social life and in contributing to the economic life of the country in industry and commerce.

Generally speaking the range of arguments falls into three broad categories: educational, psychological and social. Among educational arguments are those citing cognitive benefits, continuity of learning, increased confidence and motivation. Psychological arguments include increased self-esteem and status and an improved sense of identity, whilst social arguments encompass better communication within the family and maintenance of the child's cultural heritage.

These arguments largely relate to the benefits of bilingualism for bilinguals themselves but gradually the rationale for sustaining mother tongues has been broadened to include the whole school and even the wider society. For example, in one of the Project's early publications, *Supporting Children's Bilingualism* (Houlton and Willey, 1983), the benefits of supporting bilingualism are listed not only for bilingual children but for *all* children, and also for the teacher and the school. In a similar vein the Swann Report recommends that 'All schools should impart an understanding of our multilingual society to all pupils.'

Recently, economic and political arguments have been added to the list. The *Times Higher Education Supplement* (2 September 1983) commented that if children do not maintain their bilingualism 'Britain loses thereby a storehouse of potential speakers of Greek, Cantonese, Turkish, Gujerati, etc.'. In a trading nation like Britain, the pool of community languages is beginning to be seen as an asset. Political arguments revolve around the rights of individuals and groups in a democracy. Whilst individuals may be seen as having the right to learn through their mother tongues, at the same time, where a substantial section of the community, such as the ethnic minorities, are unable to participate fully in the political life of the country for economic, social and educational reasons, then bilingual education may be put forward as a means to facilitate their involvement. Glyn Lewis (1981) in an analysis of changing rationales for bilingual education over the last century or so makes a similar point when he comments, 'At this point in modernization, bilingual education is seen as quite explicitly concerned with the redistribution of political power'.

Whilst the justifications for supporting the mother tongue outlined above are by and large shared by the ethnic minority communities themselves, very often a different emphasis may be placed on them, particularly in community run schools. Probably the single most important reason advanced by parents and community groups for sending children to voluntary classes is to maintain the language and culture of the community. A number of other reasons such as sustaining relationships within the family and with the country of origin, promoting self-esteem and supporting religious teaching may also be given (Saifullah Khan, 1980; Taylor, 1985; Tosi, 1979). In addition, practical considerations including future marriage arrangements and the availability of a safe worthwhile activity may encourage parents to send their children to classes. Educational arguments concerning cognitive and linguistic benefits may be of less significance to parents partly because they may not be aware of them and also because they may see education to be the function of the mainstream school over which traditionally they feel themselves to have little control. For these reasons, among others, they may feel uncertain as to the place of mother tongue teaching in mainstream schools and regard it as the province of community classes. But attitudes are now changing, especially as mother tongue provision increases, and parents are becoming more aware of the educational as well as socio-psychological benefits that accrue from mother tongue teaching in mainstream schools.

At the same time that ethnic minority communities are increasingly pressing for more provision for community language teaching and mainstream teachers are also becoming aware of the role of home languages in the classroom, some educationalists have begun to express doubts as to whether supporting mother tongue languages really helps the children it is intended to benefit. Some of the arguments, such as those suggesting that mother tongue provision may lead to children learning neither language as well or that growth in the mother tongue may be at the expense of pupils' needs for ESL teaching, are not new and have been largely discounted. But other issues, mainly political, need to be carefully examined. Although the EC Directive on Mother Tongue Teaching has been used to justify provision for community languages, critics point out that there is nothing in the Directive about 'acknowledging and respecting the validity of other people's cultures, languages, identities. Nothing about enhancement of esteem and self image. Nothing about cognitive/emotional/social importance of keeping children's own languages going until fluency in English is achieved.' (Brook, 1980) For these reasons the EC Directive is often seen as a red herring in the mother tongue debate, which cannot be used either to support or argue against provision for community languages.

The fear that separating children off from mainstream classes for mother tongue teaching and support will lead to isolation and exploitation is another important issue. Well-meaning teachers may feel that with the provision of mother tongue teaching due allowance is being made for home languages, whereas the very act of separation may in fact contribute to ethnic minority children's under-achievement and consign them effectively to an underclass. A similar argument is put forward with reference to the wider society; that use of minority group languages can serve the purposes of the system itself, i.e. to control and domesticate minority group communities through assimilating them into society as it is and avoiding the need for change. Indeed, some critics (Skutnabb-Kangas, 1981, for example) go so far as to say that immigrants have a new function in society – to act as a buffer at the lowest layer of society and thus protect the higher layers from experiencing the worst shocks of restructuring the economy. Promoting the use of mother tongues in schools, these critics argue, lulls minority group parents into believing that their children's needs are being met whereas in reality piecemeal provision ensures children learn neither their mother tongue nor English to a sufficiently high standard to compete either with their English or home country peers.

On the other hand, proponents of mother tongue support in mainstream schools counter these arguments by making the case for proper provision within the mainstream curriculum to avoid the risks of isolation and to provide the opportunity to involve all teachers in a discussion of the issues. At the same time they stress the importance of choice for bilingual pupils; unless children and their parents can opt for mother tongue teaching, many of the benefits will be lost and ethnic minorities relegated even more effectively to a subordinate position.

Obviously there is no single answer to the complexities of the issues that surround the rationale for mother tongue teaching. It seems clear, however, that if children from ethnic minority communities are to take their rightful place in the education system alongside their English-speaking peers then due acknowledgement and support for their backgrounds, including the languages they speak, needs to be made. Some of the basic principles on which British education rests, such as equality of opportunity and the recognition and development of the skills children bring to school, indeed necessitate such an approach. But the way in which these principles are translated into realities for ethnic minority children remains a matter of debate. The establishment within educational circles has taken and still continues to take (see the Swann Report, op. cit.) a moderate approach, accepting in principle that community languages should be valued, although largely within the private sector under the aegis of community groups. While some consider this an important advance, others are disappointed that a more radical stance was not adopted and that the *right* of pupils to tuition in their mother tongue was not endorsed. Supporters of bilingual education take a more forthright approach, calling for proper provision within the mainstream curriculum whilst acknowledging at the same time the important role community run schools will continue to play. In this situation, where battles still have to be fought and won, it is to be hoped that the work of the Project will be able to go some way to clarifying the principles and practicalities on which mother tongue teaching and support is founded.

The mother tongue debate

It is only relatively recently that ethnic minority pupils' mother tongues, in addition to their cultures, have been seen as having a place in the multicultural curriculum. There are a number of reasons for this. One of the most important has been the traditional dominance of English, especially in the wake of British imperialism, and this has, if anything, gained in ascendancy as trade in the English-speaking world has increased. Immigrant parents in the early years of arrival in Britain were preoccupied with the socio-economic conditions of settlement and likewise gave the acquisition of English priority. Many came from countries where learning two or three languages was not considered unusual or likely to cause difficulties, and where parental involvement in formal education was discouraged. They therefore looked to voluntary provision for their children to maintain their mother tongues and have only recently turned to the state education system as the appropriate authority to provide mother tongue teaching. Part of this shift in attitude derived from a concern about the length of the school day for pupils who attended classes after school and at weekends. Parents were also anxious about the loss of the minority language and culture among pupils who rejected this sort of extra-curricular activity because it involved them in extra time and was perceived as having low status by their peers at school.

At the same time that ethnic minority parents were beginning to regard the state education system as having responsibility to provide for home languages, many educationalists were coming to share parental concerns and to realize that multicultural education necessarily includes language, due to the central role language plays in supporting culture. Alongside this shift in approach, and indeed in some respects part of it, has been the wider change in attitudes to English and its dialects and growth in support for bidialectal language policies in schools (Trudgill, 1975).

Official support for mother tongue teaching

The origins of official support for community languages in Britain have traditionally been traced to the Bullock Report, published in 1975. In a now famous paragraph the report states:

> In a linguistically conscious nation in the modern world, we should see mother tongue as an asset, as something to be nurtured, and one of the

agencies that should nurture it is the school. Certainly the school should adopt a positive attitude to its pupils' bilingualism and whenever possible should help maintain and deepen their knowledge of their mother tongue.

However, despite the rhetoric, the Bullock Report gave little advice about what this meant in practice and it was not until 1980 – 81 when reports on compliance with the EC Directive (1977) had to be made that most LEAs began to look seriously at the implications for their pupils.

Article 3 of the EC Directive on the Education of Children of Migrant Workers states:

> Member States shall in accordance with their national circumstances and legal systems, and in co-operation with states of origin, take appropriate measures to promote, in co-ordination with normal education, teaching of the mother tongue and culture of the country of origin for the children referred to in Article 1.

Although originally conceived to apply to children of migrant workers in the Member States of the EC, the final Directive was more broadly interpreted in Britain so as to apply to immigrants as well as migrants. Indeed, the then Secretary of State, Mr. Mark Carlisle, made this clear in his opening speech of the EC Colloquium of the Bedford Pilot Project on Mother Tongue Teaching (24 March 1980):

> First let me stress that we intend to apply the Directive without regard to country of origin of the children concerned. That means that we will be concerned about provision for about 650,000 pupils, only a small proportion of whom will be from community countries.
>
> (CRE, 1982)

Fears that the Directive was intended as a disguised method of repatriation have now been allayed but the DES response, which has to date amounted to little more than surveys of provision and research into how the educational benefits of bilingualism can best be secured, has been disappointing. Although a few courses have been mounted, occasional circulars issued and funds made available through Section 11 and Urban Aid Programmes, support has tended to be minimal and *ad hoc*. Indeed, a Report prepared by the European Commission on the implementation of the Directive (Commission of the European Communities: *Report on the implementation of Directive 77/486/EEC on the Education of the Children of Migrant Workers,* 1984) showed that Britain comes out near the bottom of the league compared with other countries which have large proportions of migrants in their schools. Compared, for example, with the

Netherlands where Dutch primary schools organize mother tongue teaching at school for 80 per cent of their primary age immigrant pupils, in the UK only about 2.2 per cent of children from non-English-speaking backgrounds have such teaching.

The DES makes some acknowledgement of the importance of children's home languages but in practice it is disinclined to take on responsibility for them, preferring to leave this to voluntary organizations outside the state system. A DES document, *The School Curriculum,* 1981, states:

> Far more pupils than in the past have a first language which is not English or Welsh. This constitutes a valuable resource, for them and for the nation. How should mother tongue teaching for such pupils be accommodated within modern language provision so that this resource does not wither away and the pupils may retain contacts with their own communities?

However, a definitive answer was not given and a DES circular issued in the same year (DES Circular 5/81 – Directive of the Council of the European Community on the Education of Migrant Workers, 31 July 1981) described its responsibilities in cautious terms as 'sponsoring research related to the provision and educational implications of mother tongue teaching, as well as taking a close interest in EC-sponsored initiatives in this country'. Reference was made to the Rampton Committee of Inquiry into the Education of Children from Ethnic Minority Groups (later known as the Swann Committee), set up in 1979, presumably as one of these activities.

In recent years the DES has continued to pursue a similar approach to mother tongue teaching. In a consultative paper, *Foreign Languages in the School Curriculum* issued in 1983, only two paragraphs out of a total of 60 referred to minority community languages. Again a questioning approach was adopted and schools were exhorted to 'consider whether it is appropriate and practicable to offer also one or more of the local community languages as part of the curriculum'. The HMI Inquiry into mother tongue teaching published in 1984 (*Mother Tongue Teaching in School and Community*) took a very cautious view of developments in the field, commenting 'There is evidence that . . . provision is increasing but it is by no means clear that there is total agreement that it should and, if it should, in what form and at what levels of education'. The survey, which took place in four LEAs, concluded that initiatives were still at an early state of development and left much to be desired in terms of quality. Stress was laid on the possible role of ethnic minority communities as an important element in the cultural and educational development of their children and these, together with many LEAs and schools, were said to be

CLPE–C

'at various stages of determining what role, *if any* [my italics], the educational system at different levels might and should play in responding to children's first languages'.

The Secretary of State for Education, Sir Keith Joseph, at a speech given to the EC Colloquium held by the SCDC Mother Tongue Project in March 1984, reiterated the official view that mother tongue tuition cannot be offered to pupils *as of right* and that community-based provision may be the most effective response to the needs of linguistic minorities. He did, however, add that in areas of the country where a single mother tongue other than English was spoken by substantial numbers, then it became feasible to make some provision in state schools. The role of the state school, in this situation, is seen as encouraging respect for other cultures and languages, using the mother tongue to aid transition to English during the early stages of schooling, teaching minority languages to examination level in secondary schools where there is sufficient demand, and providing financial and moral support to voluntary schools engaged in mother tongue teaching. The Swann Committee, reporting in 1985, again echoed the official view that mainstream schools should not provide mother tongue maintenance, which should be left to community groups, although LEAs should help these groups by providing premises, materials and in-service training for teachers. However, the committee felt that minority languages should be included in the language curriculum of secondary schools where there is sufficient demand and all pupils should be encouraged to think of studying them.

Other developments in support of mother tongue teaching

Despite the lukewarm response of the DES to mother tongue teaching, a number of other developments have served to move the debate forward. The erstwhile Schools Council took a leading role in stimulating curriculum development in the field by funding several projects. Although Perren, writing in 1978 (Perren, 1979), commented that the Schools Council 'has expressed no clear views on this issue' (role of mother tongues in schools), at a conference in 1984 Alma Craft described a number of projects undertaken by the Schools Council concerned with supporting children's bilingualism, as part of the Council's multicultural programme, including a review, *Community Languages at 16+* (Broadbent *et al.*, 1983), a survey, *Bilingual Nursery Assistants* (Rathbone and Graham, 1983), and of course the Schools Council Mother Tongue Project itself (1981–5).

Developments have also been taking place in the field of teacher training. A report on the Training of Teachers of Ethnic Minority Community Languages (Craft and Atkins, 1983) was carried out for the

Swann Committee and although it revealed very little in the way of specific provision for members of ethnic minorities who wish to gain qualifications in teaching their languages, it did show a pool of goodwill which might be drawn upon in both initial and in-service teacher training should this become part of future policy. In fact positive steps have already been taken towards the training of community language teachers with the setting up of the Royal Society of Arts Pilot Course in Community Languages, initially in five centres but available at the time of writing in seven.

At the same time a number of interested organizations have put forward policy statements on the issue of mother tongues or community languages. One of the first in the field, set up specifically to further the promotion of mother tongue teaching, was the Co-ordinating Committee for Mother Tongue Teaching which later became the National Council for Mother Tongue Teaching (NCMTT). The NCMTT views 'the fostering of bilingualism, among both adults and children, as an essential element of, and contribution to, our multicultural society' (NCMTT, 1985). It has seven aims, including the provision of community language teaching for both bilingual children and 'those children of the majority community who wish to learn', as well as more general aims to do with exchange of information, development of learning resources and strengthening of links with sympathetic public bodies. These aims are pursued through promoting discussion, collecting information, monitoring provision, supporting existing initiatives, and encouraging contact and co-ordination between all those interested in promoting mother tongue teaching.

The National Anti-racist Movement in Education (NAME), in a submission to the National Congress on Languages in Education, asserted:

> This Association believes that children who can use their mother tongue and English equally effectively are in a position to make a unique contribution to our society, and therefore encouragement and resources should be provided to support development of the mother tongue.

It then went on to detail educational, psychological and social reasons for supporting the issue of the mother tongue (Perren, 1979). The Congress referred to above was held under the aegis of the Centre of Information on Language Teaching and Research (CILT), itself a supporter of mother tongue maintenance as part of its wider language policy. Indeed a Linguistic Minorities Information Officer was appointed to CILT in 1982 with the purpose of collecting and disseminating information about linguistic minorities in Britain.

Teacher unions have also taken up the cause of mother tongue teaching; the NUT in 1982 issued its own statement on mother tongue teaching (NUT, 1982), stressing the importance of schools according a higher status to the home languages of ethnic minority pupils. It recommended the teaching of pupils' home or community languages in the ordinary classroom where possible but where lack of staff prevented this, LEAs were urged to rectify the situation and improve provision. Finally the Commission for Racial Equality (CRE) published a statement on *Ethnic Minority Community Languages* (CRE, 1982) which states, 'in the interest of good race relations and equality of opportunity in education there should be provision for teaching ethnic minority community languages through a planned programme of development'. After a careful analysis of the current situation, a number of strategies for change were suggested as well as recommendations for action by the DES, LEAs, examining boards and other related bodies.

Provision for mother tongue teaching

Provision for mother tongue teaching largely reflects current attitudes towards the place of home languages in education. Whilst there has been a considerable and growing number of schools and classes organized by community and voluntary agencies, support for mother tongue teaching within the mainstream curriculum is a relatively recent development and varies considerably from area to area, depending both on the numbers of ethnic minority pupils and the approach taken by local education authorities.

Voluntary provision

Virtually from the time the various immigrant groups arrived in this country during the post-war years and even before, classes were formed to teach children the language and culture of their country of origin. Probably the earliest were the Jewish 'cheders' which taught Hebrew for the purpose of Biblical study, and which now also teach modern Hebrew for communicative purposes, followed by the East European schools such as the Ukrainian, Polish and Latvian, many of which were founded in the late forties and early fifties. As each successive wave of immigrants have put down their roots here, so classes have sprung up to cater for the linguistic, cultural and religious needs of their children. Statistics are hard to come by and complicated by widely varying provision and the tendency for provision to change with time. Saifullah Khan, writing in 1976, referred to the 'startling number of children belonging to Britain's ethnic minorities who were attending classes outside the normal school system'.

She reported, for example, that in Bradford classes existed to cater for tuition in Hungarian, Italian, Latvian, Polish, Ukrainian, Gujarati, Arabic, Urdu, Panjabi and Hindi (Saifullah Khan, 1976). In a national survey in 1970, 37 out of 71 LEAs reported that 'the immigrant community' in their areas provided 'opportunities out of school hours for pupils of school age to learn immigrant languages' (Townsend, 1971). In 1979 the Little and Willey survey found that 40 out of 70 LEAs reported languages being taught by the ethnic minorities (Little and Willey, 1981). Taylor (1985), in a detailed review of community mother tongue teaching schools and classes for Asian languages, draws on many little known studies to provide a comprehensive picture. In her opinion, the existence of so many Asian community mother tongue schools and classes points to a felt need to provide support for mother tongue teaching, although she acknowledges that provision for mother tongue teaching, even if greater recognition were to be accorded in mainstream schools, would still be required within the community in order not only to meet the full demand but also to satisfy needs for community identity and coherence.

The Linguistic Minorities Project (LMP) provides some of the most comprehensive information about voluntary mother tongue teaching. Their Mother Tongue Teaching Directory survey (MTTD) in three localities, Coventry, Bradford and Haringey, was developed in collaboration with the NCMTT and drew attention to the large number of classes run by the communities in a wide range of languages. Provision for 18 different languages in 1981–2 was reported (LMP, 1984a) although the full range was not catered for in each locality, with the individual figures for each area being as follows: 106 classes in Coventry, 183 classes in Bradford and 143 classes in Haringey. Two recent national surveys give a less detailed but more wide-ranging picture of the existence of voluntary mother tongue classes. In Tsow's (1983) survey, 47 per cent of authorities responding to a questionnaire reported some provision in the voluntary sector covering 17 languages, whilst the Schools Council survey (Tansley and Craft, 1984) reported voluntary schools in 53 LEAs providing for 28 different languages. Between them, these LEAs listed over 500 schools which they knew about but interestingly a comparison with LMP figures, which give a considerably more comprehensive list for one of these areas, shows that the figures are probably a gross underestimate of the number of schools nationwide.

Not only are LEAs ill-informed about community schools in their areas, but large numbers of teachers hardly know of the existence of community schools, even those their children attend. Saifullah Khan commented in 1976 (op. cit.), 'Few teachers and others concerned with the mainstream school system know of the existence of weekend schools or evening classes for the mother tongue of such children' (members of linguistic minorities). The situation remains much the same today; even the teachers in the

in the Project worked, who were largely self-selected and
ore than usually receptive to mother tongue teaching, had
a about local community schools and were not able in most
which of their children attended these schools, or name the
oncerned.

Mainstream provision

Mainstream schools naturally have been much slower to respond to the
community languages brought to the classroom by their ethnic minority
pupils. Partly, as suggested earlier, this has been due to the predominance
of the view that English and English as a Second Language (ESL) were
the most pressing priorities for young non-English-speaking pupils, and
partly due to the ambivalent response of the DES to children's home
languages. As educational opinion has changed, LEAs and schools have
sought, however, to make appropriate provision within the curriculum for
mother tongue teaching and support. The earliest examples of this type of
provision occur in the late 1960s. Goldman (1967), for example, refers to
one or two enterprising heads who introduced British primary children to
Panjabi at about the time of bilingual education programmes in the USA.
Such initiatives were generally in the form of using Asian staff to tell
stories from India or Pakistan in Panjabi to younger pupils during the last
period of the day or discussing topical events in Asia with older children.
In an NFER national survey (Townsend and Brittan, 1972) it transpired
that no primary schools and only four secondary schools provided tuition
in the languages of pupils' countries of origin. In addition some pupils
took O-levels in minority languages although there was no tuition for
these subjects in school. There were a few reports of local initiatives
during the seventies in Birmingham, Coventry and Bradford, largely
concerned with minority languages being taught as examination subjects.

By 1979, however, Little and Willey's survey (published in 1983)
numbered 13 LEAs who reported teaching ethnic minority pupils'
languages and over half the schools with 30 per cent or more ethnic
minority pupils wished to start or extend mother tongue teaching if
constraints of staffing and timetabling could be removed.

Tsow's (op. cit.) survey of mother tongue teaching in local education
authorities carried out in 1980–82 found that 26 per cent of authorities
responding to the questionnaire (15 LEAs) provided evidence of mother
tongue teaching in the maintained sector, catering for 12 languages,
mostly under the auspices of 'Modern Languages' departments and
therefore presumably largely examination orientated. In a later survey
investigating primary school provision only, Tansley and Craft (1984)
found that 23 LEAs provided mother tongue teaching as part of the

primary school curriculum, involving 252 schools, with three LEAs mentioning plans for more schools in the immediate future.

It is difficult to compare these two surveys as the data have been collected differently, but close analysis reveals that provision for mother tongue teaching in primary schools has been steadily rising in recent years. Tansley and Craft's survey also gives details of other forms of support for mother tongue teaching: 18 LEAs paid for community teachers, 34 provided free premises for community schools, 27 rented premises to community schools, 27 gave *ex gratia* payments and/or help with materials and 23 gave other assistance including in-service training and advisory support.

The Mother Tongue Project

The foregoing account traces the historical development of changing attitudes and provision for the support of children's mother tongues. Although immigration to this country has been taking place on a significant scale since the Second World War and in increasing numbers in response to the Immigration Act 1971, the implications for children's home languages have only gradually been recognized. Whilst the ethnic minorities themselves were quick to realize the importance of maintaining their children's home languages and cultures through voluntarily organized schools and classes, it was left largely until the 1980s before the education system itself began to acknowledge the place of community languages in schools, and to make appropriate provision.

The role of curriculum development projects in both reflecting and stimulating change is well known. The Schools Council Mother Tongue Project was part of the changing climate of opinion but in addition helped to inform attitudes and stimulate further developments. As the outcome of a proposal put forward by the Schools Council and funded by the EC, it combined interests from both organizations. For the Schools Council it was one of several projects concerned with pupils of ethnic minority origin. For the EC it was one of a number of pilot projects set up in different European member states to examine the 'administrative solutions and adaptation of language teaching methods and materials' to enable member states to study the implications of the EC Directive for the children of migrant workers in their countries. Indeed it was one of a series funded in Britain; other examples being the Bedfordshire Mother Tongue and Culture Project (1976–80), the Language Information Network Co-ordination (1981–4) (attached to the Linguistic Minorities Project), and Course Design for Community Languages (1984 – 7).

As the second EC mother tongue project to be set up in Britain, it differed from the first and other EC-funded projects on the continent in certain important respects. In the first place it was a materials development project: that is to say, its major aims were concerned with the development of curricular materials to support children's mother tongues, whereas in Europe the main focus has been on direct mother tongue teaching, arising from the assumption of the possible return of migrants to their home country (though it is becoming increasingly obvious that the majority of migrants do *not* intend to return home but plan to settle in the host country). In the UK, mother tongue teaching has tended to be viewed as part of the multicultural curriculum and consequently wider aims to do with the curriculum as a whole and the place of home languages within it came to assume greater prominence as the Project became involved in the mother tongue debate in general.

Secondly, it is a national project with a national audience. Other EC mother tongue projects, including the Bedfordshire example, were limited to particular locations, usually an identified region or even a set number of schools. For instance, the Bedfordshire Project was based in four schools and dissemination of its findings beyond the European Commission and sister projects in Europe was limited.[9] A similar EC mother tongue project in the province of Limbourg in Belgium was also confined to four schools, although the Minister of Education pledged continued and expanded support for mother tongue teaching on completion of the project.

The Schools Council Mother Tongue Project, however, had a national perspective from the outset. Not only did the team work with teachers and schools in many different parts of Britain during the course of the Project, but the published outcomes have an even wider audience, potentially all teachers in primary schools and community mother tongue schools. Even the materials developed in the two target languages, Bengali and Greek, were intended to have applications for a range of other community languages.

A final respect in which the Mother Tongue Project was distinctive has already been implied above. It was not restricted to bilingual teachers *per se,* but addressed itself to all teachers whose work involves regular contact with children from a range of linguistic backgrounds, whether they speak any of these languages or not. Unlike other projects, whose main aim has been to support and extend children's mother tongues through direct teaching of the languages themselves, this project took a broader view by including the child's usual (mainstream) teacher as well as the mother tongue teacher in developing strategies and materials to support children's mother tongues in the classroom.

One further point needs to be made here. This project had another unusual feature. Unlike many other EC projects (although similar to the LINC project (op. cit.) and indeed unlike most other British projects, it attempted to span education in both the maintained and private sectors.

The materials developed for teaching the mother tongue were the outcome of collaboration between teachers from many different backgrounds including both mainstream and community schools.

As part of its endeavour to explore the methodology of teaching community languages in different situations and to develop materials for both mother tongue teachers and all teachers who wish to support the home languages of children in their classrooms, it was able to re-examine current approaches and at the same time break new ground.

The ways in which this was done, the problems encountered, the Project's impact and the issues which arose are analysed in subsequent chapters.

Notes

1. A recent House of Commons Home Affairs Committee Report (1985) gives a figure of 200,000.
2. Compare, however, with the Mother Tongue Project's estimate of 200,000 Greek speakers, given in Chapter 6.
3. EC: Many readers may be more familiar with the initials EEC which stand for the European Economic Community. The Mother Tongue Project was funded by the European Commission, which is the administrative arm of the European Community, and it is therefore correct to refer to it as an EC-funded project. Since about 1980 the European Community has preferred the initials EC to be used as they reflect more accurately the broadening of its scope beyond the economic treaties which were its original starting point. The use of both EEC and EC are correct but the latter initials are used throughout the book for the sake of uniformity.
4. 'Multilingual' is used here to mean primary schools with at least ten per cent bilingual pupils.
5. In *submersion* programmes, children from a linguistic minority of a country with a low status mother tongue are educated through the language of the linguistic majority. There is no element of choice and the teachers are normally unilingual whereas teachers in immersion programmes are bilingual.

   In *immersion* programmes, children from the linguistic majority of a country (with a high status mother tongue) choose to be educated through the medium of a foreign language.
6. Bilingual education programmes in Wales, although not mentioned by Mitchell, have also proved successful (Price, 1984).
7. When tested in English the bilingual experimental group performed better than controls in decoding (listening) performance in both schools and better than controls in encoding (speaking) performance in one school but worse in the other. When tested in Panjabi the bilingual experimental group performed better than controls in both encoding and decoding performance in both schools. All the tests were oral and were based on modified versions of various PICAC tests adapted for both the English medium and Panjabi

medium sessions.
8.   For this account of multicultural education I am indebted to the Open University Third Level Course in Educational Studies – 'Ethnic Minorities and Community Relations', E354, Block 4, Units 13 + 14.
9.   There are, however, three evaluation reports covering the first three years of the project obtainable from CILT. The evaluation report of the final year of the project was not published but a copy is held by CILT. Some of the materials produced can be seen at the Multiracial Education Resources Centre, Acacia Road, Bedford MK42 0HU.

Chapter 2
Supporting Community Languages

Introduction

When the Project started in 1981 the idea of supporting children's community languages in the primary school classroom was still relatively new. Maintenance of the child's mother tongue was regarded as the responsibility of the family and the community and in fact the prevailing view was very often that any support for the home language would be at the expense of the acquisition of standard English and consequently would be likely to hamper progress through the education system.

In recent years, however, this traditional response has begun to give way to a view of the child's mother tongue as a set of skills and resources that can be tapped by the teacher as an aid to learning, as a means of establishing closer links between home and school, and as an acknowledgement of the range of cultural experiences that make up our multicultural society.

It was against this background of increased interest in the role of mother tongue learning, and indeed as part of this blossoming of enthusiasm that the Project carried out its work. The material outcomes of the Project are described in the next chapter but what we will do here is to set the scene by bringing together the accumulated experiences of the teachers, schools and LEAs with whom the Project worked to show how children's home languages may be supported in the primary school.

Innovations can enter into the education system through a variety of mechanisms. They may be introduced in a formal way as part of a new policy or they may develop more informally, starting from an individual teacher or school's initiative. Both approaches, and they are not mutually exclusive, have varying degrees of success depending on complex factors which are not always strictly educational.

The field of mother tongue teaching is no exception in this respect. It was stated earlier that the growing interest in children's home languages derives from a number of interlinked sources. The position of ethnic communities in Britain in the wake of the Immigration and Race Relations Acts of the 1970s has given rise to feelings of insecurity and culture disassociation which have led to increased pressure from these communities for improved educational achievement for their children. One of the ways in which the pressure has become articulate has been through the call from ethnic minority parents for mother tongue tuition for their children which is seen as a way of preserving the language and culture of their communities, felt to be under threat from the majority group in society. The EC Directive has helped to give official backing to these demands. At the same time, teachers and educationalists have become increasingly conscious that the Bullock maxim, that 'no child should be expected to cast off the language and culture of the home' on crossing the school threshold, means supporting children's home languages in practical positive ways within the classroom. Furthermore, they have become aware of growing evidence that far from hindering the child's development in English, mother tongue teaching can actually aid development in the second language (see for example the MOTET Project's outcomes (MOTET, 1981)) and has a number of other benefits of an educational nature, such as improved concept development, increased self-esteem and better motivation. These advantages do not only apply to children from ethnic minorities; all children benefit from increased language awareness and sensitivity to the range of cultures present in contemporary Britain.

The demand for mother tongue teaching comes from many different roots, and it is therefore not surprising that its permeation into the school curriculum has come about in a variety of ways and at a number of levels. In this chapter we will look at the growing support for children's home languages in the school through the initiatives of three groups of innovators operating at three different levels: local education authorities, schools and individual teachers.

Local Education Authorities

LEAs are crucially important agents in bringing innovation into the classroom. This is, of course, true with respect to all educational initiatives but particularly applicable in the field of community languages as a new and politically sensitive area of curriculum. The experience of the Project suggests that in supporting community languages, unless teachers in mainstream schools have the support of the LEA the impact they can make is limited. Houlton and Willey (1983) endorse this point when they state that:

> all teachers in multilingual schools are involved and should take part in assessing what is necessary, and what can be done. They need, for instance, to sharpen their awareness of pupils' home language

experiences and examine how they might respond to these within the classroom. But to be fully effective such a process requires adequate support by the school, the LEA and national bodies.

Of course, the converse is also true; LEAs can formulate ambitious policies but unless there is agreement at the grass roots level these policies will not work successfully.

So what can be done at a local authority level to promote children's mother tongues? LEAs have tackled this in a number of ways ranging from formal policy statements to little more than token support of teacher initiatives. Some of the many ways in which LEAs can and often do support community languages are:

(a) Formulation of formal policy.
(b) Gathering information on language diversity within their local authority area.
(c) Curricular provision for mother tongue teaching.
(d) Financial support for non-statutory provision (payment of community teachers, provision of free or cheap accommodation, etc.).
(e) Provision of materials and resources.
(f) In-service training.
(g) Advisory support.

Formal policies

Many LEAs have taken very seriously the need to respond to both national and local pressures to formulate policy on issues to do with ethnic minority pupils in their schools. The gradual shift from predominantly explicit government pronouncements on multicultural pluralist objectives for society, together with growing pressures from increasingly articulate community groups has, however, led them to re-examine their principles and practices. As the focus of attention has broadened from the acknowledgement of multiculturalism to include recognition of multilingualism and, within that, the place of the mother tongue, they have sought to reflect these changes of emphasis within their policies. A further factor has been the recognition that positive initiatives are required to counter racial discrimination in society and to assess and meet the particular needs of minority ethnic groups.

Until recently LEA policies relating to ethnic minority pupils, where such policies existed, came under the umbrella of multicultural education. Houlton and Willey (op. cit.) report that 'whilst concerted approaches to education in a multicultural society are often now relatively well-developed, issues of language diversity have tended to be dealt with on a fairly *ad hoc* basis'. The languages spoken by pupils were rarely specified and policy regarding mother tongue teaching or support was embryonic. This picture is gradually changing.

The survey undertaken by the Schools Council (Tansley and Craft, 1984) revealed that about one-third of LEAs now report having a policy on mother tongue teaching, ranging from general support to various bilingual or mother tongue teaching programmes. Although some of these policies are little more than lists of ways local authorities give practical support to community languages, others are more comprehensive. Cleveland LEA, for example, gives the following reasons for supporting children's mother tongues:

a(i)   'to assist the transition of young children into school from homes where Asian languages are spoken and to promote good home/school liaison'

(ii)   'to facilitate easy concept formation across the curriculum'

(iii)   'to strengthen a child's capability to learn English by degrees from entry onward (but particularly from 6+ onwards)'

b   'to develop courses to CSE, O- and A-level in Urdu which is seen as an important community language (available for Asian and non-Asian children)'

The London Borough of Haringey, with whom the Project worked closely, has a policy statement on bilingualism which 'recognizes the importance and value of the languages spoken within borough boundaries' and outlines the part the Education Service must play 'in assisting all members of the community to maintain and develop their knowledge of oral/written fluency in the language of their home and community', which involves the employment of bilingual staff, provision of language awareness courses and specialist teaching.

But the most extensive and well thought out policy is probably that developed by the ILEA. Following on the 1981 Language Census (repeated in 1983) six principles were endorsed (ILEA, 1983b):

(i)   It is the right of all bilingual children to know that their mother tongue skills are recognized and valued in schools.

(ii)   It is educationally desirable that bilingual children in primary schools should be given the chance to learn to read and write their mother tongues and to extend their oral skills in these languages.

(iii) It is educationally desirable that bilingual children in secondary schools should be given the chance to study the language of their home as a subject on the school curriculum and to gain appropriate examination qualifications.

(iv) The mother tongue skills of bilingual children should be seen as a valuable potential channel for supporting their learning.

(v) All children should have the opportunity to learn how other languages work and be encouraged to take an interest in and be informed about the languages spoken by their peers and neighbours.

(vi) In developing arrangements for teaching mother tongue and in other ways promoting bilingualism schools should consult with the parents concerned and seek to co-operate with mother tongue classes organized by community groups and other agencies.

It is significant to note that several points in the implementation programme have in fact been exceeded: two bilingual inspectors have actually been appointed and money for 45 teaching posts has been set aside.

As part of the survey, Welsh authorities were also asked for details of mother tongue support and their replies provide interesting examples of the possible extent of support for minority languages. For example, Clwyd sets out a Welsh language policy document outlining bilingualism at nursery, primary and secondary levels. The aim of the policy is 'to ensure that pupils gain the educational stimulus afforded by second language teaching and become reasonably fluent in both languages as a process continuing into the secondary school'. Powys has a policy booklet detailing policy and provision according to a percentage of Welsh first language speakers in a school. For example, the document states:

in primary education the language has come to be a medium of instruction in Welsh-speaking areas, either throughout the school or, in some cases, in a stream within the school; secondary schools in these areas offer some courses through the medium of Welsh.

In areas where Welsh is not predominant it is included in the curriculum as a second language. Even in areas which are wholly English-speaking, in 'most of the primary schools Welsh is taught as a second language for the equivalent of 30 minutes per day'. The implications of such a policy applied to English schools with high percentages of speakers of minority community languages are staggering.

The variation in policies on community languages and the relatively unsophisticated terms in which many of them are couched reflect the uncertainties which policy makers feel in this emerging field.

The booklet by Houlton and Willey referred to above offers guidelines on aspects which might be considered in an LEA policy, including the importance of forming a clear policy on language based on firm principles as part of a general approach to multilingualism in the context of the whole curriculum, linked with policies on equality of opportunity and anti-racism. The collection and dissemination of relevant information was stressed, together with the identification of in-service needs, recruitment of bilingual teachers and the inclusion of a statement of financial commitment.

Other factors to be taken into account when formulating policy include wide consultation and maximum publicity. This is particularly important when working with members of ethnic minorities, who may not respond to formal overtures and need to be approached with sensitivity and care. The ILEA has held a series of consultations with interested parties during the formulation of its far-ranging policy and this must go some way to explaining its success so far.

Equally important is the development of an adequate information base. Indeed many local authorities have made this their starting point; for example, the ILEA Language Census referred to above led to the drafting of a policy on bilingualism. In this respect the survey instruments and data provided by the Linguistic Minorities Project (LMP, 1985) proved invaluable in the five LEAs in which they worked. Several authorities are surveying existing provision and assessing needs as a necessary preliminary step. Apart from the information gathered in this way there is the additional bonus of the raised level of language awareness in an authority as a result of the exercise.

The formulation of policy is, of course, no guarantee that it will be implemented and although many LEAs are now taking their responsibilities very seriously, there is still a substantial gap between policy and practice in others. Tsow (1983) wrote of the responses to her national survey of mother tongue teaching in local education authorities:

> it was clear from the findings that any meaningful assessment of each authority's provision for multicultural education/mother tongue teaching needed to rest on an evaluation of the policies that were *actually implemented* [my italics] in the maintained and voluntary sectors.

The survey undertaken by the Schools Council (op. cit.) showed that the number of LEAs with policies on mother tongue teaching has increased since Tsow's survey was carried out in 1980–82 (Tsow, 1983).

Many LEAs are also now taking steps to ensure that their policies are actually put into practice. The ILEA has agreed a five-point programme of implementation for their anti-racist policies, which include the six principles on bilingualism,[1] and Berkshire LEA has set up an evaluation and monitoring programme to investigate the implementation of their policy on racial equality.

Other forms of support

Many LEAs do not yet feel ready to endorse formal policies on home languages but may support children's bilingualism in a range of other ways. The Schools Council survey (op. cit.) carried out in 1983, relating to support for children of primary school age only, found that 23 LEAs actually provide mother tongue teaching as part of the primary school curriculum. Whilst Britain appears to be lagging behind her counterparts in other EC countries in providing direct mother tongue tuition[2] many LEAs may support children's home languages in other ways. Other forms of support included payment for community teachers (18 LEAs), provision of free premises for community schools (34 LEAs), rented premises to community schools (22 LEAs), *ex gratia* payments and/or help with materials (27 LEAs), other assistance (23 LEAs). 'Other assistance' included support from advisers, advisory teachers, support services or resource centres, in-service training for mother tongue teachers and class teachers, grants for specific projects, time off to produce materials, books, stationery and other resources. These forms of support fall into four general categories – curricular provision, financial support, provision of materials and resources, and in-service training.

Curricular provision is perhaps the most 'visible' form of support for mother tongue teaching, certainly as far as the public is concerned, and one which local authorities may consequently be reluctant to give. It varies considerably according to the age range in question but tends to be more widespread at either end of the age range (see p.92–3 for details) of formal schooling.

Many authorities prefer to give support to children's mother tongues in more indirect ways by making payments to local community groups, providing cheap or free rented accommodation and even paying salaries for community teachers. In some cases LEAs have been able to take advantage of Manpower Services Commission (MSC) funding for unemployed helpers in the form of Language Aides who may assist in schools or help develop materials. For example, 25 Language Aides have been appointed in Coventry, mostly Panjabi-speaking women, and similar schemes operate in Bradford, Birmingham, Walsall and Northampton. Of course some authorities support community languages in several of these ways; a few in all of them.

Financial support may extend to the provision of materials such as paper, pens, books, even a per capita allowance per number of children attending community run classes. Local authorities may make certain equipment available or allow community teachers to use their resources and attend their teachers centres (see for example LMP, 1984, 1985).

In-service training of both bilingual and non-bilingual teachers in community languages is also an expanding area and one in which local education authorities are beginning to feel they have a responsibility. Courses for teachers of English as a Second Language and courses in multicultural/multi-ethnic education are not a new development, but until recently the study of community languages and consideration of their relevance was not included as part of their programmes. Local education authorities have, however, become increasingly aware that teachers in multilingual classrooms need information about linguistic diversity and need to discuss language awareness[3], particularly since few teachers will have confronted these issues as part of their initial teacher training.

The Project's handbook *Supporting Children's Bilingualism* identified the following priorities for future in-service provision:

1.   LEA or school-based multicultural curriculum and language development courses should include a component on mother tongue issues.

2.   Schools should be encouraged to formulate a policy on multilingual education within the framework of a language policy.

3.   Opportunities, time and resources should be made available by the authority to encourage teachers to develop bilingual materials or consider how existing materials can be used bilingually.

4.   A group of peripatetic bilingual teachers should be available to support non-bilingual teachers as well as offering language teaching to children.

5.   There should be links and liaison between the teachers in community mother-tongue schools, in-service providers and mainstream schools.

A still more recent development in in-service teacher training has been the provision of courses for bilingual teachers teaching in either mainstream or community mother tongue classes. Many LEAs now have a co-ordinator for community languages (who goes under a variety of titles such as Co-ordinator for Asian Languages, Mother Tongue Co-ordinator, Co-ordinator for Community Languages), one of whose responsibilities may be to organize teacher training courses for bilingual teachers. The role of the co-ordinator is described more fully in the next section.

Advisory support

A key figure within the local authority structure is the adviser with responsibility for community languages. Such a person interprets local authority policy at school level and at the same time is able to relay the anxieties and experiences of schools back to the education committee. The adviser is also responsible for keeping up-to-date with curriculum developments in the field and applying these where appropriate at local level.

Changing policies and attitudes have meant the advisers concerned with community languages have undergone a number of changes of title and their place within local authority structure is still uncertain. As the field of multicultural education expanded, multicultural advisers found that mother tongue support became one of their duties. However, it soon came to be regarded as a specific responsibility, possibly more appropriate to a community languages expert, although still within the overall framework of the curriculum in general. Some advisers with responsibility for mother tongue are answerable to the Primary or Secondary Inspectorate, as their role is thought to infuse the whole curriculum rather than constitute a separate element. Others, however, remain under the multicultural or multi-ethnic umbrella whilst a few come under the Modern Languages Section.[4] An increasing number of LEAs have responded to the extra advisory workload arising from the provision of mother tongue teaching and support by appointing advisory teachers rather than full advisers, to take responsibility for community languages. These teachers, as well as performing an advisory function for schools (and indeed the local education authority) who require guidance on mother tongue support and its place within the curriculum, are frequently responsible for teams of community language teachers, working either on a peripatetic basis in mainstream schools or teaching in community run classes, or sometimes both.

A growth area

Support for children's home languages is at present a growth area in local education authorities; probably one of the few such expanding sectors. There are several reasons for this. One is that in these times of severe financial contingency in education the mother tongue field is oddly enough one in which money is not necessarily a hindrance. LEAs are able to obtain funding direct from the Home Office through Section 11 provision and the Urban Aid Programme, amounting to 75 per cent of the cost, thus enabling LEAs to increase provision in this area of education with little if any direct financial outlay. Another reason for the expansion in this area is the stimulus provided by the EC Directive (1977) and the necessity for the British Government to submit information to the EC on its compliance with the Directive on behalf of children of migrant workers in the United Kingdom. Although this factor has had little direct influence on LEAs due to the decentralized nature of the British education system and the low key response to the Directive taken by the British government, nevertheless it has helped to promote developments at a national and local level (such as DES regional courses, the HMI Inquiry, the LINC Project and the Mother Tongue Project itself), which has had the effect of furthering the mother tongue debate within local education authorities.

Two final factors can also be put forward. First, the changing attitudes to children's home languages within the field of education itself. Both from an 'official' perspective, starting with the Bullock Report, and from the increasing empirical evidence, it has gradually been accepted by educationalists and teachers that the mother tongues of Britain's ethnic minorities should have a place within the state education system. Second, the perceived political importance of responding to the needs of ethnic minority communities, especially after the 1981 disturbances. Both have financial and organizational implications for local education authorities and many have sought to respond in the ways outlined above.

It is, however, still the case that many of the initiatives that have been taken are on an *ad hoc* basis, even in areas where formal policies exist, apart from a few notable exceptions. It has increasingly been the experience of workers in the field that the time is ripe for a more formal structure to co-ordinate developments. At local authority level this could take the form of a central organization, probably based at a teachers' centre, which would be responsible for disseminating information about ideas and materials, housing a central resource collection, providing reprographic and study facilities and organizing in-service courses for bilingual and non-bilingual teachers.

Schools

A school policy

Schools occupy a pivotal position between local education authorities and individual teachers. They can mediate new approaches developed at local authority level by advisers and harness initiatives by particular staff. As with LEAs, one of the most effective ways to introduce support for home languages within the school will probably be through the formulation of a school policy, especially if the teachers are closely involved in drawing it up. It is particularly essential in this controversial area for all teachers to take part in full and frank discussions, in order to clarify their thoughts and resolve any uncertainties. Unless the whole staff support the policy it has little chance of success and will result in feelings of resentment and hostility. It is better to have a limited programme of support which is endorsed by all, than a full-scale policy which does not have unqualified backing.

The idea of developing a school policy is one that is currently gaining ground in the field. For example, a handbook produced by the Birmingham Multicultural Support Service (Birmingham Multicultural Resource Unit, 1983) has a section on formulating a whole school policy for multicultural education which includes references to children's home languages. Three categories for discussion are identified: attitudes, curriculum and materials, and two questions relating to children's languages raised: 'Are children's languages seen as an essential part of their lives, or is there a disjunction between home and school's expectation?' and 'Is language work effective and inclusive of (*a*) the child's mother tongue? (*b*) the languages of school and community?' *Issues in Race and Education* (1982), a magazine for teachers involved in multicultural education, also outlines a specific mother tongue policy for schools with suggestions for action by schools, LEAs and teacher unions. The recommendations for schools include: providing access to the school and the curriculum for community language speakers; considering mother tongues as curriculum subjects and funding community language teaching; and evaluating the use and role of community languages in schools. Although the first example of a school policy given here includes community languages as part of a policy for multicultural education, there is a growing tendency, paralleling a similar shift in advisory responsibility (see p.41), for community languages to be subsumed under a whole school language policy, a development which has generally found favour with the teachers most closely involved. Before discussing the Project's experiences of developing school-based approaches to mother tongue support it should be noted, however, that schools have limitations as agencies of language planning and change. Gorman (1977) makes this point when he refers to the failure to ensure the restoration and use of the Irish language despite consistently pursued educational measures as 'a telling illustration of the limitations of the school as an agency of language planning'. Much depends, of course, on the wider society and its attitudes towards ethnic minorities and their languages, as well as the other agencies involved, particularly national government, local education authorities and teachers themselves.

As part of its programme, the Project worked with both individual teachers and whole school staffs. Although very few schools were at the stage of even considering the role of children's mother tongues as part of a school policy, nevertheless it is clear that where a school was divided as to its importance or indifferent as to its value, then any support for home languages by isolated teachers would have considerably less impact beyond the individual classroom than in schools where the entire staff were united in their approach.

When the Project was setting up classes in which to try out the Bengali and Greek materials, there was quite a range of responses from the staff in the schools concerned, although all the schools were self-selected in the sense that the head teachers had expressed interest in taking part in the Project. In one school dissension amongst the staff was so great that the head reluctantly withdrew from the trials. In two others the head-teachers were very ambivalent from the start about the value of according recognition to children's home languages and despite the enthusiasm of some of their staff remained sceptical and decided not to continue the experiment after the trial year. However, in some schools the whole staff became caught up in the trials which were used as an opportunity for them to examine their policies on multicultural education in general and mother tongue in particular. In these schools recognition of children's home languages became an essential and integrated part of the school curriculum valued by teachers and children alike.

Further experience of introducing support for children's home languages was gathered during the trials of the handbook of strategies for teachers in multilingual classrooms. This was tried out in three different ways: as a basis for in-service education, by individual teachers usually through a local teachers' centre, and by whole schools.

The most successful was the last, in the sense that all teachers in a school became involved and children benefited from knowing that the whole staff valued their languages. One head-teacher where the whole school co-operated said of their work with the Project 'it's drawn all of our threads together and has drawn us together in our thinking and opened up staffroom discussion'. In cases where individual teachers worked with the Project they had to face indifference and sometimes hostility from other staff which made their job harder and their impact more contained. Without a whole school policy or united approach isolated initiatives are likely to remain at the individual classroom level and may even be forgotten altogether if the teacher should move on. One head-teacher felt that the Project's handbook should not be used by an individual teacher looking for 'something to do with my class on Monday' but as 'part of a deeper analysis of what teachers are about in this field'.

A whole school approach also helps to maintain momentum and leads to new ideas and initiatives as teachers learn from each other. Unless the school has a united policy which is regularly re-examined and evaluated, there is a danger that enthusiasm will wane and the whole exercise will become little more that tokenistic. A further anxiety is that any bilingual teachers, particularly if they are peripatetic, will become isolated without the support of a whole school approach and mainstream teachers may feel that the mother tongue teacher is solely responsible for supporting home languages and consequently they need not bother themselves.

Developing a whole school approach

So what can a school do if it feels it should be giving support to children's home languages but it is not sure how to go about doing this? The first step will undoubtedly be initial discussion with all the staff either as part of a staff meeting or at a specially called meeting. Here the staff can decide what their views about this are and what action they feel they should take. Probably they will need to meet together several times before they can decide exactly what to do. They may choose to find out more about what is going on in this field of education elsewhere, they may plan a few activities to try out in their classrooms, they may decide to draw up a school policy, perhaps as part of a wider discussion on the implications of a multicultural society for language policy.

If they take the last option, schools should include explicit reference to the community languages spoken by the children. It can form part of the enrichment and extension of language work currently being undertaken in the development of 'language-across-the-curriculum' strategies rather than being the responsibility of a specialist or subsumed under support for multicultural education in general.

Some of the questions schools will need to think about will include:

why support children's home languages?
which home languages should these be?
what kind of support is best (at what age, oral or written, etc.)?
how should the support be given (as part of normal classwork, in a separate room)?
who should provide the support (class-teacher, ESL teacher, bilingual teacher, helper)?

Some of these questions are ideological or organizational and are taken up in some detail in the section on working with schools. However, for the purposes of this chapter it will be sufficient to confine ourselves to looking at the themes the Project's seminar on supporting children's bilingualism (Houlton and Willey, 1983) considered should be included in a whole school policy:

1. Reasons why pupils should see their school as an appropriate place in which to use their mother tongue.

2. Strategies for ensuring close consultation and participation by pupils, parents and local communities.

3. The range of visual responses to language diversity which should be made available within the school.

4. The range of ways in which responses to pupils' languages can be embodied in the subject areas of the curriculum.

5. The importance of integrating responses to minority languages into the mainstream life of the school.

6. The resources which should be available within the school.

7. The importance of making available opportunities for teachers who want to inform themselves about language diversity.

8. The value of seeking ways of involving bilingual adults and others in responses to bilingualism.

9. The necessity of constantly reassessing pupils' language needs and of monitoring the provision made to meet them.

It was implied above that schools themselves might take the first step in considering their attitudes to supporting children's bilingualism and subsequently the ways in which they could implement their decisions. Obviously, it is best if teachers themselves take the initiative in opening up new areas of the curriculum, but it is not always the case that the impetus for working at this area comes from the school staff. If this is the case, schools may be stimulated to appraise their approach to community languages by outside influences.

At the seminar held by the Project to consider policy issues for primary schools and local education authorities, representatives from five LEAs reported on the interest aroused among schools and teachers by recent initiatives in the mother tongue field. One of the most well-known of such initiatives is the MOTET Project in Bradford which has been instrumental in opening up discussion about mother tongue teaching locally. A DES regional course in Berkshire, 'Language Needs of the Multicultural Classroom', involved many teachers in looking critically at their classrooms whilst a sister project to the Mother Tongue Project, the Schools Council Language in the Multicultural Primary Classroom Project, stimulated interest in language diversity among teachers from schools in Bradford, Cardiff, Haringey and the ILEA.

The Project's own experience of trying out community language materials in London, and materials for teachers in the multilingual classroom in 22 LEAs, also found that the exercise resulted in many teachers becoming aware for the first time of resources the bilingual children in their classes bring to school. One teacher from Northamptonshire wrote:

> As teacher responsible for integrated study planning in our school the effect of being involved has had an influence on the whole school – while we knew we had children from other cultures we had not given their cultures the recognition they deserved . . . We now hope to value them.

Another from Newham commented that working with the Project reminded her 'that the children's home languages have a real place in the classroom – something I had felt instinctively, but was wary of acknowledging.'

Teachers

Although it has already been said that it is difficult for individual mainstream teachers to develop far ranging and successful strategies for supporting children's home languages if they do not have the backing of their school, nevertheless many teachers are anxious to accord respect to children's languages and cultures within their own classrooms. The role of mother tongue teachers is considered elsewhere; here the emphasis is on the far greater number of teachers who do not speak the languages of their pupils or who may be faced with a class where many different languages are spoken by the children, and yet still feel they wish to build on children's experiences and expertise by bringing community languages into the classroom. This section looks at strategies teachers have evolved; some were collected from teachers who had already been using them over a long period, others were developed during the Project in response to the Project's work in this field.

There are many ways of acknowledging children's languages, ranging from labelling objects in the appropriate language, to encouraging children to speak and write using their mother tongue during normal classroom work. As part of a study of teachers' attitudes to mother tongue teaching carried out in the mainstream trial schools where the Project's Bengali and Greek materials were tried out, class teachers were asked to indicate support accorded to home languages in their school along a range of dimensions. As many as 90 per cent of the teachers reported that teachers in their school were 'generally aware of the range of languages and dialects spoken by the children' (these were, as reported earlier, self-selected schools in which children from ethnic minority backgrounds represented a substantial proportion of the intake). Among the most popular activities for according recognition to children's languages were school assemblies, used as an opportunity to reflect home cultures, presentation of stories and songs in children's own languages and using the visual environment of the school (e.g. books, pictures, play materials, displays) to reflect home languages.

However, there was less support for the direct use of home languages in the school. Only five per cent of the teachers responding to the questionnaire in the schools trying out the Greek materials said that ethnic minority children were encouraged to use their languages in school, although 57 per cent of teachers responding to the questionnaire in the schools trying out the Bengali materials encouraged ethnic minority children to use their language in school at the start of the trial year. By the end of the trial year teachers responding to the questionnaire in both groups of schools had markedly increased their support for this behaviour. Similarly, over half the sample of teachers for both the schools trying out the Greek materials and the schools trying out the Bengali materials generally expected children to speak English in the classroom at the start of the trial year. By the end of the trial year only a quarter of the teachers responding to the questionnaire in the sample of schools where the Bengali materials were being tried out generally expected children to speak only English in the classroom, but by the end of the year the percentage of teachers in the Greek trial schools expecting pupils to speak English in the classroom had actually increased. This finding may, however, be affected by sampling problems.

In all the schools there was a tendency for community languages to be seen as the province of ethnic minority children rather than as a resource for *all* children. Only one-fifth of the teachers in the Bengali trial schools reported that there was 'provision for *all* children to learn about each other's languages' and only 14 per cent of the Greek trial schools reported such provision at the start of the trial year. By the end of the trial year the percentage of teachers in the Bengali trial schools reporting provision for all pupils had more than doubled (45 per cent) but the percentage of teachers reporting such provision in the Greek trial schools remained virtually the same (15 per cent). On the whole the experience of working with the Project over the course of the trial year seemed to have the effect of increasing positive support for children's languages in general, whilst at the same time providing mother tongue tuition for some children.

The Project's work with teachers in multilingual classrooms focused more directly on developing practical strategies which individual teachers could use to support children's home languages. One of the most natural ways for teachers to begin bringing children's home languages into the classroom is to start by discovering which languages the children actually know. This is an activity in which all the children in the class can participate and will not only help children to feel that their home background is welcome at school but will also help teachers to find out important information about the children in their class, which will have benefits far beyond the immediate exercise. It can be used as an opportunity for many different learning tasks such as constructing simple questionnaires, making matrices, reporting evidence, etc., as well as being ideally suited to collaborative and topic work. Collaborative learning techniques are particularly appropriate for this type of work as children themselves have much to contribute and learn from each other, but it does mean the teachers themselves are put into a learning situation. Most of them do not speak their children's language(s) and therefore are in a position where they have to learn from their pupils. This can be both a rewarding and sometimes unnerving experience. It can provide valuable opportunities for teachers to appreciate their pupil's skills at first hand. One teacher said:

> I learn a great deal from children in my class. They are only too willing to extend my knowledge of their languages by teaching me new vocabulary and phrases and explaining grammatical rules . . . Apart from helping my relationship with the children it also helps me become more aware of the skills they possess but which, for various reasons, they have often kept hidden in school.

On the other hand, it can make teachers feel they are not in control of a particular part of the curriculum if children are using languages which they do not understand. Teachers need understanding and support to help them come to terms with these aspects of the work.

Many teachers reported that not only do bilingual children feel more confident and have increased self-esteem after such work but monolingual children become interested in other languages and develop a greater understanding of their speakers. One teacher wrote, 'The children have gained in confidence and have a greater appreciation of each other's achievements and a greater understanding of each other's difficulties'. It is of course most important to explain the reasons for the activity and to build up an atmosphere of trust and confidence in order to avoid misunderstandings and to encourage children to speak about their experiences.

Another popular way to introduce home languages into the primary classroom, especially with younger children, is through the use of stories in the mother tongue. Although teachers have been accustomed to using stories from different cultures for many years, especially in multi-ethnic schools, stories told in the mother tongue itself are a relatively recent addition to the curriculum. They are a particularly valuable way of giving recognition to community languages as not only do they confirm for children the teachers' valuing of their language and culture, but they represent an enjoyable activity that all children can share. A teacher from Berkshire wrote, 'We realized we all enjoy the same story even if we don't know the same language'. Many teachers have tried different ways of making and introducing mother tongue stories with the help of bilingual teachers, parents and even older children. Sometimes they have translated existing stories, sometimes they have written down traditional tales; in some cases children have written and illustrated their own stories. Once the stories are produced they can be used in a variety of ways. A group of ethnic minority children can listen to a story together; individuals can listen to a story on tape; or the whole class can participate even if they do not all understand the particular language in which the story is told. During the trialling of the handbook several teachers tried telling a story to the whole class in the mother tongue first and then English and reported a good response.

The material in the handbook was largely collected from schools having significant numbers of children from ethnic minority backgrounds, but the example of storytelling illustrates one of the underlying tenets of the Project: that *all* children can benefit from the linguistic diversity around them. This can have not only cognitive and social benefits but can be an element in combating racist attitudes in schools. Not only do multi-ethnic schools need to take account of the range of languages and cultures present in their classes but all schools, including all-white schools, should equip children to take their place in the multicultural and multilingual society in which we live.

Although this was not the focus of the Project, a few examples can be given of ways in which this could be done. Some teachers have found that language awareness topics looking either at the range of languages spoken in Britain or at language as a symbolic system (including, therefore, other communicative systems such as Braille, morse code, shorthand, etc.) can be helpful as an introduction to the scope and range of linguistic diversity. Others have started by looking at different varieties of English such as Cockney, Sheffieldese, Yorkshire English, formal and informal English, before going on to consider similar variations within other languages. A few schools in all-white areas have sought to give their pupils the experience of being in a multicultural environment by arranging exchange visits with schools whose children come from many different ethnic minority backgrounds.

Many teachers feel that the mother tongues of children cannot be introduced in a piecemeal fashion or as a single subject on the curriculum, but rather that language diversity should permeate the whole atmosphere of the classroom and be a part of all the children's work. Of course topic work, which is central to the primary school curriculum, provides a great deal of scope for language work. Teachers working with the Project frequently incorporated language work into ongoing topics or specifically chose topics which would give scope for such work. Some examples of the topics they chose are: celebrations, ourselves, weather, clothes, food, homes, the neighbourhood, harvest, and people who help us.

Apart from topic work teachers were able to bring home languages into the classroom in mathematics (mostly through counting activities, time and measurement), cooking, music and singing, geography, games and as part of general classroom displays of such items as days of the week, weather charts, numbers and letters, etc. In addition, teachers have become accustomed to labelling objects and pictures in their classroom with the appropriate languages as well as English.

A particular problem that arose in connection with this work but which applies to the visible use of the mother tongue in the school in general is the question of 'correct' language usage. Many parents may dispute the spelling or grammatical features of words or sentences used in displays and written materials and teachers may have difficulty in finding out the 'correct' version to reproduce, especially when they have no personal knowledge of the language. Some teachers feel that this is not crucial; the main point is to show the children's languages with the understanding, as when displaying any children's work, that there may be mistakes. Others, and particularly mother tongue teachers, may feel offended if incorrect labels or writing arc displayed as models for children to learn.

Some teachers have tried to overcome these problems and to show children how seriously they view their linguistic heritage by learning one or more of the languages of the classroom themselves. This may be done at an informal level as opportunities arise with teachers simply asking children and parents to teach them the words for everyday items, the phrases for greeting and simple questions. Or several teachers may group together to prepare simple lists of words and expressions or even to make a phrasebook. Alternatively, teachers may choose to take it up at a more formal level by attending a course for learning community languages. LEAs are finding there is an increasing demand for such courses not only from teachers but also from nurses, health workers, police officers and others.

Of course, not all teachers have the time to take on evening class commitments and many are faced with multilingual classes where they may feel the choice of a particular language might lead to adverse reactions from the speakers of other languages. Working with parents and the local community is a particularly fruitful avenue for teachers to explore. Making a place for home languages in the classroom helps bring parents who may normally be difficult to reach into the school. By sharing information with parents about children and their backgrounds, school policy and practice and the work and progress of the pupils, parents and teachers can learn from each other. It is important, however, to ensure that this is a genuine two-way exchange if mutual benefit is to be derived.

It is vital to ensure parental understanding of the issues, particularly why their children's languages are being acknowledged at school, and their support for any activities undertaken. Some ethnic minority parents may misunderstand the motives for introducing community languages into the school and interpret them either as a means of preventing their children from learning English or even as a way of equipping them for repatriation. These parents need to be reassured that learning English is still the first priority and that acknowledgement and use of the children's home languages in school may actually help towards this goal.

Some examples of the information parents can help schools by giving are the child's first language, religion, diet and eating traditions, name and parents' names. It may be necessary to have an interpreter to help give the information. Schools in turn can ensure that information about the school is available to parents in the language they prefer, and through both formal and informal contact ensure that the atmosphere of the school is such that parents feel free to ask for information and make their views known. In addition, parents could be asked to contribute more directly by helping with storytelling, games, songs, music, cookery, number work, etc. through the mother tongue although it is important not to abuse or exploit the goodwill of parents.

It is important to bear in mind in this necessarily brief account of the ways teachers can value and use children's home languages in the classroom that this is still a very controversial area. Not only may parents of ethnic minority children be uncertain of the aims of such activities but other parents may also feel threatened and unsure. If children's mother tongues are going to be displayed in the classroom and used as part of the everyday experience of the children then *all* parents should be aware of what is happening and why. Many teachers working with the Project reported ambivalence or even hostility on the part of both white and ethnic minority parents, usually based on the anxiety that the children were missing out on learning English. Although parents' worries can generally be overcome they need to be seriously considered before embarking on activities which may cause a carefully built relationship to crumble.

This chapter has looked at ways in which community languages can be supported by local education authorities, schools and teachers. Although each of these agencies can take the first step towards acknowledging pupils' home languages, they are likely to have a limited impact on changing attitudes and practices in the classroom unless they work in collaboration with the others.

The following case study, taken from the Project's trials of its handbook for teachers in multilingual classrooms, is an example of the way in which all three groups can work together in order to translate a curriculum innovation into reality. It describes the actual mechanisms by which this was done, the processes undergone, the mutual benefits accruing to both the national Project and local teachers and the way in which teachers explored the rationale and means for supporting children's home languages which they were then able to pass on to others.

A case study : by David Houlton

The authority

Leicestershire is in the East Midlands of England and has a school population of approximately 140,000. It is a county of considerable diversity, ranging as it does from small market towns and mining communities, which have very few ethnic minority families, to the medium-sized industrial City of Leicester where about 35 per cent of the children in school are of Indian sub-continent, European and Caribbean origins. The languages spoken cover the full South Asian and European range but by far the most significant are Gujarati, Panjabi and Kutchi.

For some years following the major influxes of ethnic minority families in the sixties and early seventies the authority had no formal policy for multicultural education. But in October 1981, following a considerable debate among teachers and community groups, a County Working Party was formed whose brief was to develop such a policy on an authority-wide basis. One of the earliest outcomes of this was the appointment of an adviser for multicultural education. Soon afterwards steps were taken to establish a programme for mother tongue teaching in the early years of primary school.

Setting up the groups

The Project's involvement with local teachers began in December 1981 when the team member responsible for working with teachers in multilingual classrooms addressed a meeting of primary teachers specifically convened to invite collaboration with the Project. The meeting was well attended and confirmed an impression that was emerging elsewhere in the country, that many primary teachers were ready to consider what their own role might be in giving support to the home language experience of their bilingual pupils.

From this initial meeting came a nucleus of some 15 teachers who were interested in linking in with the Project's embryonic national network of development groups. Of the teachers who came forward all were from multicultural schools but there was a balanced representation of junior and infant experience, including three head teachers. Most of the teachers would have described themselves as monolingual English-speakers.

The method of working

The method of working was that, through a combination of monthly meetings for the whole group and more frequent sub-group activities, teachers, under the guidance of their co-ordinator (an advisory teacher for multicultural education), would explore classroom strategies for acknowledging the linguistic accomplishments of their pupils. It was this focus on the pragmatic question of what might be achieved by the non-bilingual teacher in the ordinary classroom that was the underlying purpose among the groups. But more specific areas of interest were identified according to how teachers perceived the priorities of their own schools and classrooms. It was through the sub-group structure that teachers were able to examine particular themes in depth whilst the full-group sessions were the opportunity to pool experience, monitor developments and draw upon the collective advice of the group as a whole.

Areas of interest

Early discussions with the teachers highlighted several areas of interest which individuals or small groups wished to pursue further. One group was anxious to devise approaches for investigating children's patterns of language use. What is the value of using a questionnaire to find out about primary children's language experiences? How might one set about constructing a questionnaire which children in the 7 – 11 age group would be able to complete for themselves? Would it be more in keeping with primary school practice to encourage children to work in groups to discuss and investigate each other's experience of language? These were some of the questions the group set out to examine. Another group wanted to look into the contribution that bilingual parents could make to a school policy of supporting children's bilingualism. The starting point was a small survey of how local schools had been able to draw on parents' skills. The next step was to try out strategies that seemed most suited to the group members' own classrooms: for instance, involving parents as bilingual aides in cookery or as mother tongue storytellers. Indeed stories in the mother tongue were of sufficient interest to merit a separate group investigation. It is very often through stories that teachers feel most confident about acknowledging children's home languages, but there is very little advice available on how to set about doing this in a way that is beneficial to the children and rewarding to the parent or any other bilingual aide who might be available. A final group took the curriculum as its focus, examining the opportunities that particular curricular areas might be able to offer for valuing the languages of the classroom. Mathematics was found to yield a surprising number of starting points.

Supporting the teachers

From the start all the teachers involved felt themselves to be working in new and unfamiliar territory. Nobody could claim a great deal of experience in the field and, in some cases, self-doubt was controlled only by a conviction that it was educationally sound and socially desirable that children's knowledge of their home languages be granted more recognition in mainstream education. For a long time mother tongue maintenance had been seen as the responsibility of the child's community and whilst nobody in the group wished to deny the importance of community efforts it was generally felt that raising the status of minority languages, in the eyes of all children, would call for a more concerted response from class teachers than hitherto had been the case. But to do this effectively teachers would need support, especially if they found themselves working in isolation from others. Support was provided in several ways. Certainly the group members had much to offer each other and they became quite accomplished at doing so. The group co-ordinator was able to provide a great deal of back-up on a day-to-day basis through visiting teachers *in situ,* assisting in the classroom, discussing problems as they arose and offering advice on resources. It was also interesting to see just how much moral support teachers were able to derive from being part of a national network of similar groupings working under the umbrella of the Project. This latter dimension was to grow in significance as time went on and it became possible to establish channels of communication and opportunities for contact between the different LEA groupings.

Writing up

From the start the teachers had been encouraged to keep diaries of their work as it developed. In some cases these amounted to little more than regular jottings – descriptions of the ground covered and the day-to-day issues that arose. In other cases more detailed accounts were kept along with greater discussion and in-depth evaluation. All, however, were to prove indispensable when the time came for the teachers to submit case study accounts of their initiatives to the Project team for inclusion in a pilot version of the eventual teachers' guide.

Obtaining more case study accounts than can be accommodated in a proposed publication is frequently a difficulty for a Project that draws its raw material from reports written by teachers themselves. It is understandable that teachers who have taken the trouble to write up their classroom initiatives should expect that they appear in some form in the Project's published outcomes. Unfortunately this is not always possible and so embarrassment can result. In this particular authority the problem was forestalled through the group co-ordinator having the foresight to propose a local publication to complement the handbook which would be published by the Project nationally. Thus all the teachers involved knew that their case studies would reach a wider audience than their own immediate group.

A next step

Opportunity for continued collaboration between the authority and the project came when the draft handbook 'Teaching in the Multilingual Classroom' entered its trial period (April–December 1983). Apart from enabling those members of the original development group who were still interested to maintain their involvement, this trial phase was seen by the authority as a means of extending the work into a wider circle of teachers. As a result the local trial group came to comprise a small nucleus of the original participants as well as a larger group whose experience of supporting children's bilingualism was at an earlier stage of development.

There was no doubt that having access to a handbook of classroom strategies, albeit in pilot form, provided these more recently arrived colleagues with the starting point and impetus for which they had been waiting.

The group evolved an organizational structure similar to that which had existed during the development stage, only this time the plenary meetings were able to call upon the additional support of those colleagues whose experience in the field now extended back for almost two years and who were well familiar with the approaches being promoted and the thinking underlying them.

Teachers were asked to maintain diary records of their work with children and towards the end of the trial period these formed the basis for more detailed written accounts, some of which were incorporated into a revised version of the handbook. But, again, a substantial amount of material was produced and so a further small local publication became viable.

Dissemination

From the outset the team had stressed to all participating teachers that involvement with the Project should be seen as a two-way relationship. Certainly the Project's materials would gain through being able to reflect the collective advice and wisdom of practising teachers. And, equally, it was hoped that the teachers and their authorities would benefit through being helped towards a greater understanding of how the normal classroom can give more recognition to children's out-of-school language experiences. That this principle could succeed was illustrated well in Leicestershire. The Project gained in many ways, not least through the wealth of classroom experience provided by the participating teachers. Similarly for the authority, as there now became available a local core of teachers who were able to demonstrate to others how linguistic diversity could become a resource and a reality in the classroom. Needless to say, the authority was not tardy in taking full advantage of this. Materials and pupils' work emanating from the local group were put on display at the Centre for Multicultural Education. Individual teachers were asked to contribute to courses and their classrooms were visited by colleagues from other schools.

Unfortunately, there is an ever-present danger that initiatives resulting from teachers' involvement in a major Project might be just short-term and have little lasting impact on classroom practice or school policy. Mindful of this the Multicultural Adviser sought to exploit contact with the Project as a springboard for more schools to review their language curricula in order to take greater account of linguistic diversity. Two local dissemination conferences were therefore held at which invited heads and class teachers heard about the work of the Project. These were later followed up in greater depth through workshop activities. At the time of writing the workshop developments are firmly established, following the now familiar two-tier structure whereby a group of teachers attend regular meetings to report on and discuss initiatives that are underway in their schools.

Outcomes

Other outcomes are less tangible but, for the teachers concerned, no less significant. Many describe how the atmosphere in their classrooms has changed through children feeling more confident about discussing their home languages and sharing their experience with others. Children's enthusiasm is frequently commented upon as is their interest in languages other than their own. Teachers talk almost apologetically about how much, in the past, they had unwittingly devalued children's own linguistic and cultural resources through having failed to acknowledge them fully within the classroom. And, now that the situation has changed, they report on how they have become more aware of the range of language skills that all children have to offer. Head teachers often point to the different relationship that now exists between the school, its parents and the local community and comment on how they themselves now have a more positive view of the contribution that parents can make to school life.

If questioned further, teachers would continue adding to this list, such is their enthusiasm. But above all the outcome to which they are most likely to return is that they now feel themselves to have a much deeper and more sensitive understanding of their pupils and an ability to meet the many language needs of the multilingual classroom.

Notes

1.   This is soon to be superseded by a more comprehensive statement on bilingualism and education.

2.   See the Report from the Commission to the Council on the Implementation of Directive 77/486/EEC on the Education of the Children of Migrant Workers, Brussels, 10 February 1984.

      However, direct comparison of numbers of children receiving mother tongue tuition, although unfavourable to Britain, may be misleading. Provision of mother tongue teaching in other EC countries may look impressive on paper but, since it often takes place on a withdrawal basis and may not be supported by a general multicultural-multilingual ethos, may actually increase divisions rather than accord children's bilingualism a genuine place within the curriculum.

3.   i.e. the recognition that pupils' language needs extend beyond the traditional emphasis on teaching English and furthermore that their language experiences should be acknowledged and capitalized upon as part of an overall strategy for language development in the multicultural context.

4.   The Swann Report (op. cit.) in fact recommended that responsibility for ethnic minority community languages should rest with LEA advisers for modern languages.

Chapter 3
Developing Materials

Background

The need for appropriate materials

A major problem faced by teachers concerned with supporting children's mother tongues is the lack of appropriate materials, and it was principally to meet this need that the Mother Tongue Project was set up.

The majority of available books and resources come from abroad and are generally unsuitable for children living in Britain, either because the culture they reflect is different from that experienced by children living in this country or because the age group for which they are intended does not match the peer group here, who are growing up in an English dominant environment which does not offer the same opportunities for the development of the mother tongue. Often the subject matter and content of the books are also inappropriate or irrelevant to children living in Britain. Another problem is the poor quality of many of the books, especially when compared with the materials pupils use in their mainstream classrooms.

These difficulties have been increasingly recognized by workers in the field. In a series of regional consultations with local minority community groups carried out by the Commission for Racial Equality (CRE, 1982), lack of appropriate resources was repeatedly cited as a major difficulty and available texts were criticized as being out of date and inappropriate. The recent HMI Inquiry (DES, 1984) referred to the 'problem for certain languages' of the availability of materials of quality appropriate to the needs of the pupils'. It went on to say, 'This problem, where it exists, is compounded by teachers' uncertainty about what is available in this country and how to acquire stocks'. The Swann Report (*Education for All*, 1985) likewise draws attention to the inadequacy of many of the available materials for teaching community languages, often produced abroad and ill-suited to the needs of pupils growing up here. Other critics have pointed out that existing materials are frequently unsuitable for the different levels of language competence encountered among pupils in a typical mother tongue class and many endorse sexist and racist attitudes which teachers find unacceptable.

Underlying principles

During recent years, materials have begun to be produced to meet these shortcomings and a number of underlying principles and objectives have been evolving which form part of the context within which the Project's materials were developed. A first consideration is, of course, the purpose of the mother tongue teaching, which will have a considerable bearing on the nature of the materials required. Taylor (1985) identifies four aims: to facilitate school reception; for language development and literacy; as media of instruction; and as languages available to all pupils including English speakers.

Materials developed for transitional purposes will obviously have a very different linguistic content from those intended for maintaining and developing the mother tongue. Likewise, where languages are to be used as media of instruction, this assumes a basic competence in the languages concerned and will not be relevant to pupils who speak only English or a different mother tongue.

A further issue, and one which was of crucial importance to the Project, is the situation in which the materials are to be used. Materials developed for use in mainstream schools may well be different from those required in community mother tongue schools. For example, production of language-neutral materials, as suggested by Ure (1981) may help reduce costs and be of use in mainstream classrooms where children speak a range of languages, but will be of little value in community-run classes where the focus is on a specific language and culture. Another consideration is the context within which the mother tongue teaching is taking place. The CRE (1982), for example, stresses the importance of teaching mother tongue in a bilingual context, whilst Tosi (1984) refers to the process of 'mother tongue development in the context of second language learning' and suggests the following factors need to be taken into account when developing materials: linguistic factors, the curriculum objectives, the age group, the learner's initial competence, skills and subjects to be taught and the cultural component.

Whatever the purpose the materials are intended to support or the situation in which they will be used, certain common principles are coming to be shared by those responsible for selecting and developing resources for supporting community languages. Some of these have already been implied in the preceding section: that materials should reflect the lives of children growing up in Britain, that they should be of a quality equal to those to be found in mainstream classrooms although home produced materials have their place, they should be appropriate to both the language competence and age of the pupils concerned, and they should avoid sexist or racist stereotypes. Other principles highlight the importance of reflecting pupils' interests, as well as paying attention to linguistic correctness, and point to the need to take account of changes in languages; for example, where an English word has become more widely used than the original community language equivalent.

In addition, many teachers are conscious of the importance of avoiding segregation of pupils by giving them different treatment, including the provision of special materials, and stress the need for integration with mainstream classwork, either through topic work, which can be developed in parallel using different languages, or through shared materials where possible. Variety in subject matter and type of material is also a common requirement and this includes the provision of resources for stimulating and developing oracy as well as literacy in the mother tongue. There is an increasing trend to learn from the experiences of teachers from a range of language specialisms such as mother tongue teachers, ESL teachers, modern languages teachers and English teachers, so as to produce materials which take account of the many approaches to developing language.

Most of the principles described above relate to materials for use by mother tongue teachers but they are also relevant to teachers who may not be bilingual themselves but who work in multilingual classrooms and are looking for materials to use with bilingual pupils in their classes. Although these teachers may not be able to understand the language content of the materials they select, similar principles apply, except that teachers in mainstream classes may teach children from many different linguistic and cultural backgrounds and may wish to ensure a balanced representation of those backgrounds in the materials chosen. They may also wish to choose materials which show a multicultural or world view rather than promote a particular cultural perspective, although this need not be at the expense of accuracy or prevent the different cultures from being allowed to speak for themselves.

Some recent developments

As the importance of mother tongue support for ethnic minority children has been more widely recognized and teachers have become aware of the lack of suitable resources, attempts have been made to produce materials specially designed for children growing up in Britain in an environment which offers limited opportunities for them to develop their mother tongue. In some cases materials have been developed by enterprising individuals or groups, such as the series 'Learn Your Language'[1] produced by a Bengali teacher in London, or the set of six Panjabi primers plus various other materials in Panjabi and Urdu prepared by the Panjabi Language Development Board.[2] With increasing frequency local education authorities have become conscious of the dearth of suitable materials and have attempted to rectify the situation by producing their own. Some of the more well known include the Minority Groups Support Services in Coventry, which has devised a number of books in various community languages, the Newham Women's Group, which has produced bilingual story books, the London Borough of Waltham Forest, which has prepared four story books in parallel bilingual text, and Wolverhampton local education authority, which has developed a graded series of work books in four languages. As well as materials in various community languages there are examples of resources for teachers in multilingual classrooms who wish to explore linguistic diversity, such as *The Languages Book*[3], published by the ILEA English Centre, and *Language Variation in the Multicultural Classroom*[4], based on material prepared for a DES regional course.

Although many LEAs have been busy producing materials in and for community languages, their involvement is variable. In Tsow's national survey of LEAs in 1980 – 2 (Tsow, 1983), of 41 per cent of LEAs responding 28 per cent had in hand arrangements for developing mother tongue teaching materials, largely in Hindi and Urdu, mostly at either end of the age range i.e. for beginners or at A-level. Rathbone and Graham (1983), writing about resources for bilingual nursery assistants, commented, 'The availability of material varied between local authorities and reflected local concern about multicultural education in general and the role of bilingual speakers in particular'.

Even where local authorities are enthusiastic and committed to supporting community languages, they do not often have the facilities for producing bulk copies or the mechanisms for marketing them and as a result materials which could have widespread use remain unheard of or unobtainable.

One way of overcoming these problems is to aim for national publication. A few educational publishers are now venturing into the community languages field and producing books with bilingual texts or even single language texts, covering a range of minority languages. For example, Methuen's 'Terraced House' books are available in Bengali, Panjabi, Turkish and Urdu, and a series of books published by Nelson for mother tongue learners in Australia under the title 'City Kids' is obtainable in Greek, Italian, Turkish and English. Books with bilingual texts produced by other publishers include Bodley Head's 'Ezra Jack Keats' books, some of which are available in Turkish, Gujarati, Greek and Spanish, all with parallel texts; Franklin Watts' 'People' series, which includes a bilingual Urdu/English and Gujarati/English version of the

'Nurse' book; and Ladybird's 'Talkabout' books which have accompanying notes in English and Arabic.

Large-scale projects

Another solution is to set up large-scale projects which both stimulate curriculum development and generally result in published and nationally available materials. Baker (1984) describes two models for curriculum development in minority languages and although he is writing about the Welsh situation, much of what he says is applicable to the development of materials for ethnic minorities in England. The first model he describes is the project model which is a large-scale development where a team of curriculum researchers is funded to produce materials. Although this is an effective means of developing materials, the economics of the exercise (production and publication of materials is too costly) and the possibility that the materials developed so carefully at national level may not be taken up locally must be borne in mind. The difficulties commonly faced by all centre-periphery models of curriculum development will also apply; viz. they have to operate within the limits of a conservative school system, the materials often become distorted once they are in the classroom, and they are non-democratic.

Baker, therefore, prefers the second model, which he terms the 'action research and development' model, as more appropriate for the production of materials for ethnic minorities because it can represent different geographical and linguistic variations. In this model teachers have responsibility for development and evaluation of the materials but whilst this may ensure more appropriate materials, tailor made for particular classes, these cannot by virtue of their limited audience be anything other than hand-made and therefore cannot meet the 'need for glossy, attractive publications, books with professionally produced artwork and sequential schemes of work' which Baker himself identifies. His solution is to recommend centralized oversight and concern combined with action research.

In England where the audience for individual minority language materials is much smaller (Baker refers to '*only* 550 primary schools' as the potential users [my italics]), the issues are more acute. For example, the Project's booklet *Supporting Children's Bilingualism* describes several teacher-generated activities (p.33) in materials development but points out that these sorts of initiative can only achieve limited impact unless they have substantial financial and structural support.

Several large-scale projects have in fact been set up to develop materials in minority languages. The Bilingual Education Project for Secondary School Pupils set up in 1977 at CUES in the ILEA produced

packs of materials in eight languages. Another project, also located at
CUES, was the Bilingual Under Fives Project (BUF) which was
established in 1978 and which aimed to provide opportunities for children
to communicate through their home language and resulted in some
published materials. The Reading Materials for Minority Groups Project
(1982–5) at Middlesex Polytechnic has collected taped or written stories
from linguistic communities and compiled bilingual story books in a range
of mother tongues and English. The first title was published by Middlesex
Polytechnic and six more titles were published by Luzac, with further
titles in the pipeline. And, of course, a final example is the Mother
Tongue Project itself which was the first project set up to develop a range
of curricular resources for supporting the home languages of primary age
children.

The Mother Tongue Project

In Chapter 1 some of the distinctive features of the Mother Tongue
Project compared with its sister projects on the continent were described.
These were its national perspective, its focus on materials development,
its potential audience of all teachers whether bilingual or otherwise
working with ethnic minority children, and its intention to span both the
maintained and voluntary sectors in education in order to reach as many
teachers and children as possible.

In addition, there were two further aspects of the Project that need
stressing at the outset, particularly in the context of the other large scale
projects outlined above. In the first place, it was a project aimed at
primary aged children although in some respects it was not possible to
draw an arbitrary cut-off point at either end of the primary school age
range. And in the second place, its overall intention was to provide
exemplar materials rather than either a complete language course or
teachers' manuals. These features will be discussed in greater detail later
in the chapter.

The Project had three main interlinked aims, two involving bilingual
teachers and one, non-bilingual teachers, or, as the Project came to call
this target audience, teachers in the multilingual classroom. The first aim
was to develop resources for bilingual teachers of Bengali and Greek.

These two languages offer interesting linguistic contrasts and
similarities which parallel those that exist among other community
languages. From the Project's point of view this was an important
consideration because the intention was always to build upon the
experience of materials development in Bengali and Greek so as to
provide a framework for preparing materials which would accommodate
other language groups and thus enable bilingual teachers generally to

adopt a common approach and share in each other's work. This became known as the transferability dimension and was the Project's second aim.

A third and equally significant strand of the Project involved working with teachers in multilingual primary schools. Many of these teachers wish to respond to the language diversity in their classrooms but are not sure how to accomplish this so the Project's third aim was to develop guidelines on appropriate materials and strategies for use in multilingual classrooms.

The Project's aims were realized through a fairly conventional model of curriculum development.[5] Although the EC provided the bulk of the funding, the Schools Council (and later the SCDC) was responsible for the Project's overall management and it consequently followed the usual Schools Council model of curriculum development. After an initial orientation period when the Project team familiarized themselves with developments in the field, teacher groups were set up to develop teaching materials and strategies. These were then tried out in schools, revised and prepared for publication. There was also a small allowance of time for dissemination of the outcomes of the Project.

Each strand of the Project's work reflected this general pattern but followed a different chronological sequence, as shown in Chart 3.1.

Bengali and Greek materials

AIMS

As we saw earlier, Bengali and Greek were chosen as the two target languages for the development of mother tongue teaching materials due to the size of their populations in London and because they present linguistic contrasts and similarities which parallel those found in other community languages. Materials developed for Bengali- and Greek-speaking teachers, it was therefore felt, might have potential applications for teachers of other community languages.

A second aim was to provide resources for community languages teachers wherever they might be, which seemed initially straightforward, but ran into difficulties as it became clear that the two situations (mainstream and community mother tongue schools[7]) in which bilingual teachers operated were quite different, with differing needs and expectations. However, sufficient resources were not available to develop two parallel sets of materials and so a single set of materials was produced.

Another objective was 'to enable children to achieve literacy and further extend their competence in their mother tongue' through 'direct mother tongue teaching'. Whilst this was already an ongoing process in community mother tongue schools it was a very new concept in mainstream primary schools. Teachers were becoming familiar with the

Chart 3.1 Project timetable May 1981 – August 1985

	1981	1982	1983	1984	1985
Bengali and Greek materials	Initial orientation Setting up of development groups of Bengali-speaking and Greek-speaking teachers in the London area Development of common framework for materials		Trials finish Summer 1983 Materials revised Leaflet Guides and Teachers' Guide produced Video of trial classrooms made	Dissemination of materials through local and national meetings Publication of materials	Published materials sold through the Project office
Strategies for teachers in multilingual classrooms	Identification of local development groups of teachers in LEAs around the country	Setting up of local development groups National Seminar for LEA policy makers. Outcome: Project publication *Supporting Children's Bilingualism* Development of Children's Language Project Cards National Seminar for members of local development groups. Outcome: draft handbook 'Teaching in the multilingual classroom'	Trials of draft handbook in 22 LEAs Trials of Children's Language Project Cards in 9 schools Revision of the cards	Handbook revised and prepared for publication Children's Language Project Cards published	Handbook published under the title *All Our Languages*

	1981	1982	1983	1984	1985
Transferability	Exploration of the concept of transferability within the two target languages: Bengali and Greek		LEA trials of selected items of Bengali and Greek materials adapted for other languages e.g. Gujarati, Panjabi and Urdu	Revised draft handbook produced	Third draft handbook produced and prepared for publication. In addition, a guide to text-free materials: 'Look – No Words!' prepared for publication
	Adaptation and trials of Bengali and Greek materials with Portuguese children		Seminar for teachers of 10 community languages. Outcome: draft handbook	8 local teacher groups set up to develop materials in a range of other community languages	Work of local teacher groups culminates in a final exhibition
Evaluation	Formative evaluation. Outcome: 'Initial Evaluation Report'	Evaluation of Bengali and Greek materials trials through data collection, school visits, questionnaires, meetings, pupil tests and case studies		Evaluation Report	Report of Project's work produced by the evaluator and prepared for publication under the provisional title: 'Community Languages in the Primary School'
	Evaluation procedures for trials of Bengali and Greek materials planned	Handbook for teachers in multilingual classrooms – evaluation procedures for trials drawn up	Evaluation of trials of handbook for teachers in multilingual classrooms – through visits, meetings, forms		
			Evaluation of Children's Language Project trials		
			Evaluation of trials of selected items of Bengali/Greek materials adapted for other languages		

use of the child's mother tongue in order to ease transition into school but the idea of teaching children their mother tongue as part of the normal curriculum was and remains a controversial topic. This difference in objectives between mainstream and community mother tongue schools made the development of a single pack of materials a difficult task.

A final objective was to produce 'exemplars of pupil materials' rather than a comprehensive language and literacy course. Realizing the impossibility of developing such a course within the limitations of time and personnel allocated to the Project, it was decided instead to aim for pupil materials together with teachers' guides, which would be designed to meet specific needs or fill gaps in existing materials as identified by the teachers concerned. However, many teachers in the two types of schools found the term 'exemplar' difficult to understand and accept, and there were very different expectations as to the type of materials which the Project should produce.

Teachers in community mother tongue schools are concerned to teach the children who attend their classes literacy in the mother tongue together with an understanding of their culture. They have limited time and generally poor facilities available and therefore look for materials which can help them to do this in the quickest and most effective way. Bilingual teachers in mainstream schools on the other hand must fit in with the aims and approaches of primary school pedagogy. Current thinking sees the acquisition of language taking place as part of the overall development of the child rather than as a specific area of the curriculum. A comprehensive language course would therefore have little place in modern primary school classrooms (see also p.74).

PRINCIPLES UNDERLYING THE MATERIALS

Within this broad framework of aims the Project team sought to develop principles on which to base the materials bearing in mind the two target audiences. In attempting to produce materials suitable for use in mainstream schools, the team selected a multicultural setting as crucial to reflect the reality of children's lives in modern Britain. Illustrations were designed to show multicultural settings and stories were frequently written in such a way as to incorporate children from different cultural backgrounds.

Another way in which the team sought to uphold principles long cherished in mainstream schools was to stress the importance of oral as well as written language development at all stages of learning, a principle particularly important when working with ethnic minority children who are struggling to maintain their languages in the face of the overriding dominance of English. The team produced text-free materials specifically

designed to support oral language development and they emphasize
both in the teachers' guides and in the notes accompanying the materials,
the importance of using these materials not only in the pre-literacy stage,
but at all levels of language development (with appropriate adaptations).
Variety and flexibility were considered important guiding precepts
throughout the materials and a sufficient range of items was provided so
that teachers could choose a picture, story or activity to fit in with their
overall plans for a particular lesson whilst at the same time flexibility was
incorporated to allow the materials to be used in different ways with
varying age groups and abilities. This was not only useful in mainstream
schools where a wide variety of approaches and activities may be followed
but also in community mother tongue schools where teachers may be
faced with a complex array of pupils and situations.

The Project also sought to meet the needs and aspirations of teachers in
community mother tongue schools. Particularly important was a concern
for the special features of the individual languages and the influence this
might have on the materials produced. The Project likewise aimed to
accommodate community school interests through representing the
children's home cultures in the materials. At the beginning of the Project
there was more stress on representing the life of the child growing up here
in a multicultural society but strong pressure from both ethnic minority
communities for specific cultural elements associated with the child's
home language to be incorporated led to their being built into the
materials during the later production stages.

Another important principle adopted by the Project concerned the
place accorded to non-standard and standard versions of the languages in
question. The majority of both Bengali and Greek speakers in this
country do not speak the standard form of their languages but a
non-standard variety. In the case of Bengali the variety most widely
spoken is Sylheti as most of the speakers in Britain come from the Sylhet
region of Bangladesh. In the case of Greek most settlers in this country
come from Cyprus and speak the Cypriot dialect. Since the majority have
been here some time they now speak what is termed the 'London Cypriot
dialect' (see *Greek Outside Greece* (Roussou, 1984)). Parents, however,
are generally anxious that children should acquire literacy in the standard
form and the Project therefore decided that all the written materials
should be in the standard form of the language but that teachers should
accept the child's oral use of different varieties of the language without
criticism, gradually leading the child towards oral and written competence
in the standard form of the language.

Finally, two other more general principles also helped guide the
development of the Bengali and Greek materials. First, the team aimed to
produce materials free from racial or national stereotypes and which did
not present fixed views of male and female roles. Particular care was

trations and text to ensure equality of status between
and girls, together with their adult counterparts, were
in a range of situations and roles. Secondly, the
erability was a constant underlying thread to the Bengali
als and was also borne in mind when considering other
who might eventually benefit from the work of the
Project. This will be explored in greater depth in the following section.

CONTENT OF THE MATERIALS

Bearing in mind these aims and principles, the Project team decided on a three-pronged approach. First they would review existing materials in the target languages so that their usefulness and relevance could be appraised and also so that valuable time would not be spent on reproducing what was already available. At the same time gaps in provision and areas of need could be identified. Secondly, they would study materials currently in use for teaching English as a mother tongue and particularly those developed for English as a Second Language (ESL) learners. This again would avoid re-inventing the wheel and would be a means of bridging the gap between mainstream and community schools. Thirdly, the team would produce a core of original materials designed to meet the needs identified during the first process.

A great deal of time was spent gathering, reviewing, classifying and colour-coding existing materials in the home languages and, in addition, during the trials of the materials developed by the Project, each teacher was given a Book Box containing a selection of available books from the home country (amounting to the value of £10), to use as and when appropriate.

The review of existing materials for teaching English as a mother tongue was more limited, given the amount of material available. Greater use was made of the underlying teaching methodology and strategies than of the materials themselves, although one particular item which was adapted and incorporated into the trial pack of materials is of special interest: an adaptation of the 'Breakthrough to Literacy' sentence maker[8] together with translations of a number of the 'Breakthrough' readers. This adaptation was particularly popular with teachers in mainstream schools whilst teachers in community mother tongue schools, who were less familiar with the methodology underlying the 'Breakthrough' approach and faced a number of practical constraints including time and space, were more critical of the technique, preferring to stick to tried and tested methods which they felt were more suitable to their particular languages and situations. However, sufficient interest was generated for the 'Breakthrough' publishers, Longman, to ask the Project to produce final revised versions of the trial sentence makers in Bengali and Greek for possible publication (Urdu, Hindi, Panjabi, and Gujarati versions are also being considered).

Thirdly the Project developed a core of original materials which were intended to supplement or be supplemented by other mother tongue materials produced in Britain, in the countries of origin and in other parts of the world where Bengali and Greek are spoken, so as to provide sufficient resources for the full 5 – 11 age range. The materials were designed to cater for children at three stages of language development:

Stage I   children who may have some knowledge of the oral forms of the language, in some cases fluent in the Cypriot or Sylheti variations, for example

Stage II   children who are at the beginning literacy level with some need to extend the oral language, especially in its standard form

Stage III   children who have acquired a foundation of literacy skills in their mother tongue and who are ready to be introduced to some more advanced aspects of reading

In the event it transpired that nearly all the Bengali-speaking children were already fluent in the oral language although this was generally in the Sylheti dialect and therefore needed materials which would develop their spoken competence, and pre-reading materials which would introduce them to the early stages of literacy. There was little demand for materials for more advanced readers.

In the case of the children of Greek origin, most had lived in this country for some time and many had actually been born here; the majority of the children involved in the trials in fact spoke Greek as their second language. In addition, there was already a selection of good quality materials produced in Greece and Cyprus although not entirely relevant for children living here. There was, therefore, a greater need for materials to stimulate the children's oracy in Greek as a second language and for materials to extend literacy to be used with older children who had been attending mother tongue classes for some time and could already read Greek.

The core materials developed by the Project consist of six components: three text-free units, principally designed to stimulate oracy; two units designed to be used when introducing literacy in the mother tongue; and a final unit consisting of teachers' handbooks for teaching Bengali and Greek as mother tongues in Britain. A summary of these materials and the stages at which they can be used is reproduced in Chart 3.2.

Chart 3.2   Guide to Bengali and Greek materials[9]

Item Stage	Stage I	Stage II	Stage III
Project materials			
TEXT-FREE MATERIALS			
Picture Cards	←———————————————————→		
Outline Story Book	←———————————————————→		
Figurines	←———————————————→		
LITERACY MATERIALS			
Primary Readers		←———————→	
Workbooks	←———————→		
Story Readers	←———————————————————→		
Existing materials in English			
'Breakthrough to Literacy' materials	←———————————→		
'Terraced House' books	←———————————→		
'Language for Learning' materials	←———————————————————→		
Existing materials in Bengali and Greek			
Books from Bangladesh, Cyprus, Greece and India	←———————————————————→		
			——————→
Teachers' handbooks			
Teaching Bengali as a Mother Tongue in Britain	←———————————————————→		
Teaching Greek as a Mother Tongue in Britain	←———————————————————→		

RESPONSE TO THE MATERIALS

As indicated earlier, the Project decided at the outset to develop a single set of materials for use in both mainstream and community mother tongue schools. This meant that the Project was able to benefit from the experience of teachers in both types of schools and produce materials reflecting current approaches in mainstream schools, whilst at the same time taking into account the specific experience which only members of the minority language communities themselves could provide.

An example of taking the best from both sides is to be found in the phonic materials. In both Bengali and Greek there is a regular relationship between the sounds and the way they are written and the Project decided to capitalize on the regular structure of the languages by employing a phonic approach to literacy acquisition, as preferred by the Bengali- and Greek-speaking teachers, but at the same time combining it with the whole sentence approach favoured in mainstream schools. Thus the Bengali readers, for example, introduce the sounds of the language in a systematic way, but at the same time using a story as a medium. But some of the mainstream teachers still reacted to the phonic element in the materials in a critical way and many community teachers were not entirely satisfied either, considering the materials to be insufficiently based on phonic principles.

Whilst mainstream teachers were generally happy with the multicultural settings adopted in the materials, community teachers were not; both Greek-speaking and, particularly, Bengali-speaking teachers felt the materials did not sufficiently reflect the culture of the children's countries of origin. Other criticisms voiced by both community and mainstream teachers concerned the quality of the materials, although most were based on the draft versions which were of course inferior to the final products. The Project team decided early on to produce black and white illustrations both for reasons of cost and for flexibility. However, both mainstream and community teachers felt that black and white illustrations compared unfavourably with the full colour books available to children in their mainstream schools and often in their community classes[10], and indeed might even be considered unintentionally racist as an example of the provision of poor materials for less important pupils, although many teachers were won over to the idea of black and white illustrations as they realized their potential during the trials. Interestingly, it was the teachers rather than the children who voiced the complaints. Observation of the children showed that they did not necessarily go straight for the highly coloured materials; in fact they often picked up the Project's materials with interest, especially if they noticed words written in their own language.

The Project's European evaluators made several comments concerning the quality of the materials which are of relevance here. They pointed out that full colour books have to do with the interest of publishing firms who need to catch the eye of adults if they are to make sales. In fact, many of the criteria teachers use when demanding full colour materials are not supported by significant evidence. Furthermore, an expensive comprehensive publication would actually reduce competition and might therefore inhibit simultaneous and future development. At present, since it is not possible to judge future developments in the field of mother tongue teaching, the materials might quickly become outdated, especially as the patterns of language use in minority communities tend to change rapidly. They concluded that an active approach to minority languages (rather similar to Baker's 'action research and development' model) was preferable, with which the Project's materials fit quite well, enabling children to appropriate the materials and thus appropriate their languages.

Perhaps a more serious criticism was that the materials were dull and unexciting. Comments such as 'the mother tongue materials are okay, but not riveting' and 'the materials are not very exciting to look at' certainly cropped up but at the same time it was accepted that this was the first time a concerted attempt had been made to produce materials for mother tongue teaching in both mainstream and community schools. One critic commented that they were 'mediocre but pioneering in the circumstances' and another that it is easy to criticize what someone else has done but that a very real service had been done by providing materials of this nature at all and this in itself was an achievement.

Indeed, some commentators felt that an important model for materials development had been provided which would have far reaching effects. One organizer of teachers in East London stated 'People have seen the model and know it is possible'. He went on to explain that many teachers had been influenced by the Project's work and the standards of materials produced by teachers had been raised as a result. Another teacher organizer from the Portuguese Consulate, with whom the Project worked fairly closely, felt that the model of materials development was original and would be useful for all languages as a basis for development. In fact, the materials package was used in this way in the final year of the Project's work.

There was less general agreement over the methodology implicit in the Project's materials. Many mainstream teachers felt that the materials were too language-based, in contrast to current thinking which views language development as taking place across the curriculum rather than in a defined subject area. However, the Project team had to bear in mind that the materials would be used in community mother tongue schools where direct language teaching is commonly a major aim. Several of the teacher groups who worked with the Project in the final year, using the published materials as a springboard for their own work, in fact moved beyond a narrow language approach to include topic-based materials. And a close adviser to the Project felt that, although the materials were little different from many materials in mainstream schools, apart from the language content, they were new to community mother tongue teachers and were useful as a starting point for their own development work. Several advisory staff indeed felt that the methodology of the materials was sound and showed 'what can be done without moving outside primary practice'.

In conclusion, it must be said that any new materials are bound to attract both supporters and critics. These materials faced particular difficulties in that they were designed for a new and controversial area of the curriculum and that they raised issues far beyond the materials themselves and far beyond the scope of the Project to deal with. It is clear from the Project's experience that materials are not independent variables but that they depend on both the situation in which they are to be used and on the individual teachers who use them.

Even the best materials may not be very effective if used in situations where back-up resources are poor or other staff are not very supportive. One of the strengths of the Project's materials is in fact their in-built flexibility which enables them to be easily adapted to most situations. Teachers who do not understand the principles on which they are based or who are not familiar with the methodology underlying them or who for whatever reason feel hostile to them will not be able to make the best use of them. On the other hand, enthusiastic and capable teachers accustomed to the approaches embodied in these materials can find them extremely valuable. It is significant that the teachers who worked closely with the Project and are therefore familiar with the underlying approaches have been amongst the most eager to obtain the published versions of the materials.

The only true test of any materials is whether and in what way teachers actually use them. This will not be apparent until the materials have been on the market for sufficient time for an appraisal to be made. This is not within the scope of this book, although some early indications are given in the final chapter.

Transferability of materials

The idea of transferring materials developed in one language to another is relatively new in Britain. In some overseas countries, where multilingualism and recognition of minority languages has been an established tradition, attempts to provide materials which have applications across several languages have been made. In Australia at La

Trobe University a multilingual model has been developed which 'works on the assumption that knowledge learned in one language can be subsequently expressed with relative ease in another' (Rado, 1977). Sets of parallel texts in several languages for the 10–14 age group were devised so that students of varying ethnic language skills could learn planned subject matter and concepts using their language or languages according to *personal choice,* an important principle of the project. Thus a class of students of different language backgrounds with differing skills in these languages can all work on the same topic using whichever language they prefer and even switch from one language to another during the course of the work.

In Britain, work of a similar nature for secondary age pupils has also been undertaken. The Bilingual Education Project produced a pack of 40 bilingual work cards in eight different languages (including English) for use in the mainstream classroom. The cards, which cover topics regularly included in the humanities areas of the curriculum, are for students literate in their first language and who are in the process of learning English as a second (or third) language. Again the principle of personal choice is stressed and the cards are seen as a resource for the whole class as well as an optional resource for individual pupils. But previously the concept of transferability had not been applied to primary age pupils.

As a first step to exploring the concept of transferability, the Project team aimed to investigate the extent to which the two target languages could work together on the development of materials which could be transferred from one language to the other. Could a story written in Bengali be translated and used by Greek-speaking pupils? Could pictures designed to stimulate spoken language in Greek also be used to stimulate oracy in Bengali? If teachers of these two languages could work together and develop parallel materials then other minority language groups might also benefit from the methods, strategies and materials developed, thus helping a greater range of communities and avoiding unnecessary repetition of work. Early meetings of the two development groups of teachers – one group of Bengali-speaking teachers and one group of Greek-speaking teachers – were held jointly so that both language groups could explore shared issues and methods. Working closely with the central team, a common approach was developed. Shared principles, such as the importance of reflecting the multicultural society in which mother tongue teaching takes place, and an urban British setting were agreed on.

Beyond these general principles a common framework of materials development was used and parallel materials developed in the following way. Each teacher group selected an item from the planned materials package and developed it in their language. Then a translated version of it was passed to the other development group for adaptation into their language. For example, one of the readers, 'Andy's Toothache', was

written first in Greek. It was then translated into English and given to the
Bengali-speaking teachers' group who translated and adapted it into
Bengali. All the items were developed in this way.

The text-free materials were tackled differently. Each group chose a
picture theme or sequence story and worked out the details required for
an illustration and the accompanying teachers' notes. Then they
exchanged pictures and stories for comments.

But when it came to developing literacy materials, the two language
groups largely went their own ways although they still retained the general
principles and common framework. Each group developed similar types
of pre-reading activities – such as matching exercises, letter and word
recognition, tasks and language games – but the specific nature of each
language prescribed certain differences such as the order of introduction
of letters or the emphasis on particular sound combinations. The phonic
readers and workbooks also shared certain features, which at the same
time distinguished them from traditional phonic materials, such as the
setting, based on the lives of children growing up in Britain, and the
presentation in story form. But again the needs of the pupils and the
nature of each language dictated certain differences in approach. For
example, Greek speakers in this country frequently speak Greek as a
second language and English as a first language. In addition, there are
similarities and confusions between the English and Greek script. On the
other hand the present generation of Bengali speakers usually learn
Bengali (or Sylheti) as their first language, with English as their second
language. The Bengali script is totally different from the English script
and confusion does not therefore arise. But an additional factor which
Bengali (Sylheti) speakers have to master when acquiring literacy is the
change of vowel symbols when combined with consonants, a feature of the
syllabary system which does not occur in English.

Overall, then, transferability between Bengali and Greek was mainly in
the areas of shared ideas, parallel forms of materials and methodology.
Although at the outset there was a strong feeling that Bengali and Greek
could not be taught in the same way due to the specificity of each
language, a common set of teacher's notes for the materials was devised
although additional sections in each book proved to be necessary to
accommodate the particular features of each language.

With the experience of the two different languages working together,
the Project then attempted to extend the transferability concept beyond
the two target languages. A selection of the materials was sent to 11 LEAs
who had expressed interest in adapting them for use with children
speaking a number of ethnic minority languages: Gujarati, Hindi,
Malayalam, Panjabi and Urdu. The Project also formed links with the
Portuguese Consulate whose teachers were able to assess the usefulness of
the materials for Portuguese-speaking children. Finally, a two-day

seminar was held, attended by community teachers from ten different language groups, in order to discuss common issues and to formulate guidelines on materials development in community languages. A number of key issues were discussed: aims of mother tongue teaching, materials, resources, teaching methods, classroom management, and liaison. It transpired that teachers from these very different language communities had much more in common than separated them; even a possible division between bilingual teachers of European languages and those of South Asian languages, due to their differing kinds of financial support and provision of teachers, turned out to be largely irrelevant.

Both these efforts to explore transferability further with other languages, however, pointed to the importance of personal contact and support if materials such as those developed by the Project are to be used by teachers from other ethnic minority groups. Many community teachers have little acquaintance with the organization and philosophy of the British education system and face enormous difficulties arising from isolation, poor facilities and lack of suitable materials. The provision of materials and teachers' guides is not in itself sufficient for teachers to be able to capitalize on the experiences of a project such as the Mother Tongue Project.

Initial and in-service training at both national and local level, improved facilities and increased liaison between teachers and schools, both mainstream and community, are necessary if the outcomes of the Project are to be fully utilized.

DISCUSSION

People who came into contact with the Project responded to the transferability aspect in different ways. Some felt it was a way of getting things on the cheap, a sop to all the languages which could not be involved directly with the Project's work. Others viewed it in a more favourable light as a way of benefiting all languages based on the experience of two languages. A few were frankly astonished by the idea and found it a curious notion. One of the Project's advisers commented that in retrospect it was an 'admirable idea' but a naïve assumption that materials could be directly transferable from one language to another. Many participants at the Colloquium held in March 1984 to present the Project and its outcomes to colleagues in Europe had not come across the concept before and found both the idea and its application difficult to comprehend.

Most of the comments turned on the extent to which it is possible to transfer materials from one language to another, given that languages are very culture bound and that relevant materials are very much dependent on the language and situation for which they are intended. Many of the Bengali- and Greek-speaking teachers with whom the Project worked found the transferability aspect of the Project restricting, necessitating, as it did, a good deal of translation of the materials from one language to another which was not only time consuming but also resulted in a loss to the quality of the language. It also meant that much of the specific culture associated with a particular language was diluted, which caused dissatisfaction not only amongst teachers working with the Project but within the wider community as well.

Many teachers and advisers working with the Project nevertheless felt the experience was worthwhile and that the notion of transferability has some future. Teacher groups working with the Project in its final year have been able to explore the concept of transferability with a wider range of languages. They have found they have many shared difficulties and that the solution to their problems may lie in co-operating with others in similar situations to develop joint or parallel approaches. In this way the wheel may not need to be completely reinvented afresh each time and the resulting materials and strategies developed may be all the richer for the broader experience.

Although direct translation from one language to another may be neither possible nor desirable, the Project team has been surprised by the extent to which different language groups have been able to utilize the Bengali and Greek materials, even the phonic elements which they had thought specific to the languages for which they were designed. It has proved possible for other South Asian languages to use the basic model and in some instances to do little more than translate and adapt the book in question. In some cases the adaptation may be minimal, such as a simple changing of the names of the main characters. In other cases more drastic alterations may be necessary, such as the redrawing of some of the illustrations to suit the particular cultural needs of another religion or language, or a completely different setting for a story, although the basic idea may be retained. Occasionally whole blocks of the materials may prove unsuitable, such as the Picture Cards, thought by several Portuguese teachers to be too multicultural. Even in these cases where common pupil materials may prove impossible, the model of the materials, plus the guidelines for teachers, may be useful for curriculum developers.

Beyond the practical advantages to be gained from the exchange of materials between different language groups, it has certainly been the experience of the Project, especially in the final year when the concept of transferability has been further explored with a wider range of languages, that bringing together teachers from many diverse language groups has been a stimulating exercise for all concerned. It has been very reassuring for community teachers to discover that other teachers from quite dissimilar backgrounds face common problems. But over and above this teachers have found that they have learned from the different language communities with whom they have come into contact and have been able to bring to bear the experiences of others on the development of materials for their particular pupils.

This is a new area of co-operation and development. At present there are still many unanswered questions about the nature and limitations of the transferability of materials developed for one language to another. At the time of writing the material outcomes of this part of the Project are still in preparation.[11] Despite the problems and setbacks encountered by the Project, a feeling of optimism remains at the end of the day. It appears to be possible to adapt a story into another language if care is taken to ensure that its essential vitality and its cultural relevance are retained. In addition, the exchange of ideas between teachers from different community backgrounds and the development of joint methodologies and shared strategies makes the experience worthwhile. Only the future will show the true limitation of transferability; for the present it seems worthy of serious consideration and further exploration.

Materials for teachers in multilingual classrooms

In many ways this part of the Project's work was the most straightforward and least problematic. Possibly this was largely due to it being in many respects a logical development of work already going on in schools. Chapter 1 described the gradual shift from the idea of assimilation of immigrants, through the concept of integration to the development in recent years of educational principles based on cultural pluralism and to some extent anti-racism. These principles envisage a society where there is room for each culture to thrive and contribute in a positive way to the society as a whole of which it is an integral part. However, whilst children's cultures have increasingly received acknowledgement in the classroom, their languages have been accorded less attention. Gradually teachers have become more aware that recognizing children's cultures necessarily involves taking account of the languages they speak and giving them a place in the classroom.

When the Mother Tongue Project was set up it was, as Chapter 1 points out, in the light of increasing information about the numbers of children in school whose home language was not English. Whilst the UK response to the educational needs of bilingual children had focused so far almost entirely on their English language learning needs, the authors of the Project felt it was also necessary to develop an appropriate response to the other dimension of these children's linguistic identity, their mother tongues.

The mother tongue materials described earlier are intended to support the development and extension of the mother tongue skills of bilingual children, but without the involvement of teachers in the multilingual classroom to provide a hospitable context in which this can take place, such materials would have a limited effect. It was regarded as important to shift the climate of opinion and to show schools how to respond to the linguistic diversity that was increasingly being identified. Not only would this aspect of the Project emphasize the need to take mother tongue seriously but it would also aim to produce detailed practical guidelines for primary school teachers, illustrating:

how schools can respond positively to the mother tongues of their pupils; how pupils' mother tongue skills can be brought to the service of the general learning and how school and home and community can collaborate to support and extend the children's mother tongue competence [taken from the Project's original brief].

Three separate publications (see Appendix C for details of publications) were developed by the Project in order to provide teachers and educators with materials for supporting home languages in the classroom, each intended for a slightly different audience. The first, entitled *Supporting Children's Bilingualism,* is a booklet designed for policy makers and was the outcome of a national seminar held by the Project. It discusses a variety of topics from an LEA perspective, including reasons for supporting children's bilingualism, the need for LEA and school policies, resources and in-service implications.

The second is aimed more specifically at teachers and is a handbook of strategies for use principally in the multilingual classroom, called *All Our Languages.* It was extensively trialled in 22 LEAs and is composed of case study accounts of classroom initiatives, examples of children's work and an overall linking commentary.

The third publication is a resource for children to use. Entitled *The Children's Language Project,* it was developed jointly with another London based European community-funded project, the Language Information Network Co-ordination (LINC) and consists of a set of four activity cards, plus teacher's notes, for pupils to use to learn more about the diversity of languages around them.

Stemming from the basic principle of wishing to build on all the experiences children bring to school, including cultural and linguistic experiences, these materials try to provide guidance on both the rationale for supporting pupils' home languages in learning, and strategies for putting this into practice in the classroom. According positive recognition to ethnic minority children's mother tongues is seen to have important educational benefits not only for the bilingual children themselves but for the whole class. Monolingual children can gain greater awareness of language and language diversity and an increased respect for the speakers of these languages. Wherever possible it was intended that *all* children should be involved rather than bilingual children should be considered odd or different from the rest of the class. Indeed, the developers of the materials felt that it was an opportunity not only to recognize ethnic minority languages but also a chance to acknowledge the diversity within English itself including dialects, regional variations and different accents.

Responding to linguistic diversity in the classroom may involve new methods of working with bilingual colleagues, older students and parents, as well as pupils. Particular sensitivity will need to be exercised when collaborating with these groups of people and understanding shown to colleagues who may find some of the strategies difficult or threatening to carry out.

There was no doubt in the minds of most people connected with the Project that this aspect of its work was the most successful. Not only did it fit in well with work already being done in many parts of the country but it stimulated teachers in other areas of the country which had only just begun to consider the bilingualism of their pupils. For many it was a justification of work they had been doing for years; for others it provided the rationale and the means for developing new curriculum initiatives in this area. It has contributed to the general debate about the diversity of languages including English; it has helped provide teacher trainers with models for looking at different languages; and it has supplied teachers in the classroom with practical strategies for responding to the needs of their bilingual pupils. It has also contributed to the changing climate of opinion in schools and helped provide a more hospitable context for mother tongue teaching.

Summary and conclusion

This chapter has looked at the development of materials for mother tongue teaching and support. At the outset we saw that there is a major shortage of appropriate materials both for bilingual mother tongue teachers and non-bilingual teachers who wish to support children's home languages in the classroom, whether this be in mainstream or community organized schools. At the same time, a number of principles on which such materials should be based have been evolving and various programmes undertaken by individuals, LEAs and large-scale projects have increased the range of suitable resources.

The Mother Tongue Project is an example of a large-scale project set up both to stimulate curriculum development and to produce published resources for supporting community languages in the primary school. It aimed to develop materials for three target audiences: bilingual Bengali- and Greek-speaking teachers and children, bilingual teachers of other community languages using the experience gained from working with Bengali- and Greek-speaking teachers, and teachers in multilingual classrooms who wish to support their pupils' bilingualism. This turned out to be a complex and demanding task due to the controversial and innovative nature of the work and the educational, political and emotional overtones associated with it.

In the event, the development of materials for Bengali- and Greek-speaking teachers was the most exacting and contentious of the three undertakings, due mainly to the often conflicting needs and demands of the dual audience of teachers in mainstream and community-organized classes. The Project chose to develop a single set of materials intended for use by both sets of teachers but in doing so had to make compromises which sometimes suited neither. Many mainstream teachers found the materials dull and in some respects old-fashioned (in their phonic aspects), and felt their black and white format forced invidious comparisons with other materials available in the classroom. Community mother tongue teachers, on the other hand, felt their specific linguistic and cultural requirements had not been sufficiently taken into account due to the pressure to make the materials acceptable to mainstream teachers. Nevertheless the Project succeeded in producing a surprisingly wide range of materials suitable for children of different ages and linguistic competence and based on broadly accepted principles shared by both mainstream and community school teachers. Indeed the Project showed that it was possible to develop materials which incorporate these principles and which can be used in different situations, thus helping to bring together teachers from very different backgrounds.

In addition, by producing a model of materials development for community languages based on the experiences of transferability between Bengali and Greek, the Project has enabled teachers to capitalize on its work and develop materials in a range of other community languages. Despite the revolutionary nature of the transferability concept, it was possible to show that teachers from many different language backgrounds can work together drawing upon each other's materials and experiences to produce a wider range of resources than would be possible if they had each worked on their own.

The production of materials for teachers in multicultural classrooms was a more straightforward enterprise. The principle of acknowledging the languages children bring with them into the classroom as a logical extension of multicultural education has been gradually gaining ground and many teachers have prepared materials and strategies to support children's bilingualism. The Project was able to extend and develop these to form a package of materials aimed at three of the groups concerned with this work: policy-makers, teachers and children.

The field of mother tongue teaching, as well as being relatively new, is highly charged educationally, politically and emotionally. The Project was set up at a time of changing attitudes and illustrates some of the complexities involved in developing materials for supporting community languages.

Despite facing a number of ideological and practical problems the Project was able to produce a wide selection of materials for both bilingual and non-bilingual teachers. At the same time it was instrumental in stimulating and informing curriculum development in the field of mother tongue teaching and support. In a rapidly developing area of the curriculum it is difficult to say how relevant and useful these outcomes will be in the long term but it is clear that the Project has made a substantial contribution to the range of resources available to all teachers wishing to support their pupils' mother tongues.

Notes

1. Buksh, Z. *Learn Your Language,* available from Z. Buksh, 38 Umfreville Road, London N4.
2. Panjabi Language Development Board, 2 St. Annes Close, Handsworth Wood, Birmingham B20 1BS.
3. *The Languages Book* by Mike Raleigh, Jane Miller and Michael Simons, ILEA English Centre, 1981.
4. *Language Variation in the Multicultural Classroom* by Viv Edwards, Centre for the Teaching of Reading, University of Reading, School of Education, 1982.
5. i.e. it was modelled largely on the Research, Development and Diffusion model of curriculum development. See Macdonald and Walker (1976) for a discussion of different models of curriculum development.
6. Developed jointly by the Mother Tongue Project and another European Commission-funded project, the Language Information Network Co-ordination (LINC).
7. A mother tongue teacher may work with bilingual children in one of two situations. She may work as a bilingual teacher in state (mainstream) schools, usually on a peripatetic basis but occasionally as a full-time teacher assigned to one particular school, whose major duties are concerned with supporting children's mother tongues, normally by working alongside the mainstream teacher or by withdrawing children for special tuition. Or she may work as a voluntary teacher in community-organized schools or classes, usually run after school or at weekends. Sometimes the same teacher may work concurrently in both situations. Community-organized schools where mother tongue teaching takes place are generally referred to as 'community mother tongue schools' in this book to avoid confusion with the term 'community schools' used in some areas of the country to mean mainstream

schools intended as centres for the local community to use by day and night for a variety of recreational/educational purposes.

8. 'Breakthrough to Literacy' (1971, Longman for the Schools Council). This approach to learning to read is based on the language experience method. There is a Sentence Maker containing the most commonly used words and children can choose the words they wish to use and make simple sentences with them. Once they can read simple words there is an attractive graded scrics of small readers for them to tackle.

9. See Appendix C for details of publications.

10. Especially in the case of some European minority languages where good quality full colour books are available free from the home country.

11. Two outcomes are planned: (a) 'Working With Many Languages' – a handbook for community teachers, dealing with the issues they share and the problems they face when developing materials and organizing classes; (b) 'Look – No Words' – a guide to text-free materials for teachers of any language.

Chapter 4
Working with Schools

We saw in Chapter 3 that the Project's main aims were to develop resources for two groups of teachers: bilingual mother tongue teachers and non-bilingual teachers in the multilingual classroom. This involved working with two separate groups of schools in which the two sets of resources, those for teachers in multilingual classrooms on the one hand, and those for bilingual Bengali- and Greek-speaking pupils on the other hand, were tried out. Both undertakings raised a number of ideological, educational and organizational issues which are of concern to all schools and teachers working in this field.

Teachers in multilingual classrooms[1]

Background

In Chapter 1 we saw that there were three major phases in the development of the multicultural curriculum: assimilation, integration and pluralism.

These shifting educational philosophies were accompanied by changes in the curriculum, reflecting current thinking. During the assimilationist phase the major emphasis was on ensuring that immigrant children learned to speak English as quickly and efficiently as possible. Educational provision took the form of teaching English as a second language to children whose mother tongue was not English. In 1967 the Schools Council Working Paper 13 (Schools Council, 1967) reported findings of a national survey undertaken in 1965, and documented different types of LEA provision including withdrawal classes, remedial groups, full-time and most commonly part-time arrangements, generally aimed at increased proficiency in English.

At about the same time further stimulus for development came from the Local Government Act 1966 (Section 11) and the Urban Aid Programme 1968 which provided funds for both projects and increased staffing levels in schools with high immigrant concentrations. During this phase, as a more integrationist philosophy was becoming accepted, the teaching of English as a second language remained important but at the same time there was an increasing awareness of the need to find out more about minority cultures. This led to an upsurge of courses for teachers on the backgrounds of immigrant children, which often placed undue emphasis on certain aspects such as arranged marriages, the racial differences between groups, low self-esteem and under achievement, which were frequently seen by the majority community in a negative light. Children's home languages were often perceived as inadequate for school purposes and contributing to their inability to benefit from schooling. Indeed, many teachers stressed the importance of immigrant children not only speaking English at school but also at home if they wished to make adequate progress. There was little conception that their mother tongues might be a source of untapped skills and a potentially valuable learning resource.

It was not until the mid to late seventies that the role of community languages in the education of children from non-English-speaking backgrounds received any recognition. Taylor (1985) writes:

> The Bullock Report, together with the CILT conference in 1976 and the EC Directive, were catalysts for a change of emphasis in approaches to E2L teaching, giving greater consideration to the role which a pupil's first language played in the acquisition of English.

A curriculum development project at the time, the Bilingual Under Fives Project (see p.64), which began in 1978, aimed to promote positive attitudes towards children's home languages in the nursery classroom and to provide young bilingual children with opportunities to communicate using their mother tongues at school. A project for secondary age pupils, World in a City, also undertook to provide opportunities for older children to use their home languages at school by producing a pack of bilingual work cards in eight different languages (including English) for use in the mainstream classroom.

The Schools Council has also been instrumental in promoting the recognition and use of children's home languages in the classroom. A number of recent projects, whilst focusing primarily on English language, acknowledge the role played by the children's first languages, such as Language for Learning (1981 – 3), concerned with language development across the curriculum for primary and secondary pupils especially those whose first languages are not English (Ackland, 1985; Smythe, 1985); Communication Skills (1981–3), developing materials for teachers of junior children whose language is not English; and Classroom Research on Teaching Language Skills in Multicultural Schools (1981–2) (Craig and Cox, 1983). A particularly relevant project, Language in the Multicultural Primary School (1981–3), explored the linguistic resources and cultural experiences of E2L learners, devising strategies to meet their language development needs based on the premise that their contributions could be an enriching experience for all children. In addition the Schools Council has funded several projects more directly concerned with mother tongue support and provision (see Chapter 1, p.24).

In the survey undertaken by the Schools Council (Tansley and Craft, 1984) a substantial increase in support for children's mother tongues by non-bilingual mainstream teachers was recorded. LEAs taking part in the survey (92) found it difficult to identify and quantify this kind of work and frequently made comments such as 'there is a fair amount of this in the Borough but we don't keep a list', or referred to teams of bilingual liaison workers or multicultural staff. Nevertheless, 28 LEAs reported that teachers in multilingual classrooms in their areas were already trying to provide support and encouragement for their pupils' languages, and another three said that a limited amount of work was going on in their area. Significantly, the biggest group of LEAs reporting work in this area directly referred to assisting with the trials of the Project's handbook. Tansley and Craft (op. cit.) conclude:

> In the past support of children's home languages has tended to form part of the recognition accorded to their culture generally. Gradually, individual teachers have become involved in supporting their children's languages more directly and many LEAs have become aware of the importance of this aspect of multiculturalism.

Although there has been a gradually increasing awareness and acknowledgement of the role of community languages in the education of young bilingual children, progress should not be exaggerated. Craft and Atkins (1983) found in their survey of initial and in-service teacher training courses in ethnic minority community languages that the emphasis was on training students in the techniques of E2L teaching rather than acknowledgement of mother tongue teaching. Teachers on these courses are more likely to be made aware of language differences than hitherto but less likely to be trained to offer language support.

In schools, developments are still at an early stage and provision tends to be haphazard. It is clear that a number of diverse initiatives such as ESL teachers, bilingual aides, mother tongue teachers and bilingual nursery assistants have all sprung up in an attempt to meet the challenge of multilingualism, but very often bypassing the mainstream non-bilingual teacher who is central to the whole enterprise. As a result teachers sometimes feel that supporting home languages is not a role for them, but is the concern of one of these specialists.

The Project's work

Many teachers feel uncertain about children's home languages and their place in the classroom and may also feel unsure about the role of these various 'specialists'. Indeed, during the trials of the handbook, there was some uncertainty on the part of the recipients as to whether the booklet was intended for use by mainstream class teachers or mother tongue teachers. In some cases the booklet was given to E2L teachers who were perceived as being responsible for ethnic minority children's language development, rather than the class teacher. Yet many teachers are beginning to review their classroom practice and feel that it is educationally sound and socially desirable that they should be giving more place to linguistic diversity, although they may be uncertain of how to approach this within the curriculum. At the same time they need reassurance that they are doing the right thing; the handbook was developed in order to meet these twin needs of pedagogical rationale and practical strategies. It was hoped that as a part of this process, teachers' attitudes would also be changed to provide a more receptive climate to the use of the mother tongue in school.

Since widespread provision of mother tongue teaching is unlikely in the foreseeable future it is all the more important that the class teacher should be the central linchpin in supporting home languages, linking not only bilingual teachers and helpers within the mainstream school, but also providing a focus and point of contact with community mother tongue teachers and indeed parents and other representatives of ethnic minority communities; in other words all those concerned with the education of bilingual children. At the same time they are in a position to act as the link between bilingual children and their indigenous, non-bilingual peers and ensure that linguistic diversity is a resource shared by the whole class. At a time when investigation and acknowledgement of the range of linguistic repertoires possessed by all children, including monolingual children, has achieved prominence with the recognition of English accents and dialects, this is particularly apposite.

Altogether some 22 LEAs and over 150 teachers took part in the trials. Two main organizational options were chosen for trialling purposes; the involvement of whole schools including all the staff, or individual teachers who were generally participants in a local group of teachers working with the Project. In this way it was hoped to ascertain whether the handbook could be used equally by individual teachers as well as through a co-operative approach by a whole school. Schools and teachers were chosen to represent the range of situations in which the handbook might eventually be used. Thus both infant and junior schools and even some nursery classes participated, some with high proportions of bilingual pupils and others with low proportions. In some classes one language other than English was predominant, whilst in others many languages were represented. Finally, teachers and schools were selected to represent those who had experience of this kind of work before and those who were new to the field. In the event about one-third of the teachers who took part had not done any of this kind of work before and a further substantial proportion had only done a little.

Issues

During the trials a number of issues were encountered which have long-term implications for teachers in the multilingual classroom. Many teachers were anxious to take account of all the languages in their classrooms and where there were many this presented practical difficulties. Others felt that the involvement of parents and community representatives, whilst laudable, created many difficulties which needed sensitive handling especially if teachers were not to feel under pressure. Teachers also felt threatened by the perceived lack of control they experienced when handling materials and languages they could not actually understand. The handbook called for collaborative methods of working which some teachers still feel to be an innovatory step.

Other issues concerned the reactions of parents both from ethnic minority communities and the indigenous population. Some minority community parents were ambivalent or even hostile to the idea of their children's home languages being used at school. They expressed concern that the children were missing English or other lessons and were instead being singled out as different from others. On the other hand, the majority of ethnic minority parents were delighted that their community languages were being acknowledged at school and even asked whether tuition in their mother tongues might be a possibility. Few parents from the indigenous population reacted although there were one or two adverse responses. Obviously the conclusion to be drawn is that all the parents need to be informed and involved before such initiatives are undertaken and the reasons for them fully explained. When this is done schools testify to the bonus of improved home/school relationships and greater involvement of parents in school life.

Another issue which arose during the course of the trials was the extent to which the proposed strategies could be considered tokenistic. Some teachers felt that a few isolated activities such as labelling objects in minority community languages, might show support for community languages at a superficial level but not go any deeper. They felt, and the same argument also applies to the involvement of parents, that the whole school should be concerned with according recognition to bilingualism and that it should be part of the normal curriculum rather than an isolated activity.

This last point highlights a general conclusion from the Project's experiences of trialling the handbook of strategies for teachers in multilingual classrooms – the importance of whole school involvement. The Project worked with both whole schools and individual teachers and found, not surprisingly, that the handbook was taken up most enthusiastically and was likely to have the greatest impact where the whole staff of a school was involved in the work. In this situation the innovation was likely to have a reverberating effect throughout the school with each classroom affecting the others. Where a teacher was alone in a school trialling the handbook and did not have the support of the head, it was difficult to have an impact beyond the individual classroom and the effects of the work were limited. Nevertheless, teachers taking part in the trials felt it was better for an individual, enthusiastic teacher to use the handbook than a whole staff who were uninterested or opposed to the idea. Furthermore, isolated teachers were delighted to have in their hands some practical ideas of what they could do to support children's home languages where they felt personally committed to the idea.

Beyond the individual school the support of the LEA was vital. It was not enough for individual schools or teachers to be enthusiastic if they did not have the full support of their authority, and, in fact, several co-ordinators had to withdraw or reduce their commitment to the Project's trials for this reason.

Obviously, the most successful way of introducing an innovation such as this is to work through an LEA which has a committed policy on bilingualism and the role of the mother tongue in schools, and to work in schools where the whole staff espouse such a policy and is prepared and eager to put it into practice. Before this can be done a great deal of free and frank discussion at LEA and school level involving parents and local community needs to take place, to ensure that all the parties are fully aware of the issues and implications of what is involved and are in support of the measures to be taken to put the objectives into practice.

Mother tongue teaching

Background

Although support for children's home languages in the classroom theoretically and pedagogically precedes mother tongue teaching in the classroom, this order has not always been followed in practice. Often individual teachers, schools or LEA advisers have felt the need to take account of children's mother tongues through enlisting the help of bilingual parents, aides or assistants or, increasingly, mother tongue teachers rather than through turning to mainstream teachers. As we have seen, until relatively recently mother tongue teaching was sustained largely within the communities themselves, but some teaching of community languages has now begun in state schools.

Generally speaking provision within mainstream schools for mother tongue teaching is concentrated at either end of the age range. There is growing support for the transitional model[2] at the nursery and lower infants level, and increasing support for home languages within the option system at secondary school level, with little coverage in the middle years.

Where nursery schools have introduced mother tongue teaching, bilingual teachers work alongside the class teacher, using their language as a means of instruction so that children learn through their mother tongue. These mother tongue teachers are often members of a peripatetic team serving several schools. In some schools there may be a mother tongue speaker on the staff and sometimes parents and other members of the community also help to support the mother tongue. Similar support exists for reception-age children and young infants but for older infants there is less mother tongue provision. What teaching there is usually takes place within normal classes, although in some cases groups are taught in a separate room. The mother tongue is usually used to help general learning, but there are some examples of special literacy help being given to children.

For junior-aged children, teaching is usually organized in groups in a separate room although there may be a combination of work in such groups and within normal classes. The emphasis is more on teaching the mother tongue as a language in its own right and less on using it as a medium for general learning. Teachers are usually visiting teachers but they are sometimes members of the school staff. In general there is less involvement of community helpers with this age range. At junior level mother tongue classes are now sometimes provided on an 'extended day' basis. Lessons may be held at lunchtimes, or begin before the end of the school day but continue afterwards. The focus tends to be on developing literacy skills, although there may be some attention to culture maintenance. Occasionally there is teaching of other subjects, such as history or geography, in the mother tongue. Teachers are generally from the local community although some may be supplied by Embassies and High Commissions and others may be paid by the LEA. Usually teachers move from school to school or class to class to teach but in some cases may be attached to one school only. More and more, as mother tongue teaching moves into the mainstream, an increasing number of teachers work in both environments which can involve clashes of educational philosophy, curriculum organization and teaching style. This information is presented in chart form on page 94.

Whereas provision for mother tongue teaching and support is a relatively recent development in mainstream schools, as we saw in Chapter 1, the ethnic minority communities have been running classes for many years to cater for the linguistic, cultural and religious needs of their children. Provision is extremely varied, both as regards organization of the teaching and the purpose of the classes. Teachers come from many different backgrounds, and range from those with no formal qualifications or training to those who have training and qualifications obtained in this country. The classes may be arranged and financed by any one of a number of people, from parents and individual teachers to community groups or consulates. They are generally held after school or at weekends and take place in a variety of venues, from hired rooms or school buildings to parents' homes. This information is summarized in Chart 4.2.

Provision within community-run classes generally starts at the infant level and continues right through to examination level for secondary age pupils. However, there is very little provision for nursery age children and some communities do not provide classes for children until they are aged about seven. The way in which classes are organized depends on space, numbers of pupils and teachers, and on the amount of finance available, but four models are common. There may be classes for children of the same age; for children of the same language stage; for children of two or three ages; or classes which include a wide range of ages and language levels. Frequently, the focus in community-run classes is on literacy in the mother tongue, with cultural maintenance as an inseparable part of this, but there may also be some teaching of history, geography and other subjects through the medium of the mother tongue. In some schools there is a strong emphasis on the teaching of religion.

The materials developed by the Project were designed to be of use in both mainstream and community school settings. The identification of community mother tongue schools and classes in which to trial the materials was not too difficult as classes for both Bengali-and Greek-speaking children were well established. Care was taken to select a representative sample of schools to include both religious and non-religious (or less religious) schools, differing social class intakes, a range of language

Chart 4.1   Provision for mother tongue teaching for primary age children in Britain

Age range	In state schools	Mixture of state and community provision	In community classes
	During normal school hours	Extended day (lunchtimes or last part of normal school hours and continuing into after school hours)	Evenings and weekends

Nursery/reception (3 – 5 year-olds)	– as part of the normal class
	– mother tongue used in play, mathematics, story time
	– teachers
	  – school staff
	  – visiting teachers
	  – community helpers		

Infants (5 – 7 year-olds)	– usually part of the normal class but sometimes in a separate room – mother tongue used for general learning but some literacy teaching – teachers – as above		– usually as part of mixed age classes – focus on literacy but some cultural maintenance – teachers usually from the 'community' – some LEA support – often use LEA premises

Juniors (7 – 11 year-olds)	– usually in a separate room, sometimes a mixture of both
	– focus mainly on language teaching with more stress on literacy
	– teachers
	  – school staff
	  – visiting teachers
	  – fewer community helpers
		– focus on literacy but some cultural maintenance through stories, music, dance
		– teachers
		  – visiting teachers
		  – teachers employed by the community
		  – LEA after school schemes
			– usually in mixed age classes
			– strong literacy emphasis but some teaching of history, music, dance, religion
			– teachers from the 'community' (some LEA support)
			– often use LEA premises

Chart 4.2 Organization of mother tongue teaching in community-run classes

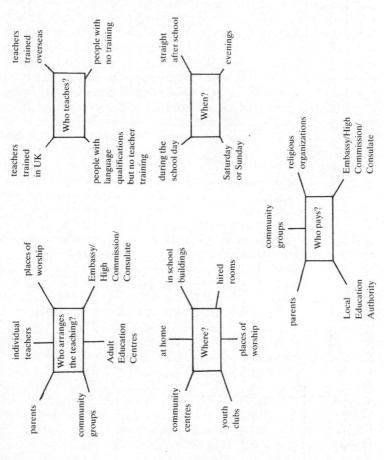

backgrounds (in particular to include both mainland Greek and Cypriot origin children in the case of Greek, and Bangladeshi and West Bengali origin children in the case of Bengali) and teachers who might mirror the possible target audience for the materials, i.e. qualified and unqualified.

Although there were sufficient classes available for a choice to be made, there were some problems in locating schools and teachers who were prepared to trial the materials. Some schools were suspicious of both the materials and the Schools Council and felt uncertain about the real intentions of the trials. Others had a busy schedule with a fixed syllabus to follow and felt reluctant to give up some of their time to trying out new materials whose value was actually the subject of the trials. It was difficult in some cases, even where the teacher was willing, to obtain the permission of the organizer of the school or his superior and the Project found itself on occasion to be embroiled in local community politics. Nevertheless, schools and teachers were found and trials eventually took place in seven Greek community schools and five Bengali community schools, with teachers generally fitting in the materials when they could alongside their usual materials.

In the mainstream system the situation was rather different. There was, as we have seen, little formal provision for mother tongue teaching and the concept itself was (and indeed still is) for most teachers still very new. When the time came, therefore, for trialling the materials, there were few ready made classes or teachers within the mainstream schools which could be used to pilot the resources; in fact classes had to be specifically set up and teachers provided. There was, in addition, no existing syllabus or materials either to slot into or to compare with. In all curriculum development projects both the materials produced and their underlying educational philosophy are put to the test during the trialling phase, especially if the materials are radically different or are for use in a new and controversial area of the curriculum. This was particularly true of the Mother Tongue Project; not only were the materials being tried and evaluated but the idea of mother tongue teaching itself was on trial.

Two areas in London were identified as possible trial bases: Haringey, where there are large numbers of Greek speakers, and Tower Hamlets (part of the ILEA), which has large numbers of Bengali (Sylheti) speakers. An attempt was made to include a representative selection of schools but as the schools were chosen primarily on the basis of their willingness to participate this was not always possible. In the event, it proved feasible to include both infant and junior schools, schools with differing percentages of ethnic minority pupils and schools in different areas with different social class intakes.

As the mainstream schools had no provision for the direct mother tongue teaching necessary to trial the materials, the Project team suggested three possible models of organization whereby this could be done:

1. The 'withdrawal' model, which could involve the mother tongue teacher withdrawing children from the classroom for regular sessions of mother tongue teaching;

2. The 'integrated' model, which would involve the mother tongue teacher working within the same teaching area as the class teacher and, whenever possible within the constraints of the materials, attempting to develop collaborative links, for example, by following similar topics;

3. The 'extra-curricular' model, which would be considered in schools where models 1 and 2 could not be implemented. It would involve mother tongue teaching being provided as a lunch time or after school activity.

In the event, none of the schools chose the third option but decided instead on the integrated or withdrawal models. In fact, rather more of the Greek trial schools[3] opted for the withdrawal model and rather more of the Bengali trial schools opted for the integrated model, but in many cases there was a combination of both models. In all cases the Project recommended four hours of mother tongue teaching for each school per week. This was considered the minimum period necessary to achieve anything of significance for the children, and would be likely to correspond to a similar time allowance LEAs might have in mind when considering introducing mother tongue teaching into schools, probably on a peripatetic basis. In addition, one hour's liaison time per school was suggested when the mother tongue teacher could discuss her work with the class teacher(s) with whom she was working most closely, and the rest of the staff if necessary. It was also an opportunity for the mother tongue teacher to talk to the co-ordinator and evaluator when they visited the school to see how things were going.

Not only did schools have to be located by the Project working through the two LEAs in question, in order to trial the materials developed, but in addition the team had to identify teachers who could be responsible for the classes and trial the materials. This proved no easy task as there was no ready-made pool of mother tongue teachers to draw upon. Those finally identified came from a wide range of backgrounds and funding authorities; some had been members of the development groups who helped to produce the materials whilst others were unfamiliar with the Project's work or its materials.

Only one of the Greek-speaking trial teachers was a mainstream class teacher with full English teacher training qualifications. The majority of the other teachers came from the Cyprus High Commission, two of whom, including the Greek co-ordinator, trialled the materials in mainstram schools, whilst the rest tried the materials out in the community schools. One teacher who worked in two mainstream schools was provided by the Greek Embassy whilst other teachers were amongst those who normally worked for the Greek Parents Association in community schools. One of these had graduate status but no teacher training qualifications. Finally, one teacher, who worked voluntarily in a mainstream school with reception and nursery age children, was an untrained, unqualified but enthusiastic parent.

The Bengali-speaking trial teachers covered a similar range of backgrounds although none of them had Embassy or High Commission support. All the teachers who worked in mainstream schools received payment from the Local Adult Education Institute, and those in the community schools represented various community organizations including the Bangladesh Centre, the Bangla Education and Cultural Centre, the Asian Centre (where pupils are mainly of West Bengal origin) and a mosque. Three of the Bengali-speaking teachers were mainstream class teachers although only one trialled the materials in a mainstream school, whilst the others tried them out in community schools. Several other teachers had qualifications in other subject areas and a few had teacher training qualifications gained in the home country. One teacher had no formal qualifications but a great deal of dedication.

Issues

During the school year the trials were carefully monitored by visits to the schools when classes were observed and all the staff involved (mother tongue teacher, mainstream class teacher and head teacher) were interviewed. In addition, regular evaluation meetings were held when both mother tongue teachers and mainstream staff from all the schools were invited to discuss their experiences.

Teachers and schools faced a number of problems and issues arising mainly from the innovatory nature of the exercise rather than the content of the materials themselves. This section looks in detail at these experiences, particularly as they relate to mainstream schools, where the experiment was regarded as new and controversial.

The issues can be divided into three categories for analytical purposes: ideological, educational and organizational, although they overlap in many respects.

IDEOLOGICAL ISSUES

These had mostly to do with the reasons why children's mother tongues should be supported in the curriculum, and the effect this might have on the school as a whole, and the wider community of which the school was a part. Although most of the schools which participated were, by definition, in favour of mother tongue teaching, in the sense that they had volunteered to take part, this willingness to co-operate in the trials concealed a range of attitudes and beliefs. Mother tongue teaching is a very broad term and teachers in the Project schools had different views regarding the reasons for including it in the curriculum. For many, the prime aim of mother tongue teaching was to aid transition to English and indeed some made it plain that learning English was the only priority as far as they were concerned. Others saw it as part of wider educational objectives, applicable to all children but previously denied in full to ethnic minority children, such as equality of status, self-esteem, acceptance of what children bring to school, etc. In a few cases teachers looked upon it as intrinsically valuable for the children concerned, and as a basic right. Yet again, some teachers had not thought very much about the pros and cons of mother tongue teaching and in this situation head teachers saw the Project as an opportunity to convince less eager teachers about the value of supporting children's mother tongues, albeit for largely transitional purposes.

Two of the schools felt morally obliged to take part, as they had a significant number of second language learners of English in their schools and thought they should be doing something to support these children's learning. Interestingly, both these schools declined to continue the experiment at the end of the year for different stated reasons; in one the head teacher queried whether the state system was the best place for children to learn their home language and culture and considered the teaching of English to be a priority; in the other the staff were disappointed the children had made no significant progress in English as a result of the experiment and in addition drew attention to what they perceived as shortcomings in their mother tongue teacher.

Other schools, however, were convinced by the end of the year of the value of mother tongue teaching, although there was an increasing concern for children from other language groups who had not been included in the Project. If you are going to support home languages, they argued, why just choose Greek or Bengali? In some ways they felt it was worse to pick one language than to support none.

This raised the issue of which mother tongues should be selected for attention, which led in turn to consideration of the relative status of the various community languages. Greek was perceived by many indigenous parents as having a higher status than Bengali, due probably to its prestige as a classical language and the historically lower standing of Bengali deriving from association with Britain's colonial past.

In one Greek trial school with a high intake of children from middle class, often intellectual backgrounds parents were eager for their children to join the Greek classes, whereas in some of the Bengali trial schools white parents did not see the value of their children's being exposed to Bengali language and culture. Parents of trial children were caught in a similar dilemma. Whilst most of them were delighted at the chance for their children to learn their mother tongue, others worried that their progress in English might suffer and their children might be isolated. The relative status of languages became an issue in some schools during the trial year, when teachers became aware that by withdrawing children from classes or relegating them to corners of the classroom with teachers who were obviously regarded as of lesser status and often with a poorer command of English, they were in fact helping to downgrade community languages instead of elevating them. One school realized that by calling the mother tongue teacher by her first name in front of the children she was perceived as being inferior to other teachers and they consequently took steps to ensure she was accorded the same status as the regular staff.

EDUCATIONAL ISSUES

Often ideological issues are not raised as such during curriculum innovations but tend to be converted into educational questions. One of the most common of these concerned the effect of mother tongue teaching on progress in English. Teachers frequently queried whether the children's learning of English was being hampered by their mother tongue classes, especially in the early months of the experiment when children were often having to adapt to new timetables, different teaching styles and experimental materials. By the middle of the year, however, it became clear that the children's learning of English was not being held back and teachers felt reassured. They seemed less interested, however, in the children's progress in their mother tongue, seeing the major benefits of the exercise as greater language awareness for the whole class, the acknowledgement of ethnic minority children's culture through their language, and increased confidence and motivation of minority children. Some teachers had hoped that support for the child's mother tongue might actually give a boost to English language learning and felt disappointed that this did not seem to occur. Others were pleased with the boost to overall learning that the Project seemed to give to the children involved.

Another educational question raised by teachers concerned the children not involved in the Project. They believed that accommodating mother tongue teaching in the curriculum inevitably meant separating out certain children for special provision. Some teachers felt this to be unacceptable. If a new item was to be added to the curriculum they felt it should be offered to all children, and also that all children should benefit. In some schools it was possible to include children who did not speak the languages for which the materials were designed, but in others, especially where withdrawal groups operated, it proved difficult to accommodate other children. Obviously, this is an issue that needs careful thought before mother tongue teaching is initiated in a school.

An issue that was of particular importance in the Greek trial schools related to the use of teachers funded by what are sometimes called extra-territorial agencies, i.e. Embassies or High Commissions. All the Bengali trial teachers were employed within the state education system and were, therefore, subject to the conditions of employment and code of professional conduct this entailed, but the Greek teachers employed by the Greek Embassy and Cyprus High Commission were subject to no such control and derived their codes of practice from non-governmental agencies. This caused problems of two kinds. First, teachers were apprehensive about the content of the mother tongue classes, as children were often taught outside the classroom and mainstream teachers could not in any case understand the language. They were also concerned that children might be receiving political or religious instruction. Secondly, head teachers were unhappy about the presence of teachers in their schools who were not responsible to them and over whom they had no official control. In the case of one school this did cause considerable problems with lasting repercussions.

A related issue that involved all the trial teachers was that of teaching methods. Details of the backgrounds of the trial teachers (see p.97–8) show that whilst the majority had either teacher training qualifications or academic qualifications or sometimes both, these had generally been obtained overseas. Most had little or no experience of teaching primary age children and few had experience of teaching in mainstream schools in this country. This led to a number of problems with teachers trying out the Project's materials in mainstream schools.

Most of the teachers used teaching methods which mainstream teachers perceived as traditional and old-fashioned, although they were not explicit about what they meant. Some mainstream teachers talked about 'formality'; one contrasted the mother tongue teacher's 'teacher-directed' approach with the 'discovery methods' used by the class teacher. Others referred to the mother tongue teachers' stress on reading and writing, with insufficient attention being paid to developing children's oral skills, particularly at the infant level. Some felt the mother tongue teachers were too quiet and 'retiring'. As well as references to different teaching methods, mainstream head teachers in several schools complained about the lack of discipline in the mother tongue classes and felt any teacher should be able to handle large groups or whole classes without support, and that standards should not be compromised just because teachers were mother tongue teachers. One head teacher remarked 'being a good teacher is as important as being bilingual'. Not all the mainstream teachers agreed. Some recognized that the difficult conditions in which most of the mother tongue teachers worked, including the short time allocated to each group of children, the uncertainty of their role, and the peripatetic nature of their work, as well as the constraints imposed by the trialling of the materials, were responsible for some of the problems. Others felt that traditional methods were not in any case necessarily unacceptable as no one method is right.

On the other hand, the mother tongue teachers themselves often felt their methods were particularly appropriate for teaching their languages, each of which is characterized by a regular relationship between the sounds and they way they are written, which they felt dictated certain teaching styles. One Greek-speaking teacher spoke of her method as 'analytical-synthetical' which she believed suitable for teaching Greek to children growing up here, taking into consideration the constraints of time and space. A Bengali-speaking teacher felt that with a language where there is a regular relationship between the sounds and the way they are written the signs and symbols have to be learned first. Several mother tongue teachers referred to the pressures of time which dictated a more formal method. Some of the teachers were, however, open to different methods and very ready to adjust, given the chance.

Whichever teaching method is preferred, it is important to preserve a continuity of teaching style where teachers are working alongside each other in the same room if both teachers are to work effectively. There are also good arguments for mainstream and community mother tongue teachers exploring and exchanging views about teaching approaches. But this does not necessarily mean that the adaptations of teaching methods should be all one way. Learning is a collaborative process and there is much to be gained from the two groups of teachers sharing ideas and experiences with each other.

Of course, one of the implications of the Project's experience with mother tongue teachers is the need for increased in-service and initial teacher training not only for community language teachers but also to inform mainstream class teachers about the background, problems and strengths of their community language colleagues and children. This issue is discussed more fully in the last chapter.

An educational issue which was linked in some respects to teaching methods was the question of when and how to introduce literacy in the mother tongue. There was a general feeling in the trial schools at the start of the year that children should not be burdened with learning two languages at once and should consolidate reading in one language before tackling another. This proved a suitable approach in the case of the Greek origin children who were generally second language speakers of Greek, but in the case of the Bangladeshi origin children many were actually more fluent in their mother tongue than English and it seemed appropriate that they should learn to read in both languages simultaneously, which, in fact, they did without detriment to either. Many mother tongue teachers were accustomed to teaching children to read and write by introducing them first to simple sounds (in some instances in alphabetical order), and gradually building up to words and then sentences. Mainstream schools, on the other hand, and certainly the schools in the Project's sample, tended to use the look and say approach which stresses meaning and understanding in reading and focuses on the whole sentence, only at a later stage introducing the child to the component parts. As it turned out, mainstream monolingual teachers did not find 'traditional' methods for introducing literacy in the mother tongue to be as unacceptable as the Project team had anticipated, and were quite prepared to accommodate phonic approaches, although preferably as one of a range of methods. As with other educational issues a spirit of compromise seemed to be the best solution.

ORGANIZATIONAL ISSUES

Very often the ideological or pedagogical arguments for a particular new curriculum development are long and hotly debated but it is the translation of the ideas into the practical realities of the classroom situation that decides whether or not an innovation will be adopted. After the initial meetings with schools and teachers when the rationale and possible benefits of mother tongue teaching were discussed, it was the organizational issues that caused most concern.

A major concern was the type of organizational model best suited to mother tongue teaching. Earlier in the chapter the two favoured models of organization – the withdrawal and integrated models – were described. Although at the start of the trial year the majority of the Project schools started with the integrated model, by the end of the year many had either switched to a withdrawal system or a combination of the two approaches. Many teachers felt instinctively that it was right for the mother tongue teacher to work alongside the mainstream class teacher in an integrated way. They felt that this avoided separating the bilingual children from their classmates and encouraged communication between mainstream and mother tongue teachers, as well as encouraging a sharing of experiences between the project children and the rest of the class. A mainstream class teacher commented that different languages were a 'lovely mix' in the classroom and one of the bilingual observers thought that the indigenous children benefited from seeing and hearing other languages. Teachers also felt that working together in one classroom encouraged continuity of teaching content and method and allowed collaborative work, such as the following of parallel themes in the two languages, to take place.

However, a combination of pedagogical and practical disadvantages emerged as the trial year progressed. Certain types of activity whether relatively quiet, such as reading, or noisy, such as singing a song, being carried out by one teacher might conflict with the type of activity in progress with the other teacher. Some mother tongue teachers felt that to be surrounded by a large class of children speaking English was distracting to a small group trying to hear their mother tongue being spoken. Other more practical disadvantages were aired, such as lack of space within one classroom for the mother tongue teacher to use, and the difficulty of accommodating children drawn from several different classes, possibly of various ages, in order to form a viable group.

Another serious consideration was the possibility of a mismatch in personality or teaching method between the mainstream and mother tongue teachers. Several of the mainstream teachers who took part in the trials were not used to working in an integrated fashion, and felt uneasy about sharing their room with another teacher speaking a different language and carrying out separate activities. Mother tongue teachers, on their part, had little or no experience of British primary schools and found it unnerving to be placed in a room with another teacher.

This lack of confidence and unfamiliarity with mainstream methods caused many of the mother tongue teachers to suggest a room of their own or at least a separate corner away from the rest of the class. Here they felt they could cope, away from the distractions of the class in a place which they could, in the words of one of the teachers, 'call my own'. This would also enable them to display appropriate materials and have background books in the language concerned rather than be surrounded by spoken and written English. An inherent danger of this solution, though, is that the withdrawn group will be considered inferior in some way, despite the good intentions.

Of course, many of the arguments for and against the two organizational models depend on the individual teachers concerned. In a class where the mainstream teacher is happy to share her space with a mother tongue colleague and indeed welcomes collaborative work with the mother tongue speakers, the experiment is generally successful, especially if the mother tongue teacher is accorded equal status. On the other hand, mother tongue teachers unfamiliar with mainstream schools can feel ill at ease, which may make collaboration more difficult. Even if the relationship is good and there is plenty of room in the classroom, there are likely to be occasions when both teachers may feel it is better to be in different rooms; if, for example, one is carrying out a noisy activity or the other wishes to hear children reading above the buzz of another language. By the end of the trial year a compromise had generally been reached in the trial schools, and a combination of both integrated and withdrawal classes formed. This arrangement seemed to achieve the best of both worlds and, interestingly, parallels experience with E2L teaching.

Arising partly out of the use of the integrated model of organization, also deriving from the peripatetic nature of the work, many mother tongue teachers felt they had no permanent place or secure base in the schools in which they taught. There was nowhere for them to leave their belongings, no space to display children's work and no place which children could associate with them. Mother tongue teachers not only found this inconvenient and unsettling but they also felt it reduced the status of the language they were there to teach. Like other peripatetic teachers, several of the teachers felt they were not really welcome in the schools, and could not bring themselves to ask for essential equipment such as paper, pencils or writing books. Very often this was simply due to a misunderstanding but was compounded by an invisible cultural barrier. In one school the mother tongue teacher told the evaluator that he really needed a blackboard. This request was relayed to the head who explained that she had told the teacher he could ask for anything he wanted and she would provide it. This reply was transmitted back to the teacher but he never felt able to ask directly for a blackboard and the head continued to assume that since she had not been requested for a blackboard then he didn't want one. This example serves to underline the need for continued support for mother tongue teachers if their understandable reticence, due largely to their as yet uncertain status, is to be overcome and their potential realized. It is not enough to place mother tongue teachers in schools and expect them to cope without either training or proper support.

Although each Project teacher was allocated one hour's liaison time as part of their work many were uncertain how to use this. Often, after initial meetings had been set up, mainstream teachers expected their mother tongue colleagues to take the initiative in arranging further meetings, and when they did not, liaison petered out. In other schools, formal arrangements such as attendance at staff meetings or regular fixed meetings helped to overcome problems. An initial period of familiarization, as suggested earlier, would help both mainstream and mother tongue teachers to get to know each other without the pressures imposed by teaching schedules. Often an E2L teacher can act as a bridge between mainstream staff and the mother tongue teacher. The allocated one hour for liaison did not really prove to be sufficient to ensure exchange of information about teaching plans, a necessary concomitant of collaborative work; and mother tongue teachers felt isolated despite the considerable efforts made in some schools to integrate them. Some schools and teachers suggested that a whole day's attendance by the mother tongue teacher might help overcome liaison problems, although this would not necessarily be the most suitable arrangement for language teaching, which may necessitate shorter but more regular sessions.

In fact, both mainstream and mother tongue teachers thought small doses of mother tongue teaching on several days rather than infrequent blocks were preferable. As a matter of policy, each school was allocated four hours' mother tongue teaching time, intended to be used for a single class or group, but which they chose to apportion in different ways. Whilst in some schools mother tongue teachers taught one class for two periods per week, in others their time was divided up in a much more fragmented way. Sometimes, due to pressure of numbers, a particularly acute problem in the Bengali trial schools, teachers took two groups, perhaps for two blocks of one hour each per week. In more extreme cases a teacher might see several different groups in the course of the week in order to cover all children from that ethnic minority in the school, thus allowing only a short time for each group. Added to these problems were the usual distractions afforded by break-times, school visits, PE lessons and fixed feasts. Usually these timetabling problems were discussed and resolved during the course of the year, but difficulties of a similar kind are likely to arise in any school arranging peripatetic teaching of this kind, and each school will need to work out the implications of these factors for their own situation. There was general agreement, however, that four hours' mother tongue teaching per week was sufficient for children to make reasonable progress if this time allowance was devoted to one class rather than several at a time.

Underlying the discussion of timetabling is the question of selection of children to take part in mother tongue teaching, and the accompanying consideration of the optimum size of the group. There were no difficulties of this kind with the Greek trial schools; in fact the problem tended to be to gather sufficient children to make a viable group. This created its own teething problems as the group thus formed was often composed of children from several different classes who might be of different ages. On occasions children of Greek origin whose parents did not speak Greek joined the group to make up numbers. In the Bengali trial schools, however, there were more than enough children available and selection had to be made in order that the groups did not become too large. The Project specified a top number of 12 children per group but even this proved over large as, in some instances, it constituted half the mainstream class, and in addition was difficult to handle if it contained children with widely different competencies in their mother tongue. A group of six to eight children emerged as a better size, especially if the group was working in an integrated system, but of course this is likely to involve selection problems in some schools. There is no easy answer to this question and individual schools will need to draw up their own criteria, whether based on the perceived needs of the children, their competence in English or behavioural considerations.

Both the Project and the schools were keen to encourage collaboration between the mainstream class teacher and her mother tongue colleague, but this did not always prove possible. The mother tongue teachers felt their first duty was to the Project, and they were under some pressure to trial the materials which had been developed. Sometimes this did not leave much time for collaboration with the class teacher, and there was in any case little time to plan joint or parallel activities, as the teachers were only in the school on a very part-time basis. Furthermore, many of the mother tongue teachers perceived their main task as teaching their pupils to read and write in their mother tongue, something they were accustomed to doing in their community school classes; and were not predisposed towards activities which did not lead directly to this end. Many of the mainstream teachers, although not all, would have preferred the mother tongue classes to be used to support the language across the curriculum rather than for teaching the mother tongue as a language. Despite these conflicting pressures collaboration was possible in some classrooms. Teachers found they could work together on project work, stories and mathematics and there was some exchange of cultural background.

In a sense, the question of collaboration was inextricably tied up with the role of the mother tongue teachers. Although the Project's explicit aim was to try out materials, not all the schools wished to interpret the mother tongue teacher's role in that way. Some schools felt that there was intrinsic value in children learning to read and write in their mother tongue, and that this was a right all children should have; but others preferred to look upon the mother tongue teacher as a resource for the school, to be used in whatever way the school found helpful. Indeed during the trials many of the Project's teachers were asked to undertake functions which bilingual teachers and assistants in other schools have frequently found to be part of their job, such as translating letters, interpreting for parents, and arranging cultural activities. The head of one school seemed most surprised when a mother tongue teacher did not automatically respond to her request for help with counselling although he had helped by talking to a parent.

Key variables

In an innovative and controversial area of the curriculum such as support for children's home languages it is difficult to make hard and fast judgements, since so much depends on the circumstances of individual schools, their teachers and pupils. Nevertheless, it may be helpful to identify some variables which seem to be particularly relevant when assessing the impact of mother tongue teaching, and draw some tentative conclusions.

Mother tongue teaching will obviously be more successful where teachers are in agreement as to its value. Mainstream teachers need to have the opportunity to talk through their worries and discuss the educational, ideological and organizational issues both before the work begins and as it progresses. Furthermore, it does seem to be especially important for both the head teacher and staff to concur on this issue.

Schools where the head teacher was eager but the staff not, and those where the staff was open-minded about the experiment but the head rather unconvinced, were not among the Project's successes. Mother tongue teaching, like other innovations, is more likely to take root in schools where there is plenty of staff discussion, where organization is good and where contact with parents and the wider community is successful.

The nature of the mother tongue teacher's role, the aims of her work, the expectations staff have of her, her duties and those of the rest of the teachers should be clearly spelled out if the most efficient and effective use is to be made of her time. Several schools highlighted the importance of mother tongue teachers' being committed to their role. In some cases, especially where the teacher was funded by an outside agency such as an Embassy or High Commission, as pointed out earlier, their loyalty was sometimes felt to be to the funding authority rather than the children or school with whom they were working. Even teachers who were employed by the local authority were torn between commitment to the school, the Project and loyalty to their communities. Underlying this tension, their personal attitudes to Britain and the British education system were intertwined with those of their communities.

Mainstream teachers and heads pointed to certain other aspects of the mother tongue teacher's role which they considered important. These included personal factors, such as confidence, an out-going personality and friendly manner as well as more professional qualities including relevant qualifications and teaching experience. Most of the Project's teachers had no direct experience of the British education system and many had not worked with primary-age children before. In addition, some felt less confident when speaking English than when using their mother tongue and this affected their ability to liaise and collaborate with their mainstream colleagues, undermined their confidence and had the effect of reducing their status in the eyes of the children and other teachers.

This formidable list of desired qualities serves to indicate the very high standards mainstream schools and teachers expected from their mother tongue colleagues. Many did not appreciate the very real hurdles the Project teachers had to overcome through their lack of relevant teaching experience, unfamiliarity with British primary schools and the existence of cultural barriers, many of which were perhaps intangible but deeply felt. In addition, as very part-time teachers, they were under considerable pressure to trial an ambitious range of Project materials with which they were sometimes not completely familiar, in schools and with pupils who were new to them, in just four hours per week. Partly as a result of their high expectations, mainstream teachers were sometimes disappointed, for reasons which often had nothing to do with the educational aspects of the innovation. In fairness to the mother tongue teachers, it must be said that mainstream teachers did not always give the sustained support so necessary to their new unestablished colleagues. Despite these enormous difficulties, the majority significantly advanced the cause of mother tongue teaching in British primary schools and convinced teachers that the educational benefits of mother tongue teaching outweighed the organizational complexities involved.

Counterbalancing the role and personality of the mother tongue teacher, the attitudes and expectations of the mainstream teachers and heads were crucial to the success of mother tongue teaching. Since the mainstream teachers had opted to take part in the experiment, they were, by definition, positive in their approach but even so they did not always appreciate the continual commitment and support they would be required to give. As with any teachers working alongside each other in the same classroom, complementary personality factors and teaching styles worked best. Some of the mainstream teachers felt diffident about sharing their room with another teacher whose methods and outlook might be very different from their own. The attitudes of the rest of the staff, whilst not directly influencing the mother tongue teachers' work, affected their reaction to the school as a whole. Many head teachers had hoped that the experiment would spread beyond the individual classroom to the whole school and were disappointed by its limited impact. One head attributed this to the mature age of most of her staff, suggesting that it is harder to introduce new ideas where teachers are not young enough to take them on board.

Despite the wide range of schools working with the Project, the majority of other school-based variables did not turn out to be significant in determining the success or otherwise of mother tongue teaching. There was little difference in the response from infant or junior schools, except that the lack of experience in teaching young children and the tendency for the mother tongue teachers to introduce literacy early on showed up more clearly in infant schools. The percentage of children from ethnic minority backgrounds appeared to have little effect on the experiment; schools with a smaller number of bilingual pupils (about ¼) were just as likely to be enthusiastic about supporting children's languages as those with larger number of bilingual pupils (¾). However, the latter were more likely to have already supported home languages in some way (for example by inviting mothers in to tell stories in the mother tongue or to have already started mother tongue teaching in a small way) and to show other forms of support, such as labelling in minority languages, or encouraging children to use their home languages in the classroom. Neither the age of the children in the trial groups nor the particular language concerned (Bengali or Greek) seemed to be significant factors.

Although the two languages differ in certain important respects, the attitudes of the mother tongue teachers were remarkably similar. Both, initially at least, favoured a phonically based approach to teaching reading, both stressed the importance of a cultural base to the materials, and both were under constraints of time and pressure from parents and the local community. Neither had much experience of mainstream methods, but felt their years of experience of teaching in the community were not taken sufficiently into account. Perhaps the major difference between the two language groups lay in the attitudes of the teachers and their communities to the role of mother tongue teaching. Many of the Greek-speaking teachers were employed by governmental agencies on limited contracts in Britain and did not envisage a long-term career in this country. For some their motivation in coming here was also academic, and many were enrolled on courses of study. In addition, there was a genuine anxiety within some sections of the community that their role would be taken over by quasi-governmental bodies such as the Schools Council. Many of the Bengali-speaking community also feared their role might be usurped, but, unlike the Greek-speaking teachers, they had come to Britain to stay and were therefore more inclined to go along with new developments which might be in their long-term interests.

From this account it is clear that the most significant variables to emerge during the Project's trials with mother tongue classes had to do chiefly with teachers and teacher attitudes. On the one hand, the mother tongue teacher's qualifications and teaching experience, her English language competence, her familiarity with British primary school practice, her personality and attitudes were all important factors. On the other hand, the mainstream teachers' enthusiasm and willingness to understand and accommodate sometimes conflicting approaches to education were equally vital. Added to this, the attitudes of the rest of the staff, and particularly the head teacher, to mother tongue teaching, and their expectations of what the Project's trials would achieve, all helped to contribute to their final outcome. A final example will illustrate these points.

An illustrative case study

One of the Project's mother tongue teachers worked in two schools. One was an infant school where about two-thirds of the children were from Bangladeshi Sylheti backgrounds, whilst the remainder were mainly indigenous English. Although the school acknowledged the children's cultures by mounting displays at festival times, they had done very little in the past to take account of their language background. They became interested in participating in the Project as they thought it would be a means of acknowledging the children's first language and they hoped it would stimulate their progress in acquiring English. The school was built on open plan lines and although organized loosely in age classes, children worked together in small groups on themes or particular curriculum areas. The Project teacher worked with two groups of children at a table near the mainstream classroom.

The second school was a junior mixed infant school also with a large number of Sylheti speakers of Bangladeshi origin (almost three-quarters). Here there was an enthusiastic head teacher who had been clamouring for mother tongue teaching for some time, and had actually had a part-time mother tongue teacher for a year before the Project started in her school. There was a large committed staff in this school who met frequently to discuss current issues, among them support for children's home languages. Indeed, special meetings were set up during the trial year to bring both the whole staff and mother tongue teachers together to discuss means through which both mainstream and mother tongue teachers could, in their different ways, acknowledge and use the children's mother tongue. The classes were organized into partial vertical grouping, and co-operative teaching between teachers was encouraged. The same mother tongue teacher worked with two groups of third and fourth year juniors at this school, inside their teachers' classroom.

It soon became clear that although the mother tongue teacher's work at the second school was set to become one of the major successes of the Project's trials, her work at the first school was destined to end in failure. How could the same teacher be so successful in one school and yet a failure in another? A number of complex interwoven factors seem to account for this experience.

In the infant school, the staff, and particularly the head, were noticeably ambivalent about the Project even before it started. They were not convinced about the value of mother tongue teaching and saw it mainly in terms of helping children to acquire English more quickly. Although the staff were friendly and did their best to welcome the mother tongue teacher, she never felt at home there. Problems also arose with the children she taught. She was not accustomed to teaching very young children and had to cope with a succession of groups for very short periods at a time. The mainstream teachers felt she had a discipline problem and could not control her small group of children.

By the middle of the year when Project children were showing no obvious gains in English, the school was beginning to regret its decision to participate and by the end of the year they made it clear they did not want to continue with mother tongue teaching.

In the second school the mother tongue teacher was welcomed with great enthusiasm by the head teacher and two members of staff with whom she was to work closely. Other members of staff, including several from non-English backgrounds, were friendly and interested and the staffroom was a lively, homely place where teachers became sucked into the life of the school. There was already a strong tradition in the school of supporting children's home languages, with bilingual labels and posters in evidence throughout the school. Both teachers with whom she worked were already in the habit of encouraging children to use their home language wherever possible and welcomed the mother tongue teacher's advent as a way of extending this. During the year there were several examples of both teachers working on parallel themes and a great deal of interest in languages in general was created in the classrooms, with English children becoming very curious about Bengali and the hitherto unknown linguistic skills of their peers. The mother tongue teacher was more at home with junior age children, and there was no hesitation about her teaching them to read and write Bengali as there had been in the infant school; with the constant support and encouragement of the mainstream teachers, discipline problems were not an issue.

By the end of the year the mainstream teachers' enthusiasm for mother tongue teaching had grown, as beneficial effects such as increased confidence, improved conceptual awareness and greater self-esteem amongst the Project children became obvious. One of the teachers said that the Project had helped him to see how to put mother tongue teaching into practice; it 'gave me a lot of confidence to tackle mother tongue teaching . . . made me think about things I wouldn't have done . . . I now talk to people about it'. When the trials finished the head teacher believed that the experience meant that everyone now felt it was part of normal school to be taught in one's own language although some teachers went along with this more than others. The Project's teacher was appointed full-time to the staff of the school and a number of other part-time teachers were recruited to help support Bengali (Sylheti) speakers and the few other ethnic minority group children (Urdu, Hindi, Turkish).

Summary and conclusion

In this chapter we have looked at some of the issues and complexities that arise when introducing mother tongue teaching and support into mainstream primary schools.

The first section focused on teachers in multilingual classrooms and sought to show, through the Project's experiences, the kinds of questions faced by all schools and teachers wishing to support children's mother tongues in the classroom. Past and current curriculum developments in this emerging field were traced and the place of the Project's work within this framework indicated. A number of issues raised by teachers during the Project's trials were highlighted, such as uncertainty about the place of mother tongue teaching in the classroom, the role of mainstream teachers in supporting community languages, involvement of parents and the community, and various practical difficulties. The importance of whole school involvement in innovatory developments of this kind was stressed, and beyond the individual school the support of the local education authority was shown to be vital.

The second section looked more specifically at mother tongue teaching using bilingual staff. In order to try out the Bengali and Greek materials produced by the Project, special classes had to be set up in mainstream schools, as very few were in existence at the start of the Project. In addition, suitable teachers had to be found and assigned to schools. A variety of schools, covering different age ranges, social backgrounds and ethnic composition, worked with the Project over the course of a school year, trying out the materials and at the same time assessing the value of mother tongue teaching itself. This is a complex and controversial new area of the curriculum and many ideological, educational and organizational issues were raised. These included the justification and purpose of mother tongue teaching, ways of introducing it into the classroom, the role of the mother tongue teacher, liaison between mother tongue teachers and other staff, teaching methods, and the effect of mother tongue teaching on children's progress, particularly their acquisition of English. A number of variables affecting the introduction of mother tongue teaching were examined, such as the age of the children, the percentage of ethnic minority children in schools, and the individual languages concerned. Overall, the most relevant factors seemed to be the qualities of the teachers themselves, both mainstream and mother tongue teachers; and their attitudes to each other and to the role and importance of mother tongue teaching. This was illustrated by an apposite case study.

Looking at both aspects of the Project's work in schools together, certain common themes are apparent. Mother tongue teaching and support is a relatively new and sensitive topic and much careful preparatory work needs to be done if it is introduced into schools. The purposes of mother tongue teaching, whether, for example, for transitional ends, to develop oracy and literacy in the mother tongue, or even as an intrinsic right, will need to be discussed and agreed by all members of staff in advance, with the active support of the local education authority if possible. An appropriate organizational model can then be selected to achieve the chosen objectives. It is important to give all the teachers involved, including mother tongue teachers, the opportunity to discuss the issues fully, especially their individual roles and relationships with one another. The question of teaching content and style will require particular consideration and here mainstream and mother tongue teachers have much to learn from each other. It is most important that the views of both mainstream and mother tongue teachers are taken equally into account if the mother tongue teacher, and by implication her language and the pupils who speak it, is to be accorded equal status. Sensitivity also needs to be exercised when liaising with parents and the local community in this area of work if a genuine and fruitful dialogue is to be opened up.

None of these measures is quick and easy. All involve careful discussion, adequate preparation and sustained effort and commitment. It takes time to establish any curriculum innovation. Due to the complex and controversial nature of mother tongue teaching and support, special care and additional time will undoubtedly be necessary if a successful outcome is to be ensured.

Notes

1. This account is based largely on the trials of the draft handbook for teachers, which was published as *All Our Languages,* and to a lesser extent on The Children's Language Project. The other item developed for non-bilingual teachers – *Supporting Children's Bilingualism* – did not undergo trials.
2. i.e. mother tongue teaching or support is provided with the aim of stimulating children's transition from their mother tongue to English.
3. The terms 'Greek trial schools' and Bengali trial schools' are used for reasons of brevity to apply to the schools where the Greek and the Bengali materials were tried out, respectively.

Chapter 5
Children and Parents

Throughout the Project the responses of the children and parents involved were monitored carefully. What did parents think of provision for community languages within the mainstream curriculum? Was children's progress in English affected? Did parental attitudes change during the trials? These and many other questions were put to the test during the trial phase of the Project. Although this stage of the Project was relatively brief (one year), a great deal of information was collected which gives a fairly clear picture of the effect of the undertaking on the participants. The information was gathered in a number of different ways: by visits to schools, interviews with teachers and heads, observation of classes, evaluation meetings with school staff, questionnaires, forms and tests. Most of the detailed work was carried out in the 12 mainstream schools[1] with whom the Project worked intensively, where direct mother tongue teaching was carried out; but data gathered from the large number of schools with whom the Project worked less closely on trying out strategies for non-bilingual teachers to support children's home languages without direct mother tongue teaching are sufficiently similar to allow general conclusions to be drawn. Where there are any important differences between the two groups of schools these are brought out.

Children

The reaction of the children involved in the Project was monitored in four main ways. Teachers and head teachers in their schools were asked to comment on their reactions, usually orally during an interview, but sometimes in writing. The children were observed doing their work either by local co-ordinators, a member of the Project team or the evaluator, and additionally by two bilingual observers (one Greek-speaking, one Bengali-speaking). Their progress in language development in both

English and their mother tongue was assessed using tests (this was only carried out in respect of the children receiving direct mother tongue tuition). Finally, some case studies were conducted.

General response

Many of the effects noticed in the children who participated in the Project's trials concerned their overall motivation and response to school. Virtually all the schools reported increased confidence among the children which had beneficial effects on their work as a whole. Teachers felt this was not only a morale booster to the children, but enabled them to take a fuller part in education generally. Younger children seemed to benefit especially, particularly if their English was limited; this kind of support made them feel more secure and actually prompted them to try speaking English earlier than is usual with children from ethnic minority language backgrounds. Transition to school was generally felt to be eased by according support to home languages; and schools reported that it helped children mix more easily with their English peers, who were likewise more inclined to be interested in and sympathetic to their bilingual classmates.

Most Project children experienced a rise in self-esteem as the status of their home languages was elevated through the use of the Project's materials. This led to increased pride in their home language and culture which many had felt constrained to play down or even hide in the past. One of the Greek origin children said at the end of the trial year 'Greek is my language. I speak Greek at home', whereas previously he had referred to English as his language. A teacher trying out the handbook for multilingual classrooms wrote, 'The West Indian children who initially insisted they spoke only standard English are now making up a play in Jamaican patois'.

Apart from these social benefits accruing to the children, it was obvious to all concerned how much the children enjoyed their mother tongue work. For some it was simply a time of the day when they could relax and be themselves, for others it was an opportunity to find out more about their language and culture. Many felt proud of their new ability to read and write in their mother tongue, and the increased status this gave them in the sight of their peers and their parents. Some children were enthusiastic enough to ask for homework and many took home books in their mother tongue for their own pleasure or to read to their families.

Not all children were, however, equally enthusiastic. In very general terms the Bengali- (Sylheti-) speaking Project children were more enthusiastic than the Greek origin children, probably because the majority were younger and more of them were first language speakers of Bengali (Sylheti) compared with the Greek origin children, many of whom actually spoke English as a first language. They therefore found learning Greek a harder task, though once over the initial difficulties most seemed pleased enough to be learning Greek. Some of the older Greek origin children were also concerned that they might be missing important lessons by taking part in the mother tongue trials, although schools generally made special provision to ensure this did not happen. These anxieties may derive from the age of the children concerned and their correspondingly greater awareness of the relative importance of the various components of the curriculum, or it may stem from the higher value accorded to English by Greek-speaking parents and their community. Bengali- (Sylheti-) speaking parents, possibly because they have lived in England for a shorter time, perceive literacy in Bengali as well as English to be a valid aim of the school.

Some parents and teachers, as well as the children mentioned earlier, were concerned that the pupils involved in the mother tongue teaching trials might be missing important lessons. All the schools trying out the Bengali and Greek materials were therefore asked which lessons the children missed, to see if any general pattern emerged. In fact, schools tackled this possible problem in a variety of ways. In some schools, teachers tried to avoid the children's missing basic skills lessons such as language work or mathematics, as they felt this might be detrimental to their progress. In others, teachers felt it was unfair for children to miss classes such as games, art or swimming which might lead to them feeling resentful. Some schools compromised by having the children miss some basic skills lessons and some creative activities. Even in schools where children did miss core subjects, teachers were generally at pains to point out that there were usually opportunities for them to do the work at some other time or catch up later. One school said they operated an integrated day so children could do the work later. Another said children did not miss anything because the work was organized on a workshop basis. None of the schools suggested that the time spent on mother tongue teaching adversely affected the children's overall progress; whatever arguments are put forward against mother tongue teaching in schools, missing vital lessons does not seem to be a valid one.

As well as the children directly involved with the Project, other children in the same class, or even in other classes in the same school, were also affected by the Project's work. Some were initially curious and then lost interest, as most children will with new developments that do not directly concern them, but many sustained their interest and even asked to join the mother tongue groups. In two of the schools it was possible for indigenous children to work alongside their bilingual peers following mother tongue activities, and in other schools there was a sharing of experience across language boundaries. Indeed the team of EC evaluators commented about the Bengali trial schools that 'oral expression and the work achieved indicate a firm interchange between Bengali and English'.

Many teachers trying out the handbook for teachers in the multilingual classroom wrote about the greater awareness and interest in languages and their speakers which had resulted from the Project. Speakers of other languages felt confident enough to talk about their languages and even to ask about the possibility of mother tongue classes in their own languages. Teachers also felt that all children were now more aware of each other's needs and more tolerant of individual differences. Many felt that the Project had contributed towards good race relations in the classroom and had helped indigenous children to see their non-English-speaking peers in a new light. It had also fostered a new respect for bilingual teachers.

It is important, however, not to exaggerate these effects. Although it is true that many of the children developed a more tolerant view of other races, others remained ambivalent or even hostile. One school head spoke of racism 'just under the surface' and another encountered strong reactions from white parents to the increasing numbers of Bengali origin children at the school. Perhaps it is best summed up by the response of an English boy watching Bengali-speaking children write Bengali words on the blackboard. When asked if he wished he could read them he replied 'I half do, I half don't'. Progress has been made, but there is still a long way to go.

Much depends, of course, on the attitudes of the teachers concerned towards mother tongue teaching when they report the response of the children they teach. Most of the mother tongue teachers involved in trying out the Project's bilingual materials reported much enthusiasm amongst the children they taught, with rather more interest being reported by the Bengali-speaking teachers than the Greek-speaking teachers. This may reflect the attitudes of the teachers rather than the actual response of the children.

Most of the mainstream teachers felt the children had enjoyed the experience, but there were distinct differences from school to school, often depending on the school's overall approach to mother tongue teaching and the particular mother tongue teacher concerned. Schools which had been very keen on mother tongue teaching from the start generally reported considerable enjoyment and enthusiasm among the children, whereas schools which had been ambivalent were more inclined to speak of discipline problems among the children or a certain amount of indifference. In two schools where the particular mother tongue teacher was perceived by mainstream teachers to be awkward and old-fashioned, the children were reported as bored and the teachers were uncertain as to the benefits they were deriving. In fact, the Greek-speaking bilingual observer noted that these children made particularly good progress in learning Greek.

The two bilingual observers, together with the evaluator, provided a more objective view through direct observation at all the schools concerned. Overall their reports show that most children involved enjoyed the work and felt pleased at the interest taken in them and their language. One of the bilingual observers wrote of the 'happy and co-operative atmosphere' she observed in several schools, whilst the other was a little more cautious, pointing out that much depended on the teacher concerned, but that the children generally seemed to be gaining benefits from the classes and in some cases showed considerable pleasure. On the whole there was more open enthusiasm amongst the younger children, as might be expected, and probably more sustained interest amongst the Bengali (Sylheti) origin children who, as first language speakers of their community language, took to learning it more easily and enjoyed widespread support from their parents and community.

In schools trying out the multilingual handbook it was not possible to observe all the Project classes. In those that were seen the children seemed interested and involved, and teachers generally reported much enthusiasm, although there were instances of children feeling uncertain about the purpose of the work and embarrassed by the sudden interest in their languages. Of course, the teachers reporting the children's reactions were all committed supportive teachers; it is probable that less enthusiastic teachers would have got a much less positive response from children.

Overall, then, it seems that support for children's home languages can create enthusiasm and enjoyment among both bilingual and indigenous children if handled carefully by committed teachers. But does it have any impact beyond these rather general social and educational benefits? This is the focus of the next two sections.

Progress[2]

Teachers were pleased that the Project children's confidence and self-esteem were increased, but many felt that a major purpose of providing mother tongue teaching was to assist their linguistic development generally in both their mother tongue and, hence, English. Although many teachers felt it was right that children should have the opportunity to learn to read and write in their first language, they might have taken a different point of view if it had transpired that this entailed falling behind in English or other basic skills.

It was therefore considered important to monitor the progress of the children. This was done in two main ways; by collecting teachers' impressions, and through the use of a series of tests.

Almost all the teachers felt that the children's progress in English had not suffered, although, without control groups, it was difficult to be sure.

Some felt there had been a marked improvement both in the children's proficiency in their mother tongue and in English and that children learned English better and faster. They commented that learning two languages helps children to look at the structure of languages and use the experience gained in one language to help acquire another. Some even thought mother tongue teaching assisted children to build and retain concepts better, as concepts they might have failed to acquire through the difficulty of understanding in the second language they could pick up in the first language and then transfer to the second language. Little confusion between the two languages was reported and the additional bonus of children being able to read and write in two languages at the end of the trial year was pointed out by some.

Others thought it was difficult to be certain whether the experience had actually helped children's development in English, which some teachers had hoped for, although they acknowledged that it did not appear to have held it back. It should, of course, be pointed out that over such a short testing period very few gains in English would be expected in any case. There was some disagreement as to whether progress in English and the mother tongue was correlated, so that children who were good at English also turned out to be good in their first language, or whether the children who were poor in English showed most signs of progress due to increased confidence and the opportunity to demonstrate their skills in their mother tongue. Certainly teachers were sometimes compelled to reappraise their perceptions of their ethnic minority children as a result of working with the Project. One said 'I thought Michael was very poor at language but now I find he is fluent in Greek'. Others found that children they had thought to be withdrawn and uncommunicative blossomed when given the opportunity to talk in the language they found most natural, with beneficial spin-off effects on progress in English. During the course of making the Project's video a child, earlier judged a possible ESN case, was seen on film by the school's head who was surprised at seeing her ease and fluency when speaking Bengali (Sylheti), which led her to reconsider her assumption that the child's poor performance in English and other school work was indicative of low intelligence. These impressions supplied by teachers about the children's progress are largely borne out by the results obtained from tests given to the children which are described below.

TESTS[3]

Children were given a series of tests at the beginning and end of the trial year in order to provide a fuller picture of the effect of mother tongue teaching. They were not intended to yield research type results, and due to difficulties that arose during the course of the testing and to the experimental nature of the tests themselves, the results should be treated with caution. Nevertheless, they do provide some supportive information and afford some interesting insights into the feasibility of assessing children in their mother tongue. In addition, they aroused interest in the field of mother tongue teaching in general and formed part of the materials package produced by the Project (they were not, however, published). Indeed, the EC team of evaluators wrote of them 'In our view the appeal of these tests also lies at least as much in their instructional as their diagnostic function'.

Three main types of assessment were drawn up: an oracy test, a reading test and a writing checklist, all chosen to be applicable in both English and the child's mother tongue. The oracy test was designed to assess children's spoken language using an everyday activity familiar to all children – storytelling. Using pictures and props (either figurines or sequence cards) the teacher, chosen to be the tester because of her/his familiarity to the child, told one of four stories, selected according to the age of the child and the language being tested, to the child. The child was then required to retell the story, using the pictures and props if preferred. In case children did not respond to the story they had a chance to show their spoken competence by answering some simple questions about themselves. The child's performance in retelling the story, in vocabulary, enunciation and fluency was then scored.

Cloze-procedure tests were used to test reading. In these tests, which principally measure reading comprehension, words are omitted at regular intervals and the child has to choose from one of four words to fill the gaps. Available standardized tests in English were used to test the children's level of reading in English but non-standardized tests had to be specifically drawn up to measure the children's competence in reading Bengali and Greek. In the event many of the children tested were too young or too unfamiliar with reading either in English or their mother tongue to complete a reading test, and consequently a reading checklist was drawn up in which teachers assessed children's competence in pre-reading, word attack skills, simple and advanced reading.

Finally, a writing checklist was also completed by teachers, measuring children's performance in early and more advanced writing skills, punctuation and spelling, both in English and their mother tongue.

Altogether there were over 250 Bengali-speaking children and over 150 Greek-speaking children in the 12 mainstream schools which were involved with the Project. Six children from each of these schools were selected for testing, giving a total of 72 children. As there was no information about the children in advance of the Project's trials, it was not possible to select them in a very systematic way as pre-testing had to start almost immediately. Mainstream teachers, who would have more knowledge and access to information about the children, were therefore asked to select six children, choosing two of average ability, two of above average ability and two of below average ability, basing their estimations on the children's performance in their basic skills in English. The mother tongue teachers were asked to test the same six children in their mother tongue.

Although control groups would possibly have shown more clearly the impact of mother tongue teaching, it was not within the scope of this Project to arrange for the inclusion of such groups and so the data that follows relates only to the children included in the Project.

Before turning to the outcomes of the tests, however, it is important to draw attention to some factors that need to be borne in mind. The children who worked with the Project's materials received a maximum of four hours' teaching in the mother tongue per week and in some cases only half this.

Furthermore, the work took place over rather less than one school year as the Project did not get under way in some schools until October 1982 and finished in June 1983 in others; great changes were not therefore expected. In addition, the tests were only experimental tests developed specifically for the trials, and suffer from certain shortcomings, such as ceiling effects and imprecise wording. The administration of the tests was also problematic. It was difficult to identify children to be tested in the initial stages of setting up the mother tongue classes in schools when practical issues of a pressing nature had to be faced: classrooms had to be found, children chosen and teachers introduced. Most of the mother tongue teachers had never worked in a mainstream school before and in addition had a complete new set of materials to trial, with which they were only barely familiar, and only four hours a week to do this in! Both mainstream and mother tongue teachers were unfamiliar with the testing procedures and had little time in which to carry them out. Furthermore, the mother tongue teachers did not really have a chance to get to know their pupils before they had to test them.

Despite this rather formidable list of problems it did prove possible to test a sample of the Project children at the beginning and end of the trial year. Complete data was obtained for between 20 and 30 Bengali-speaking children and a similar number of Greek speakers.

The Bengali-origin children involved in the Project were generally fluent speakers of Bengali[4] and so it is not surprising that their oral skills were stimulated during the trial year, resulting in improvements not only in measured fluency but also in enunciation and their ability to retell a story. Altogether, 23 out of the 26 tested improved their overall oral skills in Bengali. Fewer children were tested in English, but, of the 12 whose oral competence in English was tested, all except three improved their performance. Although their competence in English was not as good as their competence in their mother tongue, their spoken fluency particularly improved and so did their ability to retell a story.

Virtually all of the Bengali-speaking children were unable to read in their mother tongue at the start of the trial year and teachers consequently completed reading checklists for their pupils. None of the children tested did less well by the end of the year and 15 out of the 20 tested made gains, some of them quite large. Most children graduated from the pre-reading stage to being able to read, some at quite an advanced level. At the same time the children's proficiency at reading in English was improving; the 13 children tested using a Cloze procedure test obtained an average score of 39 per cent in the pre-test and 62 per cent in the post-test, an increase of 23 per cent.

The children's writing skills were tested using a writing checklist, although due to the amount of pressure on the teachers, they were not asked to assess the children until the second term and consequently the assessment is based on only six months' work. Nevertheless, the children showed a marked improvement in writing Bengali. Out of the 25 children tested, only one did less well and 19 made gains, some of which were quite substantial. Although most children could write a little when tested first, as they had been working with the Project for three months, most were at an early stage in writing. By the end of the trial year, nearly three-quarters were able to write simple sentences and one-third of these could write short stories in Bengali.

The Greek-speaking children included in the Project were mainly second- and third-generation speakers of Greek and while their understanding of Greek was good, their spoken fluency lagged behind. This affected their performace in the oracy test so that their vocabulary was usually good but they found it difficult to retell the story. Nevertheless two-thirds of the children tested made an overall improvement over the trial year, whilst one-third stayed at the same level or did less well. This picture was paralleled in the children's performance on the test in English. Two-thirds improved their standard and one-third remained at the same level or did less well. However, the oracy test for Greek children in English was particularly affected by ceiling effects; that is to say, most children's vocabulary and enunciation was judged to be in the top category both in the pre- and post-test and there was consequently no opportunity for progress to be shown. The results are therefore undoubtedly an underestimate of the progress actually made by the children.

Complete data for the reading assessments in Greek are only available for a small number of children. Whereas those not able to tackle a reading test in Greek seemed to stay at a similar level, probably due to the teacher's emphasis on oral development, those able to complete a reading test made very good progress, increasing their average percentage score from 38 per cent to 70 per cent. Although numbers were small, more data was available for children tested in English, where again they made good progress, increasing their average percentage score from 55 to 74 per cent.

The writing skills of 27 children were assessed in Greek and 23 of these were found to have improved over the test year. When they were first tested, over half of the children could not write a simple sentence on their own, but in the post-test all the children could, and some could write short stories in Greek. Seventeen of the children had their writing skills in English assessed. Most of them improved, although ceiling effects in this test again underestimate the amount of their progress. All the children except one could write simple sentences without help in the pre-test. By the post-test they had all advanced sufficiently to be able to write a short story in English.

Looking at the results for both the Bengali-speaking and Greek-speaking children together, it would appear that most of the children tested improved their oral, reading and writing skills both in their mother tongues and English over the course of the trial year, despite the short interval between the two testing times and the limited time available for mother tongue teaching. Although it is difficult to measure the effect of mother tongue teaching on progress in English without control groups, there does not seem to be any evidence from these tests that mother tongue teaching hinders progress in English: in fact progress in both languages seems to develop at a similar pace, a fact which is borne out by anecdotal evidence from the teachers in the schools. However, too much reliance should not be placed on these conclusions as the tests were only experimental. The performance of the Greek-speaking children in particular was affected by ceiling effects, so that little opportunity was provided for improvement by the more advanced children to be shown; their progress was therefore undoubtedly underestimated and the imprecise nature of some of the assessment categories means that small gains or losses should probably be discounted.

Case studies

In order to provide additional background information, some of the children assessed were also selected to be the subject of small case studies. Information about parental attitudes, socio-economic background, personality, friendship patterns, motivation and language use was collected. Both mother tongue and mainstream teachers completed case study 'diaries' for two out of the six children tested in each mainstream school. Two examples of these diaries will show the flavour of the children's experiences and progress in the two languages.

Marinella is an eight-year-old Greek-speaking girl who was born in

England but whose parents are from Cyprus. Her parents are dress manufacturers and she has two brothers, both older than herself. Although she does not attend a community school, when the Project started her parents were very keen for her to learn Greek at school. She is an outgoing child who is generally well-behaved, highly motivated and very confident. Both her mother tongue teacher and her mainstream teacher say that she mixes well with other children, is friendly and popular. When she is at home, she speaks only Greek to her grandparents, but uses both English and Greek when speaking to her parents, and English to her brothers. She usually speaks English at school but since the Project started she has taken to speaking Greek to the mother tongue teacher whenever she sees her around the school (the teacher is a mainstream teacher as well as the mother tongue teacher), and she also speaks Greek with some of her friends. Marinella's mainstream teacher wrote in her case study diary at the end of the school year:

> I asked Marinella if she spoke more in Greek to people since she has been having lessons in school or if it was the same. She said she has definitely spoken Greek much more, feels much more confident herself about the language now she knows more words, and is looking forward to her holiday in Cyprus where she will be able to speak Greek a lot.

Both her mainstream teacher and mother tongue teacher feel she has progressed well this year. She can now read simple books in Greek and write a few sentences on her own. In English she has made particular progress in her written work and now uses a wide vocabulary.

Mukith is a seven-year-old Bengali- (Sylheti-) speaking boy who was born in England. He has five older brothers (two are in Bangladesh) and two sisters, one aged six months. He comes from a working-class background where the parents are supportive but shy about coming into school. One of his older brothers comes to the school to discuss Mukith's progress. Mukith is a friendly but quiet boy who tends to play mainly with other Bangladeshi origin children, although he is on good terms with English boys. He is well motivated and his mother tongue teacher reports that he has gained confidence and self-esteem through his achievement in Bengali. He speaks only Sylheti at home with his parents, brothers and sisters, but at school speaks English in general situations and switches easily to Sylheti when talking to other Bangladeshi origin children. His spoken Sylheti is sprinkled liberally with English phrases. Both his mother tongue teacher and mainstream teacher feel he has made good progress during the year. His mother tongue teacher says he has progressed well in reading, writing and oracy and his mainstream teacher writes: 'He has made very good progress this year especially in his written work and his reading. He now sits and reads Bengali books which are available in the classroom as well as the English reading books'.

Parents

An early issue faced by the Project when introducing mother tongue teaching into the curriculum of the primary school was that of parental consent. The two Local Education Authorities with whom the Project worked in trying out the Bengali and Greek materials took two different approaches. In the London Borough of Haringey where Greek classes were set up, the local authority decided to write to all parents in advance to secure their permission for this innovatory addition to the curriculum, whereas the Inner London Education Authority, where the Bengali materials were trialled, took the viewpoint that mother tongue teaching could be considered part of normal primary school provision (and already was provided in some instances) and therefore special permission was not necessary. Schools were left to decide whether and how to inform parents of what was happening.

The different conditions prevailing in the schools in the two areas should be taken into account when comparing these two approaches. In Haringey a very wide variety of languages is spoken and the selection of one, albeit the most widely spoken, might have given cause for concern without due explanation. Furthermore, most of the children involved in the Project were second language speakers of Greek, coming from families who had been established in this country for some time. Many of their parents therefore considered achievement in English to be important, and some were a little concerned about time spent learning another language which might interfere with their progress in English. In the ILEA, an even wider variety of languages is spoken, although in the Tower Hamlets area, where the Project was focused, the main language other than English is Bengali (Sylheti). Parents of children who were involved in the Project here were more likely to see Bengali (Sylheti) as a natural learning objective, particularly as their children were fluent speakers of Bengali (Sylheti) and often knew very little English when they started school. In addition, there was already a precedent within the ILEA for mother tongue teaching and support to be encouraged within schools as part of the normal school curriculum.

The issue of permission did not arise when trying out the multilingual handbook as the strategies and activities suggested and tried out in most cases represented only a small part of the curriculum. The responses of the parents to both the direct mother tongue teaching and the mother tongue support work are considered together in this section as there was generally a very similar reaction.

On the whole, the most frequently reported parental responses were either pleasure or indifference. Most Bengali- and Greek-speaking parents who commented were pleased about the opportunity for their children to learn their mother tongues at school. A few Greek origin parents whose children were second or third generation speakers of Greek were initially concerned in case their children's progress in English suffered but were soon reassured by events. Bengali origin parents, perhaps not being English speakers themselves, were less concerned about this, and mostly very enthusiastic about mother tongue teaching. In fact, many parents whose children were not able to be included in the Project asked why their children could not learn Bengali as well. Parents from other language groups were also frequently reported to be pleased, excited and interested. Many came into school, brought artefacts from home and even participated in the activities being tried out (for example storytelling, cookery, music). Some schools reported that parents from ethnic minorities were more likely to come to meetings, talk to each other outside the school and bring friends along to the school than before. Some ethnic minority parents expressed a new sense of belonging to the school. It led in some cases to a greater mixing between parents from different ethnic groups, including English. In one school a Bengali-speaking father was seen explaining a poster written in Bengali to an English father. In another, mothers shared an after-school class on cooking in different cultures.

At the same time, many parents were reported to have shown little response, even though they might have been informed by letter of what was happening. In some cases, despite this notification, parents seemed unaware that anything different was actually going on. There are a number of factors which help account for this reaction. Often, parents genuinely did not know what was going on (sometimes because they could not read the letter or were not able to read the language in which the letter was written), or even if they did, felt it was not something for them to comment on. Many ethnic minority parents come from cultures where what happens at school is seen very much as the province of the teachers and education authorities and not to be questioned by parents. The British education system, with its decentralized structure and espoused 'open-door' policy in primary schools, may be perceived as strange, although this will depend on the extent to which schools are actually in practice receptive to parental involvement and on parents' familiarity with similar approaches in their countries of origin. This cultural barrier also extends to forms of communication. Parents from many ethnic minority communities may prefer face to face or verbal communication, especially when they have not been in this country for long and occupy an underprivileged position in society, and may not respond readily to written forms of information. Even if teachers try to overcome this by talking to parents in person, there still may be language and understanding problems.

In fact, there was a clear contrast between reports of parental interest given by mother tongue teachers and those from mainstream teachers. Where mainstream teachers might report lack of interest, a mother tongue teacher in the same school, speaking the language of the parents and coming from the same culture, might report enthusiasm and interest which the parents had been too shy to express to the mainstream teacher.

There may also be more concrete reasons for an apparent lack of parental interest. Many parents, including mothers, will have jobs which occupy them for many hours a day, especially if they are piece workers, and they may have little time for visiting the school and expressing their interest in their child's education. In one school, and this may be the case in other schools as well, the population was transient and it was therefore difficult to build up and maintain parental interest in the school's work.

Generally speaking, there was little response from parents whose children were not involved in the mother tongue work. A few parents from other ethnic minority groups asked for mother tongue teaching in their language but most did not react, probably because they were not aware of what was happening. In some schools, indigenous white parents objected to the use of languages other than English at school although they were often reassured when the multicultural aim was explained. Not all indigenous white parents reacted in this way; some were happy at the opportunity for their children to find out more about other cultures, and in some cases parents in schools trying out the Project's Greek materials asked if their children could learn Greek. This did not happen in schools trying out the Bengali materials, perhaps due to the higher status accorded to Greek compared with Bengali (see p.99), or because parents were not aware of the possibility and its underlying benefits.

In the Project's experience, then, parents from ethnic minorities are generally pleased and interested when their children's languages are acknowledged in school although they may require some explanation and reassurance about the motives behind these new developments. Indigenous white parents will also want to understand what is happening. Once the aims and purposes have been discussed, parents usually see the benefits for their children and are delighted when they realize their children have learned to read and write in their home language as well as in English. Tact, encouragement and sensitivity will continue to be needed but the indications are that if handled carefully, mother tongue teaching can become a resource for the whole school to share, children, teachers and parents alike.

Notes

1. Less information was collected from the community mother tongue schools in which the Project's materials were tried out, due to lack of time, wide variation in the hours at which classes were held, and language barriers (the evaluator could speak neither Bengali nor Greek). However, the 11 schools involved were all visited and some general impressions about their work and their reactions to the Project and its materials obtained. These are incorporated into the account where appropriate.

2. This section and the following one relate only to the children involved in the trials of the Bengali and Greek mother tongue materials.

3. A small working group, composed of some members of the Project's Advisory Group (see Appendix A), was set up in order to give advice on the development of the tests used in the Project. Special thanks are due to Silvaine Wiles, Hilary Hester, Alma Craft and Elizabeth Hunter-Grundin for their help.

    Further details about the tests appear in Appendix D.

4. In fact, most of the Bengali-origin children in the Project were Sylheti speakers, but as some children did speak standard Bengali, and as reading and writing tasks were generally in standard Bengali, this term is used throughout for purposes of uniformity and ease of reference. The oracy tests were designed so that children could be assessed in whatever spoken language variety they used – see Appendix D for details.

Chapter 6
Working With Minority Communities

Introduction

Although schools, in the wake of the Plowden Report (1967) and even before, have been aware of the importance of home/school links, the development of close working relationships with minority communities has been slow to gain widespread support at an institutionalized level. There are, of course, numerous examples of individual mainstream schools building up strong bonds with parents and the local community, and many of these have explored in depth the particular needs of ethnic minority communities and the issues associated with involving them closely in the work of the school.

However, very little information exists documenting these experiences. Tomlinson (1984), in a chapter which sheds considerable light on the area, writes 'Home-school relations have never figured as a priority in education, and there is actually very little known about the purpose and effectiveness of home-school contact in general'. Furthermore she suggests that there is no general definition as to what constitutes 'good' home-school relationships. She goes on to describe a mismatch in expectations between ethnic minority homes and schools which she identifies as a crucial area which must be improved if ethnic minority pupils are to be offered a fair and equal education alongside their indigenous peers.

Teachers, on the one hand, may have little clear idea of their role in a multiracial, multicultural society and may still adhere to assimilationist perspectives. In addition, they may hold stereotyped views of working class parents as unambitious and uninterested in education and this may affect their views of ethnic minority pupils, especially when compounded by the additional factors of race and culture. Ethnic minority parents, on the other hand, may question the ability of schools to educate their children in accordance with the principles of equal opportunity and racial justice, and to take genuine account of cultural differences. Although a high percentage are, in crude socio-economic terms, 'working-class', their aspirations and educational ambitions for their children approximate more closely to 'middle-class' views.

Despite this fundamental divergence in views which critically affects the relationship between minority parents and schools, Tomlinson sees grounds for optimism. Beyond the familiar 'Plowden' type contacts such as parents' days and evenings, welcoming parents in school, pre-school groups and so on, there are now new types of links, such as the involvement of parents in educational decision making as school governors, and genuine discussion with community leaders and parents' representatives.

Little and Willey (1981), in their report on multi-ethnic education for the Schools Council, refer to innovative programmes for home/school liaison in multiracial areas, normally on a limited, exploratory scale. Eleven per cent of schools reported having home/school liaison teachers for work with various ethnic groups, and 22 local education authorities said they sent communications to parents in minority group languages. Direct involvement of minority ethnic groups tended to be limited; there was a disproportionately small number of minority ethnic group teachers and involvement of minority ethnic groups in curriculum issues was reported to be 'generally of an informal and limited kind'. Forty-two per cent of schools (60 per cent of these with a concentration of minority ethnic groups) reported forms of liaising with local minority ethnic groups usually through community relations councils or through direct contact with minority group organizations. Again, teacher attitudes were identified as a crucial variable, and the importance of helping teachers develop positive attitudes to cultural diversity and consider the implications of a multi-ethnic society for their teaching was emphasized.

Both Little and Willey and Tomlinson (op. cit.) refer to a number of local education authorities who are now beginning to formalize contacts with minority ethnic communities. Little and Willey quote an authority which refers to 'a new working party on the curriculum [which] includes teachers from ethnic minority groups'. Tomlinson refers to 'about ten LEAs' which were in the process of producing written policy guidelines to help schools in their dealings with ethnic minorities. Some of these have consulted ethnic minority organizations as part of this process. For example, Berkshire set up an advisory committee for multicultural education in 1981 to debate issues concerning 'education for equality', involving representatives from 17 ethnic minority organizations. The London Borough of Haringey has a Standing Committee which acts as a consultative committee on mother tongue teaching and consists of representatives from all minority language groups. And the ILEA has established a large-scale structure of consultation with ethnic minority communities, with a liaison committee in every division and consultation at the highest level on all functioning committees of the authority. It is important, however, to remember that consultation does not necessarily mean that the views of ethnic minority communities are acted upon, although they may be heeded; some ethnic minority groups feel that consultation of this form may be cosmetic rather than genuine.

Notwithstanding these two reports, there is still a dearth of information about working closely with ethnic minority communities. Available reports deal with a range of related issues such as gathering information on responses of schools (Little and Willey, op. cit.) or the analysis of minority parents' attitudes, particularly towards the maintenance of their children's mother tongues and possible provision in mainstream schools (Mercer and Mercer, 1979; Wilding, 1981; Kerr, 1978; Ghuman 1980; Ghuman and Gallop, 1981). There are some reports of working with parents through schools, such as Jennie Ingham's project (Ingham, 1984) on working with parents to produce traditional mother tongue stories, and also the previous EC-funded mother tongue project in Britain – the Bedfordshire Mother Tongue and Culture Project. One of the evaluators for the project (Simons, 1980) noted:

> All the Heads commented that the project teachers' liaison with parents had very positive spin-offs for improvement of home/school relations with parents generally. One noted that immigrant parents came into school more, both requested and on their own accord, another that having project teachers attached to the school even for a limited time had been very instrumental in improving home/school relations.

Although there is little concrete documentation describing working relationships between education authorities and ethnic minority communities there has been increasing recognition of the importance of gaining community support. As far back as 1976 Saifullah Khan (1976) stressed the importance of eliciting community support when making decisions about provision for mother tongue maintenance, and drew attention to the advantages in improved home/school links and increased participation of ethnic minority group parents which would be likely to result from closer links between mainstream and mother tongue schools.

The Schools Council, in a document on Multicultural Education (Schools Council, 1982), also recommended this sort of co-operation six years later in the following terms: 'Whenever there are enough enthusiastic pupils and sufficient expertise, the provision of and support for mother tongue and mother culture should be considered in collaboration with the work of community supplementary schools'. Similarly the National Congress on Languages in Education Working Party Report stated in the section on minority language teaching in mainstream schools:

it is . . . vitally important that any development of such teaching in mainstream schools should be accompanied by the fullest consultation with the minority language community regarding, for example, the language varieties to be taught, and the literacy and cultural aspects of the programme. (Reid, 1984)

There are many reasons why there has been growing recognition of the importance of developing close relationships not only with ethnic minority parents but with the wider community of which they are a part. Many of the 'immigrant' groups are now well-established members of British society who have the same educational rights as the so-called 'indigenous' population. Schools and teachers are aware that they have an obligation to provide ethnic minority pupils with an education equal to their peers and this obviously entails involving ethnic minority parents in the life of the school in the same way as other parents are involved. Although ethnic minority community groups have in the past taken a cautious approach to education and politics and even today show a reluctance to participate in political events compared with the population as a whole (30 per cent of the black community, for example, do not register a vote compared with six per cent of the population as a whole, reported in the *Guardian*, 10 December 1984), they are nevertheless increasingly aware of their needs and rights in the educational field as in others. Many ethnic minority groups have formed educational organizations which are putting increasing pressure on local education authorities and even national government.

A further factor in the increasing acknowledgement of the importance of working with minority ethnic groups has been the political situation, particularly in the aftermath of the race disturbances of the early eighties and the Nationality Act of 1981. The unrest and uncertainty caused by these confrontations has led many educationalists, as well as politicians, to review their attitudes to and provision for ethnic minorities within their schools and to re-examine their relationships in general with the wider ethnic minority communities.

Background to the Bengali-speaking and Greek-speaking communities

In Chapter 1 information was presented about the considerable range and diversity of languages spoken in Britain today. The Project chose to work intensively with just two of these languages and the communities who speak them. We saw in Chapter 3 that the two languages in question, Bengali and Greek, provide some interesting linguistic contrasts and similarities, but beyond this the Bengali-speaking and Greek-speaking communities also present social, political and economic contrasts which are of crucial significance when considering issues concerning the education of children from ethnic minority backgrounds.

There are a number of ways of classifying the ethnic minorities in Britain but, for the purposes of highlighting the differences and similarities between Bengali and Greek it is probably best to focus on the time of arrival here, motivation for the migration and place of origin.

The majority of the most recent influx of immigrants came to Britain between 1940 and 1975. The first to come were political refugees from Europe such as the Poles and Ukrainians. They were followed by other Europeans who came as migrant workers to post-war England such as Italians, Portuguese and Spanish. In the fifties, sixties and seventies many ex-colonial peoples came for a mixture of economic and political reasons such as South Asian groups, for example Panjabis, Gujaratis, East African Asians, Hong Kong Chinese and West Indians.

The Bengali-speaking community in Britain falls generally into the last category, although some Bengali speakers formed earlier links with Britain through service in the British merchant navy during British rule in India, and others migrated to this country after the partition of India in 1947 to seek employment and refuge from political unrest and economic pressure. At first single men came, then families followed as immigration laws began to impose restrictions on entry to Britain.

The Bengali-speaking community in Britain comes from the two countries of India and Bangladesh. The estimated population is 150,000–180,000 (1985)[1] and is largely concentrated in the industrial cities and dock areas of Great Britain. Of these, over 150,000 people are from Bangladesh[2] and nearly 80 per cent of them are from the small rural district of Sylhet. Most came to work in British factories as unskilled labour but independence also provided the opportunity to the rising Muslim middle class who came to Britain to gain academic qualifications for enhancing their careers. There are significant numbers of Bengali-origin pupils in over 35 local education authority areas, where the percentage of Bengali-speaking pupils may vary from ten per cent to over 70 per cent. In some schools in the ILEA the percentage is even higher.

The Bengali speakers from India came from the state of West Bengal and adjoining states, mainly for professional and academic reasons, although political instability and racial violence were contributing factors for some.

These distinctions are futher complicated by religious and linguistic differences between the two groups of Bengali speakers. Those coming from Sylhet generally speak the Sylheti variant of Bengali although a few, mainly middle-class, speak standard Bengali. Most of this group are Muslims. The Bengali speakers coming from West Bengal are mainly professional people who speak the standard form of the language and are generally Hindus.

Greek speakers, on the other hand, do not fit neatly into the pattern of migration identified above (p.134). There is an estimated population of about 200,000[3] which can be broadly divided into two groups. The first of these is the Greek Cypriot community, based mainly in North London. Historically speaking, the Greek Cypriot settlement in London started before the Second World War, following the migration of young men who came over in search of education and work. After the war, Cypriot immigrants came over in substantial numbers, males in the first instance to be followed by their families as soon as they were settled in jobs. During the 1955–60 Independence struggle a considerable number of Greek Cypriot families sought refuge in London, to be followed by further refugees during the intercommunal struggle of 1963, and a much larger number who were forced to leave home and came to Britain after the invasion of their country by Turkey in 1974. The second group of Greek speakers are from mainland Greece and come from a different socio-economic background from most Cypriots. They are mainly ship owners, big business people and middle-class professionals. On the whole they are concentrated in affluent areas of London, such as Bayswater and Hampstead. The estimated school population of Greek origin is now about 25,000[4] pupils spread in the boroughs of Islington, Camden, Haringey, Enfield, Barnet, Brent and Harrow, with a smaller number of pupils in other parts of the country such as Birmingham, Manchester, Leeds and Bradford, Great Yarmouth and Hastings.

Both Bengali speakers and Greek speakers originate from ex-colonial countries (except for mainland Greeks), whose migrants traditionally have rights to British citizenship. However, in the year the Project started (1981), citizenship became an important issue, as some Cypriot refugees were not counted as nationals of this country and were consequently deported. Many Bengali-speaking people likewise faced uncertainties about their legal status and both ethnic minorities were more than a little suspicious about the motivations behind the Project, starting as it did in the same year that the EC Directive became binding. They referred to the wording of the Directive concerning 'migrant workers', and despite assurances that they were considered settled citizens of Britain, drew the conclusion that one reason behind the Project might be to equip their children, through teaching them their mother tongue, to take their place alongside their peers in the country of origin.

The parallels between the two ethnic minorities extend beyond citizenship however. As indicated above, they are each composed of two major subgroups originating from different countries. In the case of the Bengali speakers the majority come from the rural area of Sylhet in Bangladesh, speak the Sylheti variety of Bengali and are mainly Muslims. A small section of the Bengali community come from West Bengal in India, speak standard Bengali and are generally Hindus. Most Greek speakers in Britain come from Cyprus and speak the Cypriot dialect. However, there is also a small number of Greek people from various parts of Greece who speak standard Greek or another dialect such as Cretan. In the case of the Greek-speaking community there are no religious divisions; where applicable, Greek speakers all belong to the Greek Orthodox Church.

The Greek-speaking community have, as we have seen, been in Britain longer than the Bengali-speaking community and are more well established. Many have settled here long enough to have children and even grandchildren. This means that not only is there a spread of age groups within the community, but also that many, probably most of the children speak English as a mother tongue or first language. The Bengali-speaking community, on the other hand, are among the most recent groups to settle in this country. The majority are young with young children, most of whom speak Sylheti or Bengali as their mother tongue. Most of the parents have received little formal schooling before coming here and know little about the education system in Britain, whereas Cypriot Greeks have often gone through an education system modelled closely on the British one.

Another distinguishing feature is the different ways in which the educational arrangements made by each of the two communities for mother tongue teaching operate.

The Linguistic Minorities Project (1985) distinguishes three typical forms of organization of mother tongue teaching for the main groups of languages. First, for the East European languages such as Polish and Ukrainian, who were the first to establish classes for mother tongue teaching, schools were usually set up by parents' groups, often under the auspices of the local church, in most cases with no help from LEAs.

The second group of languages includes South Asian migrants from the Indian sub-continent and East Africa, such as Bengali, Gujarati, Hindi, Panjabi and Urdu. Most of these language populations started teaching the national or regional language of the place of origin, together sometimes with languages for religious purposes, occasionally with assistance from LEAs.

The third category of languages consists of Southern European languages such as Italian, Spanish, Portuguese and Greek, whose speakers often have migrant worker status in Britain. Most of these languages have 'official' support from their countries of origin in the form of provision of teachers, materials, funds for accommodation and so on, through their Embassies or Consulates. In some cases, there is also support from the churches or from local parents' associations.

Bengali and Greek fit into the second and third categories respectively. Whereas both the Bangladesh High Commission and the Indian High Commission have an active interest in the political, social and educational welfare of their expatriates, they have neither the facilities nor the finance to become closely involved in their day-to-day lives. Most of the mother tongue schools organized for Bengali-speaking children are, therefore, organized by parents, community groups and religious organizations with meagre funds sometimes supplemented by LEAs.

The Greek-speaking community on the other hand receives support from both the Greek Embassy and the Cyprus High Commission in the form of teachers and materials. The funding of premises and the running of classes is undertaken by the various Greek Parents' Associations and Church Committees. In the past, the schools for Greek-speaking children were financed largely by the community and the two governments concerned, but LEA support is now becoming a more significant factor. These contrasts and similarities between the two communities are summarized in the following chart.

Two case studies

Two members of the Project team, the Bengali-speaking co-ordinator and the Greek-speaking co-ordinator, were responsible for developing materials in Bengali and Greek respectively, with the assistance of specially created teacher groups. The work involved them in close liaison with each of their communities, both through the teacher groups and through contacts with the wider Bengali-speaking and Greek-speaking communities. Their experiences form the basis of the two case studies which follow, and serve to illustrate some of the issues that arise when working with minority communities.

1. The Greek-speaking communities in the UK – Maria Roussou

DEVELOPING COMMUNITY LINKS

Prior to joining the Project I had already built up a network of contacts with the Greek communities in London through both professional links as a teacher of the Cypriot Educational group (KEA), and as a parent with the Greek Parents Association (GPA). Through teaching Greek as a mother tongue to children of Greek Cypriot origin, I had developed links with various parents' associations in North London, such as Haringey, Leyton, Brent, Harrow and Enfield, and my involvement broadened beyond educational issues to include social and cultural gatherings. Voluntary work in areas in which my professional knowledge was required was expected and, although it was tiring, it was an enriching

Chart 6.1   Contrasts between the Bengali-speaking and Greek-speaking communities

	Bengali-speaking communities		Greek-speaking communities	
	Bangladesh	West Bengal	Cyprus	Greece
Place of origin				
Areas of settlement	East London, Birmingham, Coventry, Manchester and Bradford		Mainly North London but also Birmingham, Leeds, Manchester, Glasgow, Edinburgh, Hastings and Great Yarmouth	
Numbers	150,000–180,000[1]		200,000	
Time of arrival in Britain	1970s and 1980s		1. Between the two World Wars 2. 1950s and 1960s 3. Refugees in 1970s	
Religion	Mostly Muslim	Hindu and Muslim	Greek Orthodox Church	
Language	Majority speak Sylheti variant of Bengali	Bengali	London Cypriot	Demotic Greek
Reasons for coming to Britain	economic and political	educational and economic	economic/political educational	economic/ educational

Socio-economic status	majority of men are unskilled labourers but also catering and small business owners (shops/restaurants), professionals, and students	majority are professionals	Men[5]: 20% self-employed (including small scale employers) 20% service workers & distributive trades, catering, etc. 9% construction workers Some professionals. Women: majority are clothing workers, many work in catering and retail with family	Students, professionals entrepreneurs, ship owners
Legal status	majority are British citizens	British citizens (some still hold Indian citizenship) political status – residents	mostly British citizens, some refugees	established residents may be British citizens. Newer residents came under EEC legalization on labour mobility
Organization of mother tongue classes	Parents' organizations		Greek Orthodox Church Greek Parents' Assns. Cyprus High Commission Education Office	Greek Orthodox Church Greek Embassy Education Office

experience. A pilot survey that I conducted among Cypriot families in Haringey added to my understanding of Greek Cypriot familial and social structures in the UK.

THE DEVELOPMENT GROUP OF TEACHERS

The setting up of a development group of teachers is a common practice in mainstream curriculum development. Materials are developed by informed, enlightened practitioners who have close contact with the population for whom the materials are produced. These practitioners, alongside other teachers, try out and evaluate the materials before they take their final form. This process is not so common in the Cypriot educational system, nor, as far as I know, in the Greek one. In Greece special groups of curriculum planners and materials developers (KEME)[6] undertake the task of developing materials, a governmental publishing house (OEΔB)[7] publishes whatever materials they develop, and the finished product is distributed to all state schools all over Greece, Cyprus and the Greek diaspora[8] free of charge. These materials generally form part of a recommended list of books issued by the ministry of education in the country concerned. Usually teachers are obliged to use only the materials on the list; special permission is required if teachers want to use other books in the classroom.

The network of contacts I had already established helped towards selecting the teachers who would form the development group and assist in producing materials for young Greek-speaking pupils. However, the task of choosing the teachers proved to be a very difficult one because of internal politics amongst the various Greek-speaking community groups, as well as their common reaction to a much delayed interest on the part of the mainstream educational authorities in young bilingual children of Greek and Cypriot origin. The fact that the Nationality Law, with its implications for the immigrant communities, came at the time of the fact-finding phase of the Project, when teachers who were willing to work with the Project needed to be identified, was an unfortunate coincidence. It made the community very cautious of the Project. In some cases members of the community who felt threatened were hostile. This delayed the process of selecting the teachers and starting the production of materials.

The teachers chosen represented different sections of the community and in addition came from varied educational backgrounds. Some of them were highly qualified and trained, while others were either untrained or unqualified. The eventual development group included teachers from the Cypriot Educational Group, seconded from Cyprus; teachers seconded from Greece; some unqualified teachers working with various parents' organizations, and some from local education authorities which co-operated with the Project.

The contacts between the Project and the Greek communities were mainly through the members of the Greek Development Group (of teachers) who, as mentioned above, were selected from various organizations and agencies involved in mother tongue teaching. The first issue which arose concerned different methods and approaches to language teaching. Most teachers in the group argued for a specific approach, basing their arguments on the lack of experience of the new methods on the part of most mother tongue teachers, the constraints of time and space, the nature of the pupil population and the resources available. The phonetic nature of the Greek language, with its syllabic characteristics and regularity, made some Greek teachers even more adamant in their argument for what has been labelled the 'traditional' approach. After long discussions and presentations of the different points of view, the Project adopted work based on the communicative approach, and prepared sample materials embodying flexibility of approach and stressing always the importance of developing oracy at the communicative level.

The transferability principle (see p.75ff) also came under analysis, doubt and fierce attack by some teachers and community organizers, especially those in the community run schools and classes: 'How could a Bengali-speaking teacher write something which could be culturally relevant to a Greek mother tongue speaker? It's impossible, non-valid, unwanted' argued those who saw mother tongue teaching as the medium for transmitting certain ideas. Their answer to possible benefits from the transferability principle was the decision to remain separatist: 'The authorities (LEAs and DES) should give us money and we will develop materials that have our culture in them. There is no time to teach the children about others. Anyway, they do it already in their English school.' A similar attitude was held by some on the issue of the multicultural nature of the materials:

> They are confusing the children. They need to concentrate on their culture, to be able to absorb its basic characteristics, which their parents value and live with. If they learn too much about other cultures there is a danger that they might rebel early in their lives before the parents have established their own sets of rules.

The opponents of the above arguments worked on the principle of persuasion and managed to convince some of the others to opt finally for co-operation with other language groups and consider the transferability principle and the multicultural nature of the materials as an enrichment to their own culture.

When practical issues of developing oracy, and introducing and extending literacy came up, the issue of parents' demands for immediate tangible results was raised. Some teachers and other community members argued that the mainstream education had failed their children by not developing the basic skills of literacy and numeracy early enough or to an adequate standard. If similar approaches were followed in the field of mother tongue, they argued, then their children would not have a chance to learn their mother tongue adequately either. Their preference was to go for early literacy in the standard form of the Greek language. In many ways these teachers, who also supported the above mentioned arguments against transferability and multiculturalism, took the conservative point of view on whatever issue was raised by others, whether these were members of the Project team or Greek-speaking teachers from various community and mainstream schools.

The debate concerning the form of the language to be used in the mother tongue class was an important one, considering the fact that 90 per cent of the target population are speakers of the Cypriot dialect. The points of view presented varied from those who opposed even mentioning the dialect as an issue, to those who considered it very important in language teaching to recognize the child's vernacular and accept it in the classroom, especially at the early stages of a student's language development. The decision taken collectively was to opt for acceptance of the child's preferred form of language in the classroom, gradually extending it with elements from the standard form. When the written form of the language was used, a simple 'standard' version of the language was introduced, including some dialect words that had strong cultural value or no equivalent in the standard.

The Project was strongly criticized at the very beginning for not working towards an initial primary reader or 'starter set' to take account of the specific needs of children who are learning Greek as 'a mother tongue in the context of a second language' (see Tosi, 1984), and for not making allowance for the need of most community teachers for a basic reading scheme on which to base their curriculum planning and which they would consider as their Bible when introducing literacy. The Project team consequently adjusted its original plan and set up a subgroup of teachers to develop suitable introductory materials. These were ready and printed in draft form by September 1982, but in January 1983 a new set of readers for levels 1 to 3, which were fully illustrated, colourful and quality produced, were received from the Greek Ministry. That immediately set the community and the Project an important question to answer: Should we go ahead with our cottage industry production of materials for the starter set, or should we drop them and list in our Teachers' Guide the reading scheme produced by the Greek Ministry? This would be distributed free to schools as the basic starter set, and the other materials produced by the Project could be used alongside this to complement and enrich it. We opted for the second alternative.

LESSONS WE LEARNT FROM THE TRIALS OF THE PROJECT MATERIALS

All the materials now published have been tried out in mainstream and community schools and have been commented upon extensively by the teachers. The process of setting up the trial classes during the school year 1981 – 2, to start in September 1983, was an interesting experience of dealing with people from various educational backgrounds and with varied degrees of commitment to the discussion on bilingualism and mother tongue teaching. The Project team hoped that the members of the Greek Development Group, who had already participated in the initial discussions and choices and in some cases produced materials, would be released by their relevant authorities to try out the Project materials in schools. Unfortunately for the Greek part of the Project, dealing with five different agencies to organize the release of the Greek-speaking teachers and the trial classes proved a time consuming and difficult task. In searching for trial schools, we were faced with indifferent or actively negative reactions to mother tongue teaching by some head teachers and mainstream staff. This discouraged parents, members of the team and Greek-speaking teachers present in the school, who had hoped that the Project's appearance would finally 'move the waters' in their school. Perseverence and hard work on the team's part, as well as receptive attitudes from some mainstream heads, helped the Project to finalize a group of five primary schools.

In the community sector, we found it easier to organize the trial classes since they were operating as mother tongue classes already. It was more difficult, though, to implement all the aims of the trials here because of practical problems concerning numbers of pupils, time, space, financial constraints, and teachers' commitment towards the agency or authority which employed them. In addition, materials were generally provided free for community teachers by their agencies and there was consequently less motivation for them to use the Project's materials.

One of the first problems that the Project faced was the fact that three of the five teachers from the Cypriot and Greek Educational groups, who were allocated to the Project for three hours per week, were recalled to their countries, having come to the end of their five-year secondment to the UK. Some of the newly arrived teachers who were allocated to the

Project for trialling the materials faced severe English language problems of their own. Some of these community teachers did not see the methodology of the Project in a favourable light, for various reasons related to other commitments, age and personal beliefs. The lesson we learnt here was that teachers' in-service training should precede any trials of new methodology and materials. A shortcoming on the Project's part which affected the start of the trials and in some cases created a negative attitude on the part of some mainstream and mother tongue teachers was the piecemeal distribution of the trial pack, as well as the absence of an overall chart from which the teachers could see the progression and integration of Project materials with existing resources.

Working with groups of teachers from various backgrounds requires much planning, time and central resources. In particular, a base with space for working in small groups is necessary, and resources for workshop activities if community teachers are to be asked to present project work and language activities of a standard equivalent to that found in the richly equipped mainstream schools. Unfortunately, very few teachers' centres have opened their doors to community mother tongue teachers. Education cuts have come at the moment when community hopes for financial help in training teachers and producing materials for teaching mother tongues have been raised. This was another unfortunate coincidence which taught us the lesson of lowering our expectations to the minimum – a very disheartening experience in itself – and of trying to give the teachers we collaborated with some courage and patience to continue.

Challenges, or problems as some people might call them, are constant characteristics of pioneering projects. We would like to believe that our Project, which had to deal with many people from different backgrounds, managed to break the ice in some areas and to suggest possible procedures. In others, debate and consultation continue. The majority of the Greek-speaking communities did not have the chance in the time available to digest all the new ideas and methodologies suggested by the Project. But we hope that, for some members at least of these communities, we offered the chance of raising further issues concerning organization of mother tongue teaching and curriculum development.

2.   *The Bengali-speaking communities in the UK – Hasina Nowaz*

The setting up of the Mother Tongue Project in 1981 with its focus on the Bengali and Greek languages created high expectations in the Bengali-speaking community. Most people failed to see that the Project's major objective – to produce teaching materials for the Greek-speaking and Bengali-speaking communities – had implications for mainstream teachers and for other language communities as well as for them. Many others questioned the appointment of an English director and the soundness of the decision to make one bilingual co-ordinator responsible for developing all the Bengali materials and liaising with the many different Bengali and Bangladeshi organizations.

Many were surprised that there was no arrangement for professional bilingual editorial support and were very critical of the whole set up. Many others were suspicious of the Project's overt intention in the long run: was it to repatriate people back to their home countries? However, in spite of misgivings and suspicions on the part of some people, there were many others who welcomed the Project and thought that it was a positive step forward.

DEVELOPING COMMUNITY LINKS

I had been working for several years with two prominent Bangladeshi organizations in setting up and running mother tongue classes and through them had come into contact with members of other local and national organizations. I also had many personal contacts with members of the Hindu Bengali Community from West Bengal, who organized classes for teaching language, music and dancing.

SETTING UP THE DEVELOPMENT GROUP OF TEACHERS

The experience of working with the community and the personal contacts proved invaluable when setting up the development group to help with the production of materials. But nevertheless it was a formidable task. To win the support of the community it was essential to select members from each of the major Bangladeshi groups working in London as well as from the groups from West Bengal. But it was also essential to look for teachers and individuals who had good academic qualifications, training and teaching experience from the home country or who had experience of teaching in mainstream schools and were familiar with British methods of teaching.

In addition it was necessary to look for teachers who were actually involved in mother tongue teaching. The Project team therefore deliberately planned to choose members from a wide range of backgrounds, interests and expertise, so as to have a balanced representation from the various sections of the community.

Neither the Schools Council nor the Project team, apart from the two co-ordinators, had experience of working with bilingual teacher groups drawn from the communities. Mainstream teachers working on other projects were either seconded or released for short periods from their schools so that the Project in question did not have to pay them. Following this procedure the Mother Tongue Project had not budgeted for the teachers in the development group, many of whom were in fact either doing part-time work or were unemployed. The whole community felt outraged at the idea of expecting these teachers to give voluntary service when the Project was being funded by the European Commission and when mainstream teachers were in fact released from their work without losing their pay. The matter was amicably settled when the ILEA offered to pay these teachers at the usual hourly tutor rate.

OTHER ISSUES

Once set up, the teacher group was eager to work in earnest. Many of the members had been working in the field for several years and had definite ideas about what they wanted for themselves and for their children; a comprehensive language and reading scheme which would represent the communities' religion, culture, history, civilization and the lives of great people and which would include modern stories, poetry and drama, together with a starter reader for mastering the basic features of written language. This, they felt, would help their children to learn their language and feel pride in their heritage.

The Project team and its advisers envisaged things in a different way. Though they realized that setting up objectives and planning the content of the materials without reference to the communities' hopes and aspirations would defeat the purpose, nevertheless they believed that mother tongue teaching in the long run would have to be acceptable to the mainstream teachers if community languages were to find their place in the curriculum. The Project team was faced with a dilemma, not only outside, but within the team as well; for each of the members had at the back of their minds the aims and expectations of their own communities – English, Bengali and Greek. Even though the common goal for all was the ethnic minority child's language development, the purpose of that development was different for each group. Mainstream English teachers had mixed views; for some the mother tongue was seen as an aid and support to the learning of English, whilst others regarded the maintenance of community languages as having intrinsic value. For the community mother tongue teachers, learning the mother tongue was generally seen as an aid to the appreciation of literature, the valuing of the cultural heritage and the development of a sense of group identity.

But even within the community there was a difference of opinion – some sections of the community believed that it was important for their children to learn about their culture and religion but that it was equally important for them to look around and ahead to fit in the society they would grow up and live in.

The teacher group worked over the course of a school year, meeting every fortnight to discuss issues and plans, and working at home to write materials. Much of the co-ordinators' time was spent in translating the teachers' work into English so that the Project team and its editor could select materials for production and so that members of the opposite language group could adapt stories into their own language for transferability purposes (see pp.76–7) for details of how this worked).

It was at this stage that the Bengali-speaking teachers began to show signs of discontent. They questioned the Project team's objectives in producing materials that would be multicultural and transferable. The mainstream schools would teach children about the different cultures and, anyway, they argued, mother tongue materials should be culture-based to help children learn about their own culture and religion. Culture specific materials could not be transferable – by trying to enforce the principle we would make the materials artificial, unnatural and even false. In addition, all the members were unanimous about the need for a starter reader for beginners, which would help children to master the sounds, symbols and basic phonetic features of the language, as in Bengali there is on the whole a regular relationship between the sounds and the way they are written.

Some members also questioned the procedure and criteria used for selecting individual contributions. They were frustrated and even angry when they realized that many of their writings would not be used for publication and pressed for an editorial board to be composed of experienced members from amongst themselves who would edit and select the materials for final publication.

The Director explained that the co-ordinator was expected to produce the materials with the help and guidance of the teacher group whereas, to date, the teacher group had been producing the materials, with the help and guidance of the co-ordinator. Obviously, in such a situation, there would be surplus production and only high quality material suitable for publication would be selected. The Project editor explained that publishers would only bid for materials which would have a market demand and enable them at least to cover their costs of production; culture specific Bengali or Greek materials could have a very small market and publishers would not be interested in them. This subsequently proved to be true when publishers, invited to bid for the Bengali and Greek materials, made no response.

However, two members of the teacher group who were still unconvinced withdrew and two new teachers were recruited to join the group for the trialling of the materials.

THE TRIALS

When planning the trials of the materials in the seven selected mainstream schools we found that members of the teacher group who were themselves mainstream teachers could not be released to do the trialling in the seven mainstream schools selected for the purpose, and many of those who were available had very little or no experience of teaching in mainstream schools, and were not familiar with the range of Project materials and/or the associated techniques used for language development. As bilingual co-ordinator, I realized that it would be unfair to expect these teachers to produce materials and trial them in a situation with which they were neither familiar nor equipped to cope. It would be equally unfair to expect the mainstream teachers to accept them in their classes without first establishing any sort of mutual link with them. I therefore arranged for the trial teachers to work part-time in the schools where they would be trialling the materials. Additional arrangements were made for these and other teachers to spend some mornings in a mainstream classroom observing classroom teaching and familiarizing themselves with teaching materials, resources and equipment, as well as establishing links with the teachers.

Discontent amongst members of the Sylheti-speaking community in Tower Hamlets resurfaced during the trials of the materials. A section of the community voiced strong complaints about the low quality of the books, errors of print, poor handwriting and illustrations, and lack of cultural content. The anger and frustration of the younger generation found a pretext to burst out against the authorities, the Project organizers and the team. Plans to incorporate more culturally relevant materials into the package were consequently accelerated and the materials were carefully revised and improved in quality and appearance.

DISSEMINATION

But while the revision was going on, both the Bengali-speaking and Greek-speaking co-ordinators were expected to follow the Project's schedule of work and launch a country-wide dissemination activity. This was one of the most trying times of my work with the Project. I wondered how I could display the draft materials to solicit the support of the community in other parts of Britain when they had already been condemned by a large group in London. Though I myself had faith in the materials and believed they would have a wide market when published I was very sceptical of the outcome at this juncture.

The national status of the Project and its EC backing made many people think twice about its future impact in the field of mother tongue teaching, and quite surprisingly encouragement and support came from many quarters; from friends and well-wishers, from members of influential organizations, from both sections of the community, and from the High Commissioner of Bangladesh and his Educational Attaché. At the same time the report of the EC evaluators helped give me confidence in myself and in the materials, especially their positive remarks about the Bengali literacy materials.

The Mother Tongue Project has run its course and like many other projects will become a part of history, but as the first national project dealing with minority communities and their languages it will have an important place in the history of the development of mother tongue teaching that is being debated all over the country at present. The books written on policy issues and guides for teachers, the ideas developed and materials produced for children's use, will all contribute to this debate and make many people think about this controversial issue in a more positive way.

Common issues

Although the two minority communities with whom the Project worked were very different in many respects, these case studies highlight a number of common issues which arose with both communities.

This is the first time a project in Britain has sought to work with speakers of two minority community languages on a national basis. Many projects, LEAs and schools have worked closely with minority groups in local areas but have not attempted, as the Project did, to include speakers of a particular minority language throughout the country. Although the Project was based in London and worked initially with Greek speakers in Haringey and Bengali (Sylheti) speakers in Tower Hamlets, it always kept in mind the possible national audience for its materials. During the course of the Project, the two bilingual co-ordinators gathered information about their respective communities and established a network of contacts with individuals and groups throughout Britain helped by the Project's survey (Tansley and Craft, 1984). Contacts with the national organizations concerned with the two communities, such as the Greek Embassy, Greek Parents Association, and Cyprus High Commission for the Greek speakers, and the Bangladesh High Commission and the Indian High Commission for the Bengali speakers, also gave a national perspective.

One of the most obvious issues, but not necessarily the most widely appreciated, concerns the complexity within the minority communities themselves. For reasons of simplicity the terms 'the Greek community' and 'the Bengali community' are often used, but in reality these conceal a range of individuals and groups, with different socio-economic situations, motivations, attitudes and linguistic characteristics.

Furthermore, groups in different parts of the country or from varied religious or class backgrounds may have quite distinct views about the needs of their children and the place of mother tongue teaching. Even within defined geographical areas, there may be wide differences within, say, the Bengali-speaking population, and within the Greek-speaking population. The Project came face to face on more than one occasion with opposition from a particular individual or group who felt they represented the community as a whole. Sometimes others from the same community, such as parents or teachers, might not agree with these community 'leaders' although they might not always voice their opposition. Some of the community groupings had changing leaderships, which made it difficult to maintain and build steady, mutually beneficial relationships.

These complexities were reflected in the composition of the teacher development groups each co-ordinator set up. Both felt constrained to include teachers representing a range of groups within their communities as well as selecting members on the basis of their suitability for the task at hand. Working with teachers from many different backgrounds made the running of the development groups a demanding job, compounded by the fact that few, if any, of the teachers, like many mainstream colleagues, had experience of working in such groups and many were not familiar with mainstream education.

Apart from the practical difficulties of gathering together teachers from geographically scattered homes (particularly acute in the case of the Bengali-speaking teachers) at a time which all could manage (many had teaching or family commitments), the question of payment for teachers attending development group meetings turned out to be an unexpectedly serious problem. The Schools Council's normal procedure of working with groups of mainstream teachers, often released from their normal jobs with no detriment to their salaries, was not so appropriate for the Project's teachers, many of whom had hourly paid part-time jobs or were unemployed and for whom, therefore, the possibility of enhanced career prospects had little attraction.

In the event, for the Bengali-speaking teachers at least, the majority did actually further their teaching careers as a result of involvement with the Project and several obtained full-time permanent teaching posts. But for others the issue was never fully resolved and, in fact, it was still a problem with some of the teacher groups with whom the Project worked in its final year. Some LEAs believe that teachers should be recompensed in full for their attendance, whilst others take the view that partial payment with the possibility of enhanced career prospects is sufficient inducement, and indeed will encourage teachers to realize that teaching involves some voluntary commitment on their part.

The political dimensions of working with community groups remained a constant undercurrent throughout the Project. Working at local level with parents or a particular local group, it is sometimes possible, though not necessarily desirable, to side-step the political issues but when government agencies are involved such issues have to be faced and discussed. To some extent the Project was put in a difficult intermediary position between the state education system and the communities. Although the Schools Council always prided itself on being a non-prescriptive organization, the two communities clearly felt that the Project had been set up in order to tell them what and how to teach their children in their mother tongue classes. This seemed not only threatening in the wake of the Nationality Act, but also rather patronizing – it was as if the Project was entirely discounting the expertise teachers from the communities had built up over their years of experience in mother tongue schools. Many teachers felt upset at what they considered to be insufficient consultation and suspicious of what the long term aims of such work might be. Many indeed felt that not only their livelihood as teachers in community mother tongue schools was at stake, but the independence of the community itself and its right to control the future for its children's education was threatened. This was, to a degree, a reflection of the imbalance of power in the total society, experienced in acute form by ethnic minority communities who are typically in a position of limited power. In respect of the Bengali-speaking teachers' group, this manifested itself through the demand for an editorial board composed of development group representatives who would edit and select the materials for final publication and thus retain control not only over the output of the Project but, by implication, over their children's education as well. The Cypriot education officer spoke openly of the danger of community schools being swallowed up as a result of initiatives like the Project, and in East London some community organizations found the popularity of their mother tongue classes was adversely affected by the rapid growth of mother tongue teaching for Bengali-speaking children in mainstream schools, stimulated in part by the Project's work.

The state education system on the other side, as represented by the Project and teachers in mainstream schools with whom the Project worked, often felt that the community teachers used methods unfamiliar to children in mainstream schools and depicted inappropriate models, such as males and females in traditional roles, religious bias and racist views in their materials. The ideals of the communities were not always thought to be compatible with those of multicultural education.

In this situation of tension and misunderstandings the two co-ordinators were in a particularly invidious position, caught between the two camps.

Inevitably they came in for a certain amount of personal criticism as representatives of particular sections of their communities, but beyond this they had to face continuous pressure and criticism about the Project's work from both their own communities and the Project's advisers.

Both co-ordinators, in their case studies, refer to a series of other common issues that arose during their work with the teacher groups, deriving in some cases from the conflicting interests of the mainstream and community sectors. In both accounts, the dissatisfaction of the communities with the multicultural setting of the materials, and their preference for materials based more specifically on the home culture of their children, is described. In each case study, the desire for a specially designed, comprehensive set of language and literacy materials was expressed, and failing that, the production of a starter set of materials for introducing literacy, based on phonic principles, was requested. Finally, work with the two teacher groups in both communities highlighted the need for teacher training.

In some respects, of course, issues arose that were specific to one of the two communities. In the case of the Greek-speaking community, for example, there were difficulties in obtaining teachers in good time for the trials, due to the organizational arrangements made by the home governments for the deployment of their teachers. In the case of the Bengali-speaking community, the question of payment for teachers was more acute as, unlike most of their Greek-speaking colleagues, the Bengali-speaking teachers were not generally employed as teachers and therefore did not have a regular salary. Despite the many important differences between the Bengali-speaking and Greek-speaking communities, which the two case studies bring out, there are nevertheless remarkable similarities in their response to the Project and in the issues that arose during the course of the work.

Conclusion

One of the clearest conclusions to come out of this aspect of the Project's work is the necessity for increased contact not only between schools and the local community, but between local education authorities and local and national community organizations. It is most important that this contact is a two-way dialogue involving real partnership rather than a token attempt to go through the motions. Unless each side, and unfortunately it is often a question of 'sides', is prepared to listen and take proper account of what the other says, progress cannot be made towards improving education for ethnic minority children which is, after all, the aim. Many LEAs and schools are already opening up such dialogues which can only be for the benefit of the children concerned.

However, in order to establish a true dialogue and understanding it is essential that more information is available to all who are involved. Mainstream teachers need to know about the background of the ethnic minority children they teach and this means not only factual information about their socio-economic situation, their linguistic expertise and their cultural heritage, but they also need to talk to members of ethnic minority communities – parents, teachers and other community representatives in order to ascertain their views about education – and visit the community schools their children attend. Ethnic minority communities on their part need information about mainstream education, its aims, context and methods. They need to understand how schools work and what special provisions are made for their children. In addition they need to know how the education system works and who to ask for help and advice, both at the school and LEA level where parents and teachers are concerned, but also at regional and national level for community organizations.

A further consideration when opening up a dialogue with minority communities is the nature of communication itself. Cultural differences in consultation and discussion procedures may lead to misunderstandings about attitudes and needs. Even amongst professionals, such as teachers, differences of interpretation can occur, arising either from lack of information about how different educational systems work or from different cultural perspectives. Variations in styles of discussion (see, for example, Kochman, 1981) may unwittingly influence outcomes and the differential status accorded to men and women in all communities may also play a part.

The Project found that the usual means of contact with groups of parents and teachers through letters and meetings did not necessarily work with ethnic minority groups, undoubtedly due in part to ethnic minority communities' unfamiliarity with British traditions and to their underprivileged position in British society. Styles of communication also differ from one cultural group to another, and some are not accustomed to formal communication and may prefer to be approached personally either by telephone or through a respected member of the community, before they feel welcome to attend meetings and discussions. Many schools have had similar experiences when trying to involve parents from ethnic minority backgrounds in the life of the school.

Rather than seeing the diffidence of such parents in a negative light, schools might more profitably re-examine their ways of reaching out to all parents. Indeed, it is vital when working with ethnic minority communities to ensure that all parents are informed and involved, not just ethnic minority parents, if misunderstandings are to be avoided and progress made. Many practical ways of building up collaborative links between schools, teachers and the wider community are listed in the Project's publication *Supporting Children's Bilingualism*.

Working with two minority communities in parallel brought both problems and benefits. It certainly gave the Project greater insights than might have been obtained by working with only one community. The Project found that parents in both the Bengali-speaking and Greek-speaking communities were anxious that the culture of their home countries should be maintained. Greek-speaking parents had, however, generally been in Britain for longer and had come to accept some aspects of British culture, particularly as their culture is closer to that of Britain than is the case with the Bengali-speaking community. For these reasons, they were not so opposed to the multicultural aspects of the materials developed by the Project as were the Bengali speakers who, as more recent arrivals, had a stronger allegiance to the culture of their country of origin. But whilst the Bengali-speaking parents were only too happy for their children to learn their mother tongue at school, seeing this as a way of maintaining their culture in a new and alien land, the Greek-speaking parents were more anxious that learning Greek as part of the mainstream curriculum should not hinder their children's acquisition of English.

Although the Project, and indeed members of the two communities, learned a great deal from working alongside each other, this style of work brought its own frustrations. It was difficult to avoid comparisons which were not always valid; and members of the communities themselves sometimes felt it would have been better to concentrate on one community at a time. Nevertheless, intercommunity links were forged and members of the two communities had the experience of learning at first hand what it was like to belong to a different ethnic minority community; probably for many it was for the first time.

Working with members of two minority communities also enabled comparisons to be made between two different languages, their structures and the methodologies required for teaching them to children. Teachers in mainstream schools came to realize that each language has its own unique structure, vocabulary, and syntax and that no one method of teaching can be applied to all languages. In particular, they were made aware of the regular relationship between sounds and the way the writing system works in both Bengali and Greek and the implications this has for introducing literacy in the mother tongue. Additionally, the differences between Bengali and Greek were brought out, and those working closely with the Project realized that although many approaches to materials development can be shared between languages, there comes a time when each has to go its own way. Community mother tongue teachers, for their part, realized that there are many ways of teaching languages other than their own, and that it is possible to benefit from different approaches, particularly when the children they teach are familiar with some of these through their contact with mainstream schools.

There were other positive outcomes of the Project's work with ethnic minority communities, which were largely unanticipated. Many parents become closely involved in the Project to the extent that they continued their active involvement in the classroom after the Project's trial year had ended, forming an ongoing resource for the schools concerned. Indeed, some parents and community teachers became sufficiently interested to join courses for the further training of community teachers, thus adding to the numbers of teachers with some training available for teaching community languages. As this is an area of acute shortage, the contribution of the Project to the pool of teachers with some training, who are then able to assist in the training of other teachers, has been highly significant.

Looking back, one is struck by the sheer scale of the undertaking on which the Project embarked, and by its unavoidable naïvety in its dealings with ethnic minority communities. We hope that, through the work of the Project, we and our colleagues in the mainstream education system and the community school sector have learned a great deal about sharing ideas, approaches and materials in order that the children, with whom and for whom we are all working, get the greatest benefit. If this is the outcome, and if the experiences of the Project can be taken on by others, then the undertaking will have been worthwhile.

Notes

1.   This figure represents only a rough estimate of the numbers of persons living in Great Britain who speak Bengali or one of its varieties. The only reliable figures are those which appear in the 1981 Census which refer to the *birthplace* of the head of household rather than *speakers* of the language. The 1981 Census gives the following figures:

Table 2.   *Persons resident in private households with head of household born in the New Commonwealth and Pakistan (NCWP), by country of origin.*

<u>Bangladesh</u>	
All persons	
born inside UK	16,939
born outside UK	47,622
Total persons	64,561

Source: OPCS, Census 1981

Smith (1985), taking the 1981 Census as his baseline, estimates that 'the total of those living in households with a connection with Bangladesh, including British born children, is something in the order of 100,000'.

The Bangladesh High Commission, in response to a telephone inquiry, gave the estimate of 150,000. Adding to these the unknown number of Bengali-speakers who come from India (West Bengal) but who are not listed separately in the Census figures, I have arrived at an estimate of 150,000 – 180,000 speakers of Bengali or one of its varieties.

2.   Based on an estimate made by the Bangadesh High Commission in 1985.

3.   Based on an estimate made by the Cyprus High Commission in 1984.

4.   Based on an estimate made by the Cyprus High Commission in 1984.

5.   The statistics quoted here are based on those given by Floya Anthias which appear in Roussou (1984).

6.   KEME stands for Governmental Committee for Curriculum Development and Research in Education.

7.   OEΔB stands for the Organization for Publishing Text Books.

8.   Diaspora is the Greek word which is used to describe the emigration of Greeks all over the world, from the USA to Australia and New Zealand.

Chapter 7
Impact of the Project

The outcomes of the Project, material and otherwise, form an important part of its legacy but its impact will largely determine whether the legacy is in fact taken up. At the end of the third year of the Project,[1] the evaluator sought the opinions of those who had worked closely with it; teachers, head teachers, advisers, education officers and so on, to assess its impact. This analysis is based largely on their responses, although information from other sources (such as published articles, sales of materials, visits to schools, etc.) has also been taken into account.

National impact

The Project's impact can be examined from a variety of different perspectives and at a number of levels. It is difficult to assess its effect at national level, due to the decentralized nature of the British system, the uneven distribution of ethnic minorities throughout the country, the differential response of LEAs to their needs, and finally due to the difficulty of separating the growing awareness of the importance of mother tongue from the work of the Project.

Certainly, during the lifetime of the Project there has been a marked change in the climate of opinion surrounding the mother tongue debate. It is now widely accepted in educational circles that there are sound pedagogic and social reasons for supporting children's home languages, whether within the mainstream classroom or through assistance to voluntary community organized schools. Indeed, as we saw in Chapter 2, there has been an increase in official LEA policies which take account of pupils' mother tongues, either in the form of a specific policy on mother tongue teaching, or as part of a more general language or multi-ethnic policy.

Whilst this is an important step forward, it does not always indicate developments at grassroots level and, indeed, to some extent it has become politically expedient to demonstrate support for community languages at a policy level, without necessarily implementing this in schools. At the same time, however, there has actually been an increase in provision for mother tongue teaching as part of the primary school curriculum (see Chapter 1) together with an expansion in various forms of support for mother tongue teaching, such as payment for community teachers, provision of free or cheap rented premises, *ex gratia* payments to teachers, advisory assistance and so on. Other developments in the field also point to changes in the climate of opinion: the emergence of teacher training courses which are either designed for community language teachers (such as the Royal Society of Arts Course), or take account of their needs and those of the children they teach; and proposed changes in examinations in community languages. (The London Examination Board has recently set up a review to investigate how minority languages are examined.)

Of course, it is difficult to assess how far the Project itself may have been responsible for these developments, although there is some agreement that it has played a significant part in contributing to the changing climate of opinion. One of the Project's advisers felt that the Project was helpful in raising the issues concerned with mother tongue teaching, and in gathering information on the various organizational models which could be used to put it into practice. Another thought it not only gave encouragement and validity to new ideas, but showed how practical difficulties could be overcome and strategies implemented. Several colleagues mentioned the importance of collaboration between mainstream and community schools, which the Project had highlighted, and the usefulness of the teacher development groups as a model epitomizing this collaboration.

LEAs

It may be more helpful to examine the impact of the Project in more detail at the LEA, school and community levels before returning to its overall contribution to national developments. The Project worked particularly closely with two LEAs, the London Borough of Haringey and the Inner London Education Authority (ILEA), trialling the mother tongue teaching materials, and, in a less direct way, with 22 LEAs trialling a handbook of strategies for teachers in multilingual classrooms.

As might be expected, the Project's work had a deeper impact on the two LEAs with whom it established strong links than with the others, partly due to the nature of the link, which involved a greater commitment on the part of the two LEAs, and partly due to the controversial nature of the work itself, concerned more directly as it was with the introduction of mother tongue teaching. Both the London Borough of Haringey and the ILEA have multilingual school populations and both had already taken steps to meet the challenges these presented. Both had undertaken borough-wide, in-depth surveys of the languages spoken in their areas, and the ILEA already had some mother tongue teaching as part of the curriculum at the primary and secondary level. However, neither had primary school classes into which the Project's materials and teachers could easily be slotted and special provision had to be arranged in both areas.

This provided a great deal of experience in facing the educational and organizational issues involved in mother tongue teaching, which has enabled both LEAs to assess the policy and practical implications of this type of work. In both cases the relevant advisers referred to the stimulus of the Project in the development of positive attitudes to mother tongue teaching in the schools where the Project worked. One said that if ten schools were selected which had taken mother tongue furthest, the Project schools would be among them. But more than this, the Project has, in effect, been a launching pad for local developments. In Haringey, the experiment was one of the contributory factors[2] leading to pressure to formulate a policy on bilingualism (which it has since done), and to the realization that the LEA itself must make a commitment to the development of mother tongue teaching, rather than relying on extra-territorial teachers or community initiatives to carry out this task as it had in the past.

The ILEA already had a policy on the role of the mother tongue, but working with the Project certainly accelerated the provision of mother tongue teaching in primary schools. Before the Project started there was very little provision, but by the end of the first phase of the Project (summer 1984) about 30 schools in the authority's division in which the Project worked had mother tongue teaching. The organizer responsible for this expansion commented that 'much of the credit for setting the ball rolling must go to the Project'. He also spoke about other aspects of the Project's local impact: the take up of the Project's methodology even among schools not necessarily using the Project's materials, the improvement in the standard of materials for mother tongue teaching, and the trying out of the suggested models of organization. Although no one model will suit all schools, the Project did enable schools to examine different options and many have adopted an integrated form of teaching (see p.97) which would probably not have happened without the influence of the Project.

Another development, at least in part attributable to the Project in these two LEAs, has been an increased provision for in-service training of teachers concerned with supporting community languages. Haringey set up a series of one-day conferences for all teachers, looking in turn at different community languages, whilst the ILEA has set up a number of different mechanisms to provide in-service support for teachers of community languages. Finally, both LEA advisers with whom the Project worked referred to the importance of links with the communities which the Project had stressed. Through the Project the importance of co-operation between mainstream and community teachers in developing materials had been highlighted, together with the need to consult with parents and the wider community about their hopes and priorities for their children.

It is more difficult to assess the influence of the Project on LEAs involved in the trialling of the handbook of strategies for the multilingual classroom. Much depended on the enthusiasm of the contact person, back-up support at official level, and previous developments in the field of mother tongue teaching and support. In some LEAs, where the Project depended on the interest of a single person or school, the impact was very limited, but in others, where involvement with the Project was part of an overall programme or regarded as a spearhead for future development, it had a more far-reaching effect. Although these trials were not intended to accomplish more than the piloting of the handbook, the Project has left a legacy in the form of a number of spin-offs. Through work with the Project, channels of communications within LEAs have been established which enable teachers with a shared interest in linguistic diversity to come together. This has resulted in a pool of expertise which is proving to be a resource for in-service training. At school level, teachers and heads have been able to develop a clearer idea of what mother tongue teaching and support means in practice, and to work through the implications for their own individual situations. Both bilingual and non-bilingual teachers have become aware of the language skills of the whole class and have developed techniques to recognize and build upon them. Children, too, have become aware of the linguistic skills of their peers and have developed a new respect and understanding for each other.

Schools

Similar outcomes for schools trialling the mother tongue materials were reported. Several schools felt that children were now more open about languages and more interested in language and culture generally. Increased staff awareness about community languages and the issues involved were frequently mentioned and head teachers felt the opportunity for considering, or in some cases re-thinking, the whole question of mother tongue teaching was worthwhile. Indeed, as one head teacher pointed out, it enabled mother tongue teaching to be better structured and extend beyond storytelling, its customary place in the curriculum.

Some of the schools trying out the mother tongue materials felt the Project's work had acted as a catalyst for developments within the school, but others, particularly where the number of children involved was small or there were difficulties in carrying out the programme, thought the trials had had a limited impact and had not affected staff who were not directly involved. Over half the trial schools continued or even increased mother tongue teaching after the year's trials ended and some of the other schools might well have continued if suitable teachers had been available.

The communities

The Project's impact on the wider community beyond the school gates is hard to judge. The trialling of the materials designed for non-bilingual teachers tended to involve only individual parents and then in a relatively peripheral way.

The majority of parents whose children were included were interested and pleased but a few were suspicious or antagonistic (see Chapter 5 for details). The Project's work with Bengali-speaking and Greek-speaking pupils and teachers did, however, involve the two ethnic minority communities in a much deeper sense. From the start, official representatives of the two communities were involved, and throughout the life of the Project the two bilingual co-ordinators were in constant contact with teachers, parents and community organizations in order to hear their views and gauge their reactions. The response of the communities is described in Chapter 6, but the possible effect of the Project on them is considered here.

When the funding for the pilot scheme was first announced there was much enthusiasm and high expectations from community leaders, tempered perhaps with a certain amount of anxiety about the real purpose of the enterprise and some misunderstanding about the distribution of the money. The two communities did not immediately realize that *two* languages were involved and that there was also an obligation to provide materials for non-bilingual teachers which would reduce 'their' share of the total funds allocated. This had implications for the nature of the work and the expected outcomes, which were not fully appreciated at the time. At the end of the day there was some disappointment within both minority communities that more had not been achieved and, specifically, that complete language programmes tailored to meet the needs of their young bilingual children had not been produced. This, they felt, limited the impact the Project's work might have on their teachers and schools. All four official bodies concerned with organizing mother tongue classes for Greek origin pupils (the Greek Orthodox Church, the Greek Embassy, the Cyprus High Commission and the Greek Parents Association) felt that the Project's materials would have a limited impact and tend to be used as supplementary materials to augment the language programme materials already supplied free (or at low cost) by their governments. However, many individual teachers, especially those working with mainstream schools, have shown interest in the materials and the thinking behind the Project's work.

Similarly many members of the Bengali-speaking community have expressed some disappointment in the absence of a complete language programme for Bengali-speaking children growing up in Britain, and many have criticized the cultural content of the materials. But a number of factors suggest that the impact of the Project on members of the Bengali-speaking community is likely to be greater in the long run. First, there is a greater need for materials for Bengali origin children. There are no free materials as in the Greek-speaking community, and many materials available from West Bengal and Bangladesh are not relevant for children growing up here. Unlike in the Greek classes, where two new sets of materials which are both attractive and suitable have recently become available to all teachers, the Bengali-speaking teachers have few materials which are cheap, easily obtainable and useful.

They are therefore more likely to turn to the Project's materials which, while not offering a complete language programme, do provide a sound basis for introducing literacy geared to the needs of Bengali origin children growing up here. This has been recognized by the Bangladesh High Commission, which has welcomed the Project's work as a useful attempt to meet these needs; and this gesture, together with the Project's revision of the materials to take into account community criticism, should ensure a reasonable take up for the materials.

The Bengali-speaking and Greek-speaking communities are, of course, composed of a number of different groups and individuals who are likely to react in a variety of ways to the Project's work. Some may feel at the end of the day that the Project's contribution was tokenistic and represented an expensive public relations exercise; whilst others remain largely indifferent or unaware of its outcomes. Yet, whilst some members may reject the Project's work, others will be thankful to have its materials at their disposal.

Ironically, perhaps, in view of the greater need for materials and support in the community sector, the Project is likely to have a greater long-term impact in mainstream schools. The Project aimed to produce materials which would be of use in both situations, but they have not had as much impact on community schools as was hoped, although there has been a closing of the gap between mainstream and community schools. There is still a lot of work to be done in developing ways of working with community mother tongue schools and teachers, so that the best use can be made of their expertise and so that, together with mainstream colleagues, they can devise materials which meet their needs in community mother tongue schools.

Despite the limited impact the Project may have, it has been seen as a first step towards greater collaboration between the two sectors (mainstream and voluntary) in the future. It provided an opportunity for those involved to become more aware of each other's situations, and produced materials which, while not perfect, represent a basis for future co-operation and development.

EC

One other aspect of the Project's impact deserves a mention: the response within the European Community. The Project's progress has been followed with interest by other Member States who also attended the EC Colloquium held by the Project in 1984. Generally speaking, in other European countries, the emphasis has been on direct mother tongue teaching, usually carried out by bilingual staff on a withdrawal basis, with minimal contact maintained with children's ordinary class teacher. European colleagues were impressed by the broader aspects of the Project's work in multilingual classrooms involving non-bilingual teachers, and felt there might be possible applications for their own situations. They were less sure about the transferability aspect of the Project's work, which they felt to be a novel idea but one that required careful consideration before its benefits could be ascertained.

The Project's materials

One concrete way of gauging the Project's impact is to look at the sales figures for the materials produced. Most of the materials designed for non-bilingual teachers have either only just been published or have still to be published, but the materials developed for Bengali-speaking and Greek-speaking pupils are all published and available. Whilst the Project team does not have figures for the text-free materials which have been published commercially, it has been responsible for the distribution of the specific language materials produced in Greek and Bengali and published by Schools Council Publications. These have been selling fairly well and at the time of writing are about to be reprinted. Take up of the materials has been almost equally divided between the mainstream sector (schools and local authority bodies) and community schools and teachers.

Conclusion

Long-term take up of a project after the initial stimulus has faded is always a problem. It is especially critical in a field which is new and controversial, and if sufficient organizational mechanisms for its continued dissemination are not set up then its impact is bound to be limited. This particular project was fortunate in coming at a time when there was a growing awareness of the importance of acknowledging children's mother tongues generally, and for this reason it has made a contribution to both the discussion of the issues and the provision of resources within the mainstream sector. As a result of its efforts, the provision of mother tongue teaching in primary schools has received a boost, and support for community languages by non-bilingual teachers has increased substantially. The Project was able to take some first steps in examining teacher training methodology applicable to community language teaching, which has been taken up more fully by both the RSA and many LEAs. It was also able to investigate possible models of organization schools could adopt when incorporating mother tongue teaching and support into their curricula, and at the same time provide opportunities for teachers to work out how they could put theories about mother tongue teaching into practice. In addition, and this may be where its major impact will be, it was able to provide a range of materials and strategies for both bilingual and non-bilingual teachers who have been trying to find ways of supporting children's community languages.

In fact the package of materials developed was put to use as the basis for the final year's extension to the Project. During this year a range of community language groups of teachers used the Project's materials as a starting point for their own development work.

Its impact in the community may well be less. Although it was set up at a time when there was increasing interest in mother tongue in general, and a steady growth in voluntary schools organized by the community, it also coincided with a decline in immigration and the passing of the Nationality Act. These factors combined to produce suspicion and even hostility. Many community members felt placed on the defensive and saw their duty as protecting their cultural priorities to prevent further erosion of their position. They were therefore less open towards new ideas and more wary about new developments. Despite these barriers, the Project was able to forge links with many members of the communities and set the pattern for future collaboration. For many teachers, probably most, this was the first time such co-operation had occurred, and as such is one of the most important legacies of the Project's work. For the community, the benefits of these links, such as information about modern British education, access to resources, financial support for teachers and classes, teacher training provision and so on, are only gradually becoming apparent and, together with the resources developed by the Project, they should provide a good starting point for future developments. In the immediate future, however, the Project's materials will provide a much needed resource which teachers can draw upon. There is every indication that, as teachers become aware of them and their usefulness, their impact will grow.

This review of the impact of the Project has necessarily been impressionistic and patchy. It is difficult to separate the Project's work from other developments in the field and to assess its effect at a time of expansion and change. That the Project has affected the people with whom it has worked closely there can be no doubt, and there are strong indications that it has made a valuable contribution to the mother tongue debate by raising the issues and providing models and materials for putting ideals into action. But it is still too early to judge its long term effects; for this we will have to wait.

Notes

1.   It was in fact subsequently funded for a fourth year to work with teacher groups developing materials in a range of community languages.
2.   Other factors included the influence of the LMP and LINC in Haringey and more general pressure from organizations like the NCMTT and ethnic minority community groups.

Chapter 8
Issues and Trends

This chapter looks at some of the main issues highlighted by the Project's work in supporting children's bilingualism at the primary age level and considers them in the context of developments taking place in the field generally. Many of the key people with whom the Project worked were asked to identify important issues raised by the Project's work, and their responses are incorporated, where appropriate, into the account which follows. Some prevailing trends are identified and future developments suggested.

Information

A fundamental need, which underlies many of the issues encountered in the field of mother tongue support, is for information. Although, as outlined in Chapter 1, advances have recently been made in charting the range and diversity of languages spoken in Britain today, much of the data is locally based and incomplete. A comprehensive national picture of the numbers of languages and their speakers, together with details of oracy and literacy figures for each of the languages, including breakdowns of the data for individual languages and local areas, would help inform policy and practice in educational as well as other spheres.

This is, of course, an ambitious programme, but it could be facilitated by the use of already existing survey instruments such as the *Schools Language Survey Manual of Use*[1] produced by the Linguistic Minorities Project (LMP, 1985).

Data also needs to be collected on the views of minority language speakers, both adults, and, where appropriate, children towards their languages; and on the question of provision for these languages within mainstream and community schools. Of course, dry statistics will not be sufficient in themselves to ascertain community attitudes; locally-based consultation procedures will need to be instituted in order to establish the nature of local demand.

Primary schools can help by collecting information themselves on the languages used by their children and on parents' views on the languages they feel should be fostered at school. Some suggestions for ways in which this could be done were made in Chapter 2, and it was pointed out that this can be a valuable exercise, not only in gathering useful information but also in showing recognition for children's home languages and in changing teachers' attitudes.

Finally there is a need for more research and investigation into bilingualism in education within the British context. Many of the well-known research studies, especially those involving immersion programmes or bilingual education projects, are not relevant to the British situation where a number of minority community languages may co-exist and where current approaches are focused on mother tongue teaching for a limited number of hours per week. Of course, there is a wealth of information available from Welsh bilingual education projects, and, although it is not always applicable to the situation of ethnic minority languages in England, more use could be made of these 'home-grown' experiences. Nevertheless, several small-scale projects, albeit largely curriculum-based, in various English LEAs, have already been set up and these need to be carefully evaluated and the outcomes compared so that useful information can be derived and accumulated. But, in addition, more rigorous research needs to be carried out. Possible topics of particular importance include: the effect of minority language mother tongue provision on the acquisition of English; 'interference' between minority community languages and English; the development of strategies for teaching community languages in a range of situations, pilot bilingual education programmes for infants and juniors, and the investigation of realistic objectives for mother tongue teaching programmes.

Resources

Problems

A common problem faced by teachers of primary age children concerned with supporting children's mother tongues is the lack of appropriate resources. In addition to the problems arising from the lack of suitable teaching materials (see Chapter 3), a number of other difficulties face mother tongue teachers, particularly those working outside the mainstream education system. They encounter obstacles when searching for premises in which to hold their classes, they lack essential equipment that would make their jobs much easier, such as a duplicator or typewriter which can reproduce individual minority language scripts. Even where community language teachers use school premises, they may have difficulty gaining access to school facilities, and may also lack information about what resources exist and which may be available for their use in the school. Mother tongue teachers who work in mainstream schools, particularly those who teach at the school during the day, whether on a part-time or peripatetic basis, are in a much better position to know about and take advantage of existing materials and facilities. Even so, they may feel reticent about asking for what they need, especially if the school is one where the mainstream teachers are ambivalent about mother tongue teaching, and community languages have a low status.

Teachers in community-organized classes are likely to be isolated and even more unaware of facilities which could be made available to them. They may know very little about existing materials and facilities and be uncertain about who to turn to for help. They may also be constrained by lack of funds.

Many of these problems have eased somewhat in the last few years as local education authorities have become more aware of the needs of community language pupils and their teachers and have provided premises and funds for mother tongue teaching. The Swann Committee Report (op. cit.), in recommending enhanced support for community-based provision, through making available school premises free of charge and by offering grants for the purchase of books and the development of teaching materials, may lead to further amelioration of the difficulties faced by mother tongue teachers, although at the same time it may be used by some LEAs as an excuse for inaction due to its stress on community responsibility for mother tongue teaching. Many of the problems will, however, remain, at least for the foreseeable future, without wholehearted government support for mother tongue teaching, and whilst much of the teaching continues in a piecemeal fashion in a variety of disparate and uncoordinated community classes.

Possible solutions

So what can be done to improve the situation? There is a growing feeling amongst workers in the field that there is a need for some form of national body, properly financed and supported, to co-ordinate developments and disseminate information. At present many individuals and groups in different parts of the country are working hard to produce materials and develop strategies for mother tongue teaching, often with very little idea of what is being done elsewhere. As a result there is both duplication of effort and needless gaps in availability of suitable materials, as specific resources developed in one area may be unknown to teachers in another area. Obviously, in a decentralized educational system this is bound to happen to some extent, but it is a particularly acute problem in the area of minority languages where suitable resources are so scarce.

There have, in fact, been a few developments in this general direction already. First in the field was the National Council for Mother Tongue Teaching, which is a voluntary organization aiming among other things to collect and disseminate information and encourage co-ordination between all those interested in promoting mother tongue teaching. Bulmershe College has established a national register of multicultural resources[2] through which individuals and organizations can find out about developments and materials in a number of specified areas. The Centre for Information on Language Teaching and Research (CILT), a national organization funded mainly by the DES and open to any member of the public, maintains a collection of mother tongue materials produced by different organizations, including some LEAs. It has a large reference library, which includes many works on bilingualism, and publishes conference papers and information booklets relating to minority languages. Finally, LEAs, under the chairmanship of the Education Officer for the Inner London Education Authority, have begun meeting together to discuss race-related issues, including the exchange of information such as the collection of materials. There is a mother tongue teaching steering group as part of this arrangement.

Despite these encouraging advances, national co-ordination is still in its infancy. The NCMTT is seriously hampered by lack of funds and the Bulmershe College Register is little known and used. Even CILT's work in the field of minority languages is not widely recognized and the exchange of information generated by the LEA meetings referred to above has not yet filtered through to the grassroots level. In fact, the individual teacher or LEA is likely to encounter great difficulty in finding out what is already available, and a national body within the Modern Languages area such as a 'clearing house' on American lines may be a possible solution. Such a body, if it is to be effective, should be nationally recognized and state funded. It could assess the needs for materials, facilitate their production and oversee their dissemination, as well as ensuring that locally developed materials are nationally available.

Other solutions, such as the suggestion for the establishment of Language Development and Training Units, as put forward by NCLE (Reid, 1984), may also need to be considered. These would be organized in the first place around the most widely-used languages of minority communities in Britain, and their functions would include syllabus preparation, the development of methodologies, materials, examinations, in-service and initial teacher training, and related research. In fact, a

National Council for Urdu Teaching was formed in December 1984, albeit with a less ambitious brief comprising 'all aspects relevant to the promotion and development of Urdu teaching'.[3] A similar organization this time focusing on Panjabi, was set up in 1985.

At the same time, there is much that local education authorities can do to assist the production and dissemination of suitable mother tongue teaching materials and resources, although their focus is likely to be on several different minority languages rather than single language groups. Again the NCLE report (op. cit.) makes a number of suggestions for LEA action including provision of facilities for local production of materials through teachers' centres. One of the Project's early publications – *Supporting Children's Bilingualism* (Houlton and Willey, 1983) – identified four areas of importance in developing resources at LEA level: a central organization which can disseminate information about ideas and materials; some centralized provision of reprographic and study resources; a central resource collection from which schools and teachers can borrow materials; and adequate in-service provision to cover theoretical and practical aspects of language diversity in the classroom.

It needs to be stressed that any procedures or organizations set up locally should cater for teachers from both mainstream and community mother tongue schools, who can then share facilities and ideas. At a series of bilingual conferences held by the ILEA in March 1983, there was an overwhelming call by all mother tongue teachers for a place where they could go to use the sort of equipment and resources available to mainstream teachers, share ideas and information and find out about recent developments in the field of language teaching. Ideally, a particular teachers' centre, or other resource-based centre with the requisite facilities, could be designated and an Adviser, probably from the Modern Languages Department, identified to be responsible for establishing and maintaining access for community language teachers. In-service provision for mother tongue teachers could be made at the same centres.

Schools also have a role to play in developing resources for mother tongue teaching and support. Even where there is no bilingual teacher, there is much that schools can do to make materials in home languages available to bilingual children. The Project's policy booklet, *Supporting Children's Bilingualism* (op. cit.), identified a number of resource priorities for schools including materials for children; bilingual support through teachers, ancillary staff and parents; additional clerical help, access to equipment such as typewriters in community languages, timetabled opportunities for discussion and workshops and links with mother tongue schools.

Individual community teachers may feel there is little they can do to develop resources for mother tongue teaching, particularly if their finances are limited and they have few links with mainstream schools.

Here the Project's experience may be helpful. In Chapter 3 (p. 70) an account was given of how the Bengali-speaking and Greek-speaking teachers tackled the problem of identifying needs and developing materials to fill any resource gaps, a model followed later by the wider range of community language groups with whom the Project team worked in the final year.

By the end of the Project, the Bengali-speaking and Greek-speaking teachers, and later teachers from the many community language groups with whom the Project worked, were able to compile charts showing the range of resources available for each language. An example is given in Chart 8.1.

Besides surveying available resources in the mother tongue itself, with a little encouragement mother tongue teachers and also mainstream English-speaking teachers who wish to support children's home languages have been able to build up their own resource collections of materials. Many are available from local community bookshops and other shops and parents will often willingly supply useful items from home such as postcards, pictures, newspapers, toys, foodstuffs, artefacts, etc, all of which may reflect the home culture and many of which may include examples of the community language script. In addition, many organizations, such as the Health Education Council, produce free leaflets in a range of community language scripts which can help build up a resource collection. There are also a large number of resources developed for other purposes which can be adapted for any language, such as text-free books, board and card games, picture stimulus material, number work materials and language development aids. A guide to these has been produced by the Project under the title 'Look – No Words!'[4]

Teachers may also find it helpful to link up with other teachers in similar situations and where possible to pool resources, even if different languages are involved. In fact, teachers from different language groups may find it useful to co-operate in order to exchange ideas and develop materials, benefiting from each other's experiences. Several teachers using the premises of one school may also be able to band together to buy a duplicator or some audio-visual materials, and thus increase the range of their resources. Of course, mother tongue teachers in mainstream schools and their mainstream colleagues who wish to support children's languages may already have access to materials and equipment which mother tongue teachers in the community are not able to use. But even they can benefit from exchanging and sharing resources – mainstream teachers can use mother tongue teachers' resources gathered from the community and probably the home country, whereas mother tongue teachers can take advantage of English medium materials used in school for adaptation and use with bilingual pupils to support their mother tongues.

Chart 8.1.   Example of the range of resources available for teaching Greek as a mother tongue

STAGES OF LANGUAGE DEVELOPMENT	BOOKS FROM GREECE	BOOKS FROM CYPRUS	SCDC MOTHER TONGUE PROJECT MATERIALS
I. Oral stage 1. Listening/ speaking	1. Patridgnosia and Posters Maths Concepts 1 and 2	1. Posters from the Cypriot Tourist Office	1. Picture Cards Our Neighbours – Figurines Story Book
2. Pre-reading	2. Greek Embassy Worksheets		2. Picture Cards
3. Writing preparation	3. I Glossa Mou (1a)		3. –
4. Assessment	4. –		4. The Lost Parrot (story and figurines)
II. Early literacy 1. Listening/ speaking	1. I Glossa Mou (1a)	1. –	1. Picture Cards Story Book Some Readers
2. Reading	2. I Glossa Mou (1b and c)	2. I Learn Greek B	2. Some Readers
3. Writing practice	3. Glossa Mou (1b and c)	3. I Learn Greek B 1	3. Greek Phonic Workbook
4. Assessment	4. –	4. –	4. The Robot – Sequence Cards
III. Extending literacy 1. Listening/ speaking	1. –	1. Tapes of Greek Myths from Cyprus Educational Broadcasting	1. Picture Cards Story Books
2. Reading	2. I Glossa Mou (2a/b/c)	2. –	2. Readers
3. Writing	3. I Glossa Mou	3. –	3. Story Book
4. Assessment	4. –	4. Spelling Books from Cyprus	4. Cloze Procedure Tests

GREEK MATERIALS FROM USA, UK AND AUSTRALIA	ENGLISH MATERIALS	TEACHER-MADE MATERIALS
1. Bilingual stories and songs on cassettes	1. Language for Learning Matching Games	1. Matching Games Tapes of stories and rhymes
2. Kyriakoudis First Reader (USA)	2. Various Picture sheets from reading schemes	2. Lotto games using alphabet
3. Kyriakoudis (USA)	3. Breakthrough method and materials	3. Alphabet Cards and Sheets
4. Papaloizos (USA)	4. –	4. Using story and figurines idea
1. Storybook from the Australian Project: a – g	1. Language for Learning No 2 and No 3	1. Tapes: stories, questions and answers, instructions to follow
2. Kyriakoudis (USA) Readers from Australia	2. –	2. Class books – pupil pictures with captions
3. Kyriakoudis Workbooks	3. –	3. Worksheets
4.	4.	4. Copy the sequence cards idea
1. Storybooks from the Australian project	1. Language for Learning 3	1. Tapes for stories; instructions to follow
2. Greek Mythology (USA)	2. LMS Actions for Word Cards	2. Instructions, like the 'listen discuss and do' on tapes and cards
3. Workbooks (USA)	3. LMS Actions for Word Cards	3. Worksheets on reading materials
4. –	4. –	4. Cloze Procedure Tests

Selection and production of materials

Apart from the practical problems of obtaining suitable resources, there are a number of other issues that arise in connection with the choice and production of materials. Very often the principles guiding the selection of suitable materials will be the same as those governing the production of original materials (see Chapter 3). Useful advice on the criteria for selection of materials can be obtained elsewhere (see Houlton, 1985, *All Our Languages*; and Klein, 1984, *Resources for Multicultural Education*), but some very important considerations include the avoidance of racism or sexism, cultural appropriacy, factual accuracy, general appeal and suitable language content.

The question of quality of the materials is another important factor. Obviously, where possible they should be of comparable quality and content to those used in mainstream classes, if they are not to be seen as of inferior status. However, where considerations of cost enter in, particularly where the market is very small, as is the case with some minority languages, it may be necessary to take a different approach, especially concerning the question of black and white materials. It was the Project's conclusion that where full colour materials prove to be impossible for reasons of cost, good quality black and white booklets are equally acceptable and may actually prove advantageous in some respects, being more flexible.

Other issues have emerged as particularly thorny problems in some cases, such as the difficulty of obtaining accurate translations or 'correct' language content. Most teachers in the field will be aware of the tortuous process of arriving at an agreed text for even a simple story. Once this has been finalized there are decisions to be made about its production; should it be handwritten for speed and cheapness or should a calligrapher or typist be brought in? Generally, the Project found that, except where class books were developed for the use of a single class, properly produced versions using a calligrapher or typist were preferred despite the extra cost. Illustrations formed another importnt consideration. Here there was unanimous agreement that good quality illustrations are vital if children's interest is to be aroused and the status of minority languages is to be enhanced. Most of these considerations apply to materials which are being developed for use by a number of teachers rather than a single practitioner; there is still, of course a place for teacher-made materials where the criteria applied are likely to be less stringent although none the less important.

Materials are, however, increasingly often produced by teachers working together in groups, and here further issues may arise in the production of materials. It is important, of course, in any teacher group that good relationships are established, but it is particularly crucial when setting up a materials development group of community language teachers, as they may come from very different backgrounds and have widely differing expertise and training. Many of the issues have already been discussed in Chapters 3 and 6, but an additional point that can be mentioned concerns recognition of the work individuals within the group have done. During the initial discussions of the group it needs to be made clear what is expected of each member and what the final outcomes are expected to be. If duplicated or published materials are the intention, then care needs to be taken to ensure that, where possible, individual contributions are included in the final selection of the materials and that, in any case, the contribution of each member is duly acknowledged.

Publication and dissemination

Once materials have been produced the issue arises of what should be done with them. Although teachers are crying out for more and better quality materials, the task of getting suitable materials to the teachers who need them is a particularly difficult one.

It is generally agreed (see the Swann Report, 1985, for example) that educational publishers should be prevailed upon to produce teaching materials relating to ethnic minority community languages. In theory, many publishers would agree but in practice a number of problems arise, not the least of which are cost effectiveness and distribution difficulties. An editor with Methuen, one of the first publishers in the United Kingdom to produce children's books in languages other than English, lists some of the problems (Collins, 1984) as including: finding suitable authors and translators, identifying the diverse yet comparatively small market, reaching the intended audience, translation problems, locating a printer with machinery able to cope with a variety of languages, and the need to extend the potential market.

Indeed, the problems are so formidable that no commercial publisher would take on the Project's Bengali and Greek medium materials which were therefore published by the SCDC, although publishers did come forward to produce the text-free materials and materials for use in multilingual classrooms, both having much wider potential markets than the language specific books.

One of the difficulties raised by Collins (op. cit.), which proved in some respects more intractable than publication for the Project, was dissemination of its materials to the intended market. As a national Project, the team was in a particularly advantageous position to distribute its materials, especially as a small time allowance for dissemination had been built into the Project's timetable. Conventional channels of dissemination such as national and regional conferences, in-service training sessions, and school-based workshops were followed. The Schools Council tradition of 'training the trainers' in order to leave contacts behind after the conclusion of the Project was possible in some cases. In addition, links were established with community-based organizations on both an official basis such as through the Greek Embassy and Bangladesh High Commission, and more informally through parents' and cultural organizations and individual contacts with teachers, schools and parents. A regular newsletter brought information to hundreds of readers and journal articles spread news about the Project's publications. In the last year of the Project an information leaflet was sent to nearly 2000 recipients carefully chosen for their interest and their potential for spreading the net wider.

Yet despite this fairly extensive publicity drive, sales of the Bengali and Greek materials have been relatively modest and are likely to drop substantially now the Project has finished and staff are no longer available to maintain momentum and take a personal interest in dissemination. Although many key people have been contacted, large numbers of community mother tongue teachers will not have been reached; for them personal contact and very localized publicity are the chief means of communication. It would seem, in the light of these factors, that an individual or a small local group would have little chance of reaching a wide audience unless they manage to work through a publisher's network or other large scale organizations.

These considerations seem to lead back to the necessity for a national body to be responsible for gathering information, assessing needs, co-ordinating initiatives and disseminating materials in the field of minority languages. In the absence of such a body, materials for mother tongue teaching and support will continue to be piecemeal, of uneven quality, difficult to locate and obtain, and remain relatively expensive.

Teacher training

Identification of needs

It is often said that teaching materials are only as good as the teachers who use them. Splendid materials, incorporating the most up-to-date theories and approaches, may be available, but if teachers do not know how to use them they may ignore them or employ them to limited effect. Where teachers, such as community language teachers, are unaccustomed to the underlying principles and strategies implicit in new materials, or unfamiliar with current mainstream primary school approaches, they may not be able to take advantage of the range of resources and techniques already available which could be adapted to their use.

Equally, mainstream primary school teachers are generally unaware the range of situations in which community mother tongue teachers work and have little knowledge of their teaching approaches and the constraints under which they operate. This sometimes leads to misunderstandings on both sides, and underlines the need for a comprehensive programme of teacher training for all those concerned with the education of ethnic minority children, both mainstream primary teachers in multilingual schools and mother tongue teachers, whether they teach in mainstream or community organized schools.

In many respects, teacher training for mainstream primary teachers in multilingual schools logically precedes teacher training for mother tongue teachers, as without their support, the work of mother tongue teachers, whether within the mainstream classroom or in community run classes, will have little effect. This has recently been pointed out in the Swann Report (op. cit.), which recommends that all teacher training should inform teachers about linguistic diversity so that teachers in multilingual schools should 'be able to recognize the language being spoken, to recognize the various scripts, to pronounce the children's names correctly and to understand enough of the structure of the language to appreciate the nature of the difficulties children may be experiencing with English'.

It is important to underline the complementary roles of mainstream teachers in the multilingual classroom and their bilingual colleagues if mother tongue teachers are not to be marginalized and their status deemed inferior. It is also important to facilitate the exchange of views about teaching approaches between the two groups of teachers, even when they teach in the very different situations of the mainstream and community classrooms. Both types of teacher need to work alongside each other and benefit from each other's perspectives and experience and indeed there is much to be said for a form of in-service training which brings the two groups together, at least for part of the time.

Frequently, however, teacher training for mother tongue teachers is seen as a more urgent priority. An HMI inquiry (DES, 1984) into mother tongue teaching in four LEAs, for example, drew attention to problems arising in relation to staffing, particularly the lack of suitable and suitably qualified teachers, which sometimes acted as a constraint on development of mother tongue work. The report stated: 'The in-service training of mother tongue teachers emerges as a matter of particular concern' and suggested that in-service training of teachers both in schools and community classes needed support, despite the complexities involved. Likewise the authors of the Swann Report (op. cit.) referred to their concern about the 'limited teaching ability of some of the teachers of ethnic minority languages whom we have met'. The committee felt that ethnic minority teachers should have recognized qualifications in the

received professional training in this country
English, if they are to merit equal status with
and hope to convince teaching colleagues, pupils
idity of the subject.

organizations concerned with community language
highlighted the need for both initial and in-service
in a discussion paper, published in 1983, on the supply
and community language teachers (NCMTT, 1983), the
NCMTT pointed out that whereas a number of LEA policy documents
and local and national working parties had advocated the teaching of
community languages, at that time only the Commission for Racial
Equality (CRE, 1982) and the National Congress on Languages in
Education Working Party Paper (*Towards a Programme of In-Service
Training for Minority Languages*, NCLE, 1981, quoted in NCMTT, 1983)
had mentioned in any detail the supply and training of teachers for these
languages.

The NCMTT document (op. cit.) draws attention to the complexity of
the needs of community language teachers deriving from the diversity of
contexts in which they operate and the wide variety of backgrounds from
which they come. In fact the teachers may fall into one or more of seven
different categories: trained as teachers of their own language in Britain
or overseas; trained as teachers of other subjects; trained as primary
school teachers; trained as E2L teachers; academically qualified in a
specific language but without teacher training or teaching experience;
academically qualified with voluntary teaching experience but without
teacher training; or may be teachers in the voluntary sector with at least
secondary education in the language they teach, but with no special
training in language teaching.

Issues raised by the Project's work

Over the four years of the Project, the team worked with many mother
tongue teachers who covered the full range of categories described above.
The main focus of the Project's work was with primary age children and
consequently the issues highlighted by the experiences of these teachers
relate largely to the training of teachers of primary age children. In many
respects it is difficult to make a distinction between mother tongue
teachers in primary and in secondary schools as they frequently face
similar situations, such as lack of facilities, marginalization and poor
career prospects.

However, in some ways, the issues which arise in connection with
mother tongue teachers are intensified in the primary school situation. It
is at this stage in education that questions concerning the purpose and

rationale of mother tongue teaching are more crucial; it is easier at the secondary stage to offer a community language as an option without a major upheaval to the curriculum, whereas primary school teachers generally feel responsible for the whole education of children in their care. Similarly, mother tongue teachers taking children for a community language in the secondary school do not need to liaise so closely with colleagues as in the primary school, where they may be working in the same classroom and following a parallel programme.

Again, mainstream teachers in the secondary school are more accustomed to working with staff teaching different subjects, including modern languages, and are less likely to question the teaching approaches they use or to feel uneasy about teachers using languages in the classroom that they do not understand.

Despite these differences, many of the issues discussed might well be shared by secondary teachers, but it should be borne in mind that they are based on the experiences of teachers of primary age children with whom the Project worked.

These teachers shared two overriding and overlapping concerns: to obtain recognized qualifications, which would place them on a par with their colleagues in mainstream schools; and to gain experience of mainstream methods. Many felt particularly frustrated when they had what they perceived as adequate qualifications and, in many cases, training overseas, but were denied qualified teacher status in Britain and therefore could not obtain a job in mainstream schools. Others were aware that their training or qualifications were considered inadequate but could not see a means by which this could be rectified, given the current provision for teacher training.

Given this range of backgrounds, the two community language co-ordinators on the Project team worked hard to provide some help in the form of a modest 'in-service' training programme. Visits of observation to mainstream primary schools were arranged by the Bengali co-ordinator, and took place on a part-time basis over the half-term preceding the Project trials. Frequent visits and meetings were held with the teachers to acquaint them with up-to-date thinking and materials, and where possible, meetings with whole school staffs were arranged so that mainstream teachers and mother tongue colleagues could exchange views and experiences.

Even so, many of the mother tongue teachers felt ill-equipped and marginal. For them, proper teaching training courses, whether initial or in-service, leading to recognized qualifications that would enable them to obtain worthwhile jobs with career prospects were of vital importance. For community language teachers working outside the mainstream sector, especially those already with full-time jobs, career prospects were less important, but information about current teaching methodology and up-to-date approaches were required.

Several of the primary schools with whom the Project worked were also concerned that many of the mother tongue teachers had not had appropriate training, which they considered essential if mother tongue teachers are not to be considered second class and their languages consequently devalued. This issue, which generally arose in connection with perceived differences in the teaching approaches used by mother tongue teachers compared with mainstream colleagues, has likewise arisen in the case of a few LEAs which have reacted over hastily to the demand for mother tongue teaching and introduced teachers into schools without adequate preparation on both sides.

Although opinion is by no means uniform on this question, with some teachers feeling it is better to have the mother tongue teachers with less than perfect qualifications than none at all, adequate teacher training provision would obviously iron out many of these problems.

Another important issue is that of conflicting expectations between the two sectors. Mainstream teachers may feel unsure about the function of mother tongue teachers who may likewise be uncertain of their role and objectives. Sometimes mainstream class teachers felt the mother tongue teacher was there to assist them, whereas the community language teacher might be under the impression she was there to teach children to become literate in their mother tongue. Again, in-service teacher training, especially where the two sectors are brought together, will help sort out these difficulties.

Linked to both the issue of teaching approaches and that of conflicting expectations is the question of teacher attitudes. Where mainstream primary teachers have entrenched views on the nature and role of community languages, at variance with current opinion or LEA policy, then the introduction of mother tongue teaching may well be counter-productive unless adequate preparation, probably including some kind of teacher training, is instituted in advance. Here again, the crucial role of the mainstream teacher is underlined as a critical variable in developing successful strategies of support for children's home languages.

It was the experience of the Project that the particular language involved was of less importance than the teacher. Despite the different situations in which the Bengali-speaking and Greek-speaking teachers operated, and notwithstanding their varied backgrounds, the personality of the teacher, her teaching experience and her attitude towards the purpose of mother tongue teaching were all crucial variables. This finding is supported by a large-scale long-term Welsh bilingual education project which concluded that 'the teachers' role was considered to be the most important factor determining the realization of a good bilingual education programme' (Price, 1984). However, for community language teachers, this finding should be interpreted with caution, as many factors which appear to stem from teachers' individual characteristics are in fact a function of their structural position within society in general and education in particular.

One group of teachers whose teacher training needs have rarely been considered are those commonly called 'extra-territorial' teachers, i.e. teachers who are not British citizens but come to this country for a period of years (generally between 3 and 7 years) under the aegis of their governments to teach children of expatriates now living in the UK. The largest group of such teachers are probably the Italian, Greek, Spanish and Portuguese. Whilst these teachers are not the responsibility of the British education system, nevertheless, since the children they teach attend British schools and in some cases may be taught in their home language during the school day, they need to be included in any discussion of community language teachers and their training needs. Although most of the Consulates and Embassies concerned provide their own in-service training sessions, closer links between these teachers and their counterparts in British schools would help to overcome some of the issues raised by their presence in mainstream schools (see p.101).

A final issue that needs to be raised is the need for information, not only about the existing developments in the field of teacher training for teachers of community languages, particularly in LEAs where in-service developments are taking place rapidly, but also to ascertain the precise numbers and location of teachers from ethnic minority communities already teaching in maintained schools. Although there are substantial numbers of such teachers (4000 – 5000 according to the CRE, 1982), it cannot automatically be assumed that they will be willing to change the nature of their teaching and take up mother tongue teaching. Their views on this issue, together with their suggestions for the kind of training they might choose, need to be ascertained, possibly through a national or regional surveys. Similarly, if concerned LEAs are to take seriously their wish to help local community-organized classes and teachers then they also need systematically to investigate local demand and facilities.

Existing facilities

Although there is growing awareness of the needs for teacher training for community language teachers, provision has not matched requirements.

A survey (Craft and Atkins, 1982) of initial teacher training institutions with a view to their existing and latent capacity for training teachers of ethnic minority community languages was carried out for the Swann Committee. Reporting on facilities for initial teacher training and specifically on PGCE courses for modern languages, the authors comment, 'Nowhere in England and Wales can a graduate in ethnic minority community languages such as Turkish, Greek, Chinese, Arabic, Portuguese, or any Asian language, obtain an appropriate training for teaching'. With the BEd situation apparently even weaker, the only possibility for study seemed to be through self-instruction facilities at language centres, where there was felt to be considerable scope for development. A large majority of institutions (over 70 per cent) claimed to offer awareness of some of the main issues, such as language and dialect differences, mother tongue teaching and bilingualism, as part of the normal PGCE or BEd curriculum but only just over a half sought to develop competencies for offering language support across the curriculum in linguistically diverse schools and less than one-third placed such work in the compulsory core.

On the other hand, there is more evidence of provision within in-service teacher training facilities. The Royal Society of Arts Certificate in the teaching of Community Languages is the only award bearing course in the country, and is currently available in seven locations.[5] In response to the need for qualifications and teaching experience which prevents some teachers from being accepted on the RSA course, Access courses are being set up in a few colleges to provide elementary training for community language teachers. In addition a number of LEAs now provide some form of in-service training for mother tongue teachers, either those working in their schools, usually on a peripatetic basis, or for community-based voluntary teachers, or both. Examples include Bradford, Nottinghamshire, Berkshire, Birmingham and the Inner London Education Authority.

Obviously, no one form of provision for the training of community language teachers will suffice. A careful and thorough investigation of the demand, needs and possible types of solution needs to be carried out, bearing in mind both short-run and long-term requirements. Both initial teacher training institutions and locally-based in-service provision will be necessary if teachers are to be offered flexibility and choice. Another possibility is the provision of courses at regionally-based institutions, such as universities or teacher training institutions serving several local education authorities. In this situation there could be sufficient demand generated for individual languages to have separate provision if necessary. Finally, the importance of proper qualifications and genuine career prospects is fundamental if community language teachers are to take a full part in the education system and if the children they teach and indeed their monolingual peers are to receive the full benefits of living in a multilingual society.

Liaison between schools, parents and communities

Although primary schools, in the wake of the Plowden Report (1967), have generally taken seriously the importance of developing good relationships with parents, establishing similarly beneficial relationships with ethnic minority parents and their communities has been a more recent and more complex undertaking, as we saw in Chapter 6. The Mother Tongue Project, through its work with two ethnic minority communities, particularly highlighted the importance of forming two-way relationships with minority communities.

Some of the issues that arose during this aspect of the Project's work are of general relevance to all who are working in the field, and it is to be hoped that by drawing attention to them, some of the problems faced can be avoided in the future.

The first point to be made concerns the establishment of links not only with parents but also with community mother tongue teachers and their schools. It is most important to forge links with community teachers if teachers in both mainstream and community schools are to build upon each other's work and ethnic minority children are to reap the benefits of their bilingualism.

Both parents and community mother tongue teachers will need to be approached with sensitivity and understanding so as to avoid misunderstandings about the purpose of the approach and to elicit a favourable response. Mainstream teachers are often surprised at the amount of input this involves, not always being aware of the different attitudes to the role of the education system in some ethnic minority communities' home countries, and sometimes underestimating the time it takes to build up relationships between different cultures. In addition, members of some communities, perhaps because they have been in Britain for a relatively short time, prefer face to face approaches, if possible from a member of their own community, to written communications (albeit in their own language) which are the usual means of contact in British schools. It is worth emphasizing that these relationships should be established on an egalitarian basis if they are to be more than a token gesture.

Making contact with parents, and beyond them with the wider communities of which they and the community mother tongue teachers are a part, involves developing an understanding of the socio-economic and political setting within which the communities are placed. It is important here to distinguish between specific communities, as each has its own linguistic, cultural and religious differences, in addition to its socio-economic and political characteristics, making it unwise to lump together children from a range of ethnic minority communities. Certainly, with the two ethnic minority communities with whom the Project worked most closely – Bengali and Greek – despite many similarities there were quite fundamental differences, many of which are described in Chapter 6.

Two interrelated differences of particular importance were the political status of the ethnic minorities concerned and the role of their home governments in this country. In the case of the Bengali-speaking community, immigrants to this country have British citizenship, and generally come to this country with the intention of making it their home. In this situation, and taking into account the relative poverty of the two home governments concerned, Bangladesh and India, very little concrete support can be given by the home governments to Bengali-speaking mother tongue teachers and their pupils, although moral encouragement is forthcoming.

On the other hand, the Greek-speaking community includes settlers, and in addition refugees, whose political and legal status is more precarious. It is further complicated by the presence of mainland Greeks whose status will become more like that of migrants from Cyprus when EC rules change as a result of the entry of Greece to the EC. Again, there are two home governments concerned, Greece and Cyprus, and both have established educational arrangements to make provision for mother tongue tuition for Greek origin children living in this country. While this is largely beneficial, it is also, in some respects, a disadvantage. The free provision of teachers and materials is, of course, of great assistance to Greek-speaking communities in Britain, who wish to maintain their language and culture. But at the same time it is also a constraining factor for both the community, and to a greater extent for the mainstream of British education, which wishes to encourage support of children's home languages.

Not only do relationships between overseas governments and their expatriate communities in this country have to be taken into account but also, in cases where more than one home government is involved, as in the two examples quoted above, the interrelationships between these have to be borne in mind. Thus, to reiterate a point advanced in Chapter 6 in a slightly different form, ethnic minority communities cannot be considered as single entities, but rather as composed of many different elements, both in respect of the people who comprise them and the organizations which exercise influence over them.

Organizational issues

In the light of the multilingual nature of contemporary British society and the changing climate of educational opinion regarding appropriate responses, many schools with significant numbers of ethnic minority children have been considering how best they can cater for the diverse linguistic needs of all their pupils.

Previous sections in this chapter have considered the availability of appropriate resources and suitable teachers, both of which are essential components in sound curriculum development. But, in addition, there are other pertinent issues which teachers must take into account when considering the place of mother tongues in their schools. Some of these are philosophical, having to do with the purpose of supporting children's home languages; these are considered in the last section of this chapter. But others are of a more practical nature, and concern ways in which home languages can realistically be supported within schools.

Earlier chapters have discussed these issues in depth and the details will not be repeated here. But a few conclusions, or more accurately, questions for further discussion, can be drawn out as part of the overall consideration of the central issues in the mother tongue debate. Probably the most fundamental concerns the place of the mother tongue within the mainstream primary school curriculum. Schools will need to decide why they wish to support home languages and how they fit into their overall policy, particularly their language policy. Closely related to this is a consideration of the stage at which the mother tongue should be supported, whether at infant, junior or secondary age, as appropriate.

Once schools have decided to support children's mother tongues in concrete ways, decisions regarding timetabling and curriculum have to be taken. Should children have a certain time set aside when they learn their mother tongue or should they learn *through* their mother tongue? If they are to learn their mother tongue, should this be carried out in the mainstream classroom or in a separate room? While they are having mother tongue tuition what are they missing? If ethnic minority children are receiving mother tongue teaching, whether in the mainstream classroom or in a separate room, what efforts have been made to link the curriculum so that children can follow similar work? What do the rest of the children think about it? Do parents, both ethnic minority parents and indigenous parents, know about it? Have they been consulted and do they understand why these languages are being used in school?

While each school will need to find its own solution, some general guidelines need to be worked out to which all schools, particularly those new to the debate, can refer. It is not enough to document practice and discuss issues as the HMI report (DES, 1984) does, hoping that 'a coherent pattern may emerge that clarifies what it is that schools can realistically do'; systematic investigation of the possibilities, together with firm suggestions of alternative courses of action based on sound educational principles and practice are what is needed.

The role and provision of mother tongue teaching for primary age children: current trends

An account of the many different arguments advanced in support of mother tongue teaching, and some against, was put forward in Chapter 1. These will not be repeated here but a few salient points need to be drawn out when considering the present and future role to be taken by mother tongue teaching within and outside the British education system.

It was pointed out in Chapter 1 that teachers and other educationalists within the British education system may have very different perspectives about the nature and role of mother tongue teaching compared with their counterparts in the ethnic minority communities.

Those responsible for state education generally put educational reasons first for supporting children's home languages, such as continuity of learning, building upon existing skills, enhancing confidence and therefore motivation to learn and, of course, stimulating the acquisition of English, with broader psychological arguments concerning status and self-esteem following close behind. More recently, other reasons have come to the fore, such as the anti-racist argument that inclusion of home languages demonstrates acceptance and respect for the communities which speak them; and considerations of an economic nature, pointing out the benefits Britain, as a trading nation, can derive from the range of community languages spoken in this country. Whatever the arguments, it is clear that mother tongue teaching has to be a matter of choice in mainstream schools if children are to be free to take advantage of the opportunity without feeling they have been assigned to a peripheral activity which reinforces their inferior status.

Parents and mother tongue teachers within the ethnic minority communities are more likely to stress social and cultural reasons for sustaining children's home languages, including the importance of retaining cultural ties through the languages, maintaining contact with the family, promoting self-esteem, with educational arguments very much in the background. For ethnic minority communities, political and economic considerations also underlie their support for mother tongue classes.

These broad generalizations, however, mask wide differences in approach within each sector. Some mainstream teachers put the acquisition of English as a first priority and do not see the extension of mother tongue support beyond that goal as desirable or relevant. Others may consider the provision of mother tongue teaching to be justified on the grounds that children have a 'right' to tuition in their first language or the language of their community. Still others may feel that children's self-esteem and status is the most important factor and that *all* children should appreciate the value of the many different languages and cultures present in Britain today.

Whatever the different rationales, provision within the state system has generally taken a fairly consistent form. As described more fully in Chapter 4, there has been support for a transitional model at nursery and lower infants level, and a growth in provision for home languages within the option system at secondary school level, with very little coverage in between the two age ranges.

Within the ethnic minority communities there is also wide variation in attitudes towards the place of mother tongue teaching. Views may differ not only between different linguistic communities but also within them.

Where communities such as those made up of Bengali speakers or Gujarati speakers have settled in Britain permanently, they are more likely to view mother tongue teaching as a means to maintain contact with the home country and to solidify relationships within the community here. But where a community, such as the Italians or Spanish, still regards its home country as a possible place for return, then mother tongue teaching may be considered a means to an end, i.e. maintaining and developing children's home language so that they can take their place in the home country should they return there. Again, within each community there may be quite diverse views. For example, the Project's contact person at the Greek Embassy saw the current aim of mother tongue teaching outside Greece and Cyprus 'to combine all Greeks abroad under the umbrella of Hellenism', a view other Greek speakers in this country might not share. Others, such as many devout Moslems, might consider the transmission of religious belief to be the major goal.

In addition to the different views about the role of mother tongue teaching, a number of other problems or issues remain unresolved. Despite the growth in interest and support for children's home languages both within ethnic minority communities and, more recently, within mainstream education, there is still much confusion and disagreement about why it should be supported, how it should be organized and who should be responsible for its provision.

There is, as yet, little uniformity in either ideas or practice beyond the broad outlines of provision referred to above although this is, of course, common in the development of any new curriculum area. Many teachers still feel uncertain about the grounds for acknowledging children's mother tongues, whilst others instinctively feel they should be valuing them but are not sure of the precise reasons or the benefits that may accrue. In the absence of relevant research findings and support from the Department of Education and Science and sometimes their local education authorities, they are neither sure of their ground nor decided about how they should proceed. On the other hand, many teachers have carefully considered the issues and have already put into practice some of their ideas, but again there is a lack of consensus about either the goals of the teaching or the methodologies entailed.

A number of local education authorities have now begun to consider seriously their responsibilities in the field of mother tongue, and this has led to the formulation of policies in some cases although, as we have seen, this is not always matched in practice by action at grassroots level. But there are still many LEAs, even in areas of high ethnic minority concentration, who have yet to enter into the discussion, despite the changing climate of opinion and the obligations of the EC Directive.

Among the problems that LEAs and schools often put forward as constraining factors is the diversity of languages present in their classrooms and how these can best be catered for. Many teachers feel they cannot support one language, even if it is a predominant one among the children in a particular class without supporting the others, and this presents considerable difficulties in organization, staffing, materials, etc. Another important consideration is the involvement of *all* children in the multicultural, multilingual society in which they live, including monolingual children in multilingual classrooms and those in monolingual schools. Tied up with this is the wider issue of anti-racism and how it can be linked to mother tongue support, especially in monolingual schools.

One issue which remains a matter of controversy concerns the question of who should be responsible for provision of mother tongue teaching, in particular whether the state education system or the ethnic minority communities themselves should be the major responsible authority. When the ethnic minority communities first settled in Britain little consideration was given to their home languages, and acquisition of English was seen as the priority. But over the years, first the ethnic minority communities and more recently the British education system have come to recognize the importance of supporting and maintaining children's mother tongues.

Whereas previously this was thought to be the responsibility of the ethnic minority communities, there is growing support from within both sectors for the idea that the state education system itself has a duty to make provision for mother tongue support.

Current DES policy, which has recently been echoed in the Swann Report, does not accord bilinguals the *right* to maintain their mother tongue, but feels that schools can make a contribution by encouraging an atmosphere which promotes respect of other cultures and languages and, where appropriate, by employing the use of the mother tongue to aid transition to English. It suggests that community-based provision can be more effective, and more responsive to the needs of linguistic minorities, and should be encouraged by LEAs through the provision of free or cheap premises and access to local in-service courses. Whereas most community mother tongue teachers and many mainstream teachers would not wish the maintained education system to take over these classes entirely, and see a continuing role for the community in so far as cultural maintenance is concerned, many feel that language maintenance should be a partnership between the state and the community, and are disappointed by the lukewarm response to their demands.

Future trends

In this context, then, what are the future trends likely to be, both in respect of educational opinion and provision and as regards long-term maintenance of the mother tongue by linguistic minority communities in future generations?

One of the Project's advisers commented that ten years ago mother tongue support was at variance with current educational philosophy, but that opinion has now changed and it is here to stay, unless philosophical views change, although it may suffer economically given current financial problems. While it is true that, in principle, many educationalists support the recognition and use of children's mother tongues as an extension of the principle of child-centred education, there is, as we have seen, no general consensus about the responsibility for, or nature of, provision.

Although there are many different views about the relative roles of mainstream and community mother tongue schools in providing mother tongue support, there seems to be agreement that provision will continue to expand in both the mainstream and community sectors, and that links between the two will also increase.

It may be that there will be a concentration on language support within the state education system, and more emphasis on cultural maintenance within community-run classes, but most people are agreed that there will continue to be a need for community-organized classes, whatever happens within the mainstream sector. Not only will vested interests within the community, particularly religious authorities, ensure it, but it is also unlikely that mainstream schools will feel able to provide the cultural content and cohesion considered an essential component by ethnic minority communities. In any case, the decision whether to take advantage of mother tongue support or not has to be, as pointed out earlier, a matter of choice; and some pupils and their parents may prefer to receive mother tongue teaching from within the community.

Expansion of provision within mainstream schools is likely to occur at both primary and secondary levels, although there is continuing uncertainty about what will happen to the junior age range, which at present is little provided for. Some feel that there will be more direct teaching of the language, whilst others believe that current support for children's home languages will result in an increase in bilingual education (i.e. simultaneous use of the mother tongue and English), already initiated in a limited form in some LEAs, as children maintain and extend their proficiency in two or more languages.

Others maintain that acquisition of literacy in the mother tongue during the junior school age range is more properly the responsibility of the community. However, with changes currently being made to public examinations in minority languages, the increased interest and demand which is likely to result may well lead to a demand for provision in junior schools in order to ensure continuity and comprehensive coverage from infants through juniors to secondary school pupils.

Another area of expansion, which in itself may lead to increased demand for community language provision, not only for speakers of these languages but also for their monolingual English-speaking peers, is the development of language awareness courses which are already provided by some LEAs. These will stimulate interest not only in community languages but also in varieties of English and in language generally. Together with expanded provision for home languages, these are likely to go some way to responding to the challenge presented by Britain's multilingual society. But much depends on sufficient funds being made available and on favourable attitudes within the educational establishment; without these progress will be slow.

It was said earlier that future generations of today's ethnic minorities would depend on present day pupils' maintaining and extending their mother tongues if tomorrow's teachers are to be available when needed. Opinion is divided as to the future of ethnic minority languages in this country in succeeding generations, and much is seen to depend on current attitudes and provision. Many people believe that without proper support from the state education system these languages will be lost and with them a potentially rich resource. At the same time their speakers, having lost a vital part of their cultural inheritance, may feel rootless and disaffected. Others feel that these languages will continue to flourish due to community support and the importance of maintaining cultural and self-identity. They point to the example of the USA where there has been something of a resurgence in ethnic minority languages as members of ethnic minority communities have discovered that a move away from home languages did not lead to assimilation and the social equality they were seeking.

Summary and conclusion

This chapter has reviewed some of the main issues that are current in the field of mother tongue teaching and support.

A major priority which logically precedes any kind of development is the need for information and research about linguistic diversity, mother tongue teaching and bilingualism in Britain. Without this, suitable policies and programmes cannot be drawn up.

Many mother tongue teachers share common issues relating to resources and teacher training requirements. They often have to rely on inappropriate materials, lack essential equipment that would make their jobs easier, have difficulty gaining access to school facilities and may be unaware of readily available resources which could be adapted for their use. A national co-ordinating body could help prevent duplication of effort and needless gaps in the availability of suitable materials, and stimulate the exchange of ideas and information. But there is still a role for Local Education Authorities in assisting the production and dissemination of suitable mother tongue teaching materials and resources, possibly through providing access to local teachers' centres.

Teacher training has been identified as a major need by both mainstream and mother tongue teachers alike. It is essential not only to promote good quality teaching but also to ensure equal status and proper career prospects for ethnic minority teachers. There are a number of issues concerning teacher training often involving the different expectations and approaches of mainstream primary school teachers and mother tongue teachers, many of which could be resolved by a form of in-service training which brought the two groups together.

One of the major outcomes of the Project's work was the highlighting of the importance of liaison between schools, parents and the communities. A sensitive approach, combined with an understanding of the socio-economic and political setting within which the communities are placed will help establish mutually beneficial relationships.

Many of the issues which arise in connection with mother tongue teaching concern the justification for its inclusion within the curriculum. There are a range of views about the purpose and function of mother tongue teaching both within mainstream schools and within ethnic minority communities. In recent years there has been an increase in support for children's home languages although there is still uncertainty about why it should be supported, how it should be organized and who should be responsible for its provision.

Current trends seem to indicate an expansion in mother tongue support in both mainstream and community sectors. Provision within mainstream schools is likely to increase at both primary and secondary levels although there is continuing uncertainty about what will happen to the junior age range. Provision in community run classes will continue to be needed to provide cultural content and cohesion. At the same time there is likely to be further development of the language awareness courses already provided by some LEAs.

It is now four years since the Mother Tongue Project was set up. During this time, attitudes towards children's mother tongues have changed significantly, and many schools and LEAs now believe that children's bilingualism is an asset to be nurtured rather than a disadvantage to be suppressed. Much, however, still needs to be done. There is a shortage of suitable materials and facilities, and even where these are available, teachers are often not aware of them. Many mainstream teachers remain uncertain about why community languages should be supported and what their role should be. At the same time, community mother tongue teachers, while firmly convinced of the value of mother tongue teaching, frequently labour under adverse conditions to help children maintain and develop their mother tongues.

The Project was set up in order to help meet some of these needs. By providing a range of materials for both bilingual and non-bilingual teachers, it has gone some way to help teachers who previously felt unsure of their ground or who lacked suitable materials to put their ideas into practice. At the same time, by raising a number of issues during the course of this work, the Project has helped to move the debate forward and contributed theoretically and practically to meeting the needs of young bilingual children. If, through the Project's work, the potentially rich resource Britain has in its bilingual children is fostered and developed, then the Project will have fulfilled its aims!

Notes

1. Schools Language Survey, University of London Institute of Education, Information Office, 20 Bedford Way, London WC1.

2. Access to Information on Multicultural Education Resources (AIMER), Bulmershe College of Higher Education, Reading.

3. Urdu Teaching: Newsletter No. 16, September – 1984 January 1985. The newsletter can be obtained from Ralph Russell, 19 Earlsthorpe Road, Sydenham, London SE26 4PD.

4. 'Look – No Words', a guide to text-free materials adaptable in any language, is being prepared for publication.

5. Birmingham, London, Cambridge, Manchester, Edinburgh, Enfield and Newham.

Appendix A
The Project's advisory group: list of members

Mr R Biswas	Teacher, Birmingham
Ms H Carter	Professional Officer, Schools Council, subsequently Professional Officer, School Curriculum Development Committee
Mrs A Craft	Research Officer, Schools Council, subsequently Professional Officer, School Curriculum Development Committee
Mrs I Fafalios	Researcher and Organizer of Greek Schools, London
Mr H Hester	Director of the Language in the Multicultural Primary Classroom Project
Mr D Houlton	Lecturer in Primary Education, University of Nottingham (from September 1984)
Mr M Kashis	Head teacher of Greek Community Schools in London, Cyprus High Commission
Dr V Saifullah Khan	Director of the Linguistic Minorities Project
Ms D Manley	Editor, Schools Council Publications
Mrs B Moore	Teacher, Coventry
Ms B Newman	Editor, SCDC Publications
Mr C Power	Multicultural Adviser, Haringey
Dr A Santos	Education Officer, Consulado Generale de Portugal
Mr J Singh	HM Inspectorate of Schools
Mr R Truman	National Council for Mother Tongue Teaching

| Mr J Wight | Inspector for Multicultural Education, ILEA |
| Ms S Wiles | Director of Language Division, Centre for Urban Education Studies, ILEA |

THE PROJECT TEAM

David Houlton	Director (to August 1984)
Paula Tansley	Evaluator (to August 1984) Director (from September 1984
Hasina Nowaz	Bengali Co-ordinator
Maria Roussou	Greek Co-ordinator
Lyn Keen	Administrative Assistant

Appendix B
List of EC pilot schemes related to the education of migrant workers' children

LOCATION		YEARS	SUBJECT/NATIONALITIES	LEVEL OF EDUCATION
Reception methods				
B	Waterschei/ Winterslag	1976–1979	Italian, Greek, Turkish	Primary education (6 to 8)
NL	Enschede	1979–1982	Turkish, Moroccan	Pre-primary and primary education. (4 to 8)
NL	Leiden	1977–1980	New arrivals – Turkish, Moroccan	Primary education
LU	Luxembourg	1978–1981	In a multilingual area – Italian, Portuguese	Primary education
DK	Odense	1977–1980	In a low immigration area – UK Commonwealth	Primary education
Teaching of the language and culture of origin: intercultural education				
B	Limburg	1979–1982	Italian, Greek, Turkish	Primary education
F	Paris	1976–1979	Italian, Portuguese, Serbo-Croat, Spanish	Primary education
F	Marseilles	1979–1982	Italian, Portuguese, Turkish, Arab	Primary education
UK	Bedford	1976–1980	Italian, Panjabi	Primary education
UK	London	1981–85	Greek, Bengali	Primary education
B	Limburg	1982–	Italian, Greek, Turkish (Moroccan)	Secondary education (12 to 15)
B	Min. Educ. (French Speak.)	1983–	Remedial teaching – Guidance	Secondary education (12 to 15)
DK	Copenhagen	1982–	Remedial teaching – Guidance	Secondary education (13 to 16)
NL	Amsterdam	1984–	Arab, Turkish	Secondary education (13 to 16)
UK	London	1984–	Italian, Panjabi, Urdu	Secondary education
Training of teachers – further training				
D	Nordrhein-Westfalen	1976–1978	Greek and Italian teachers	

LOCATION		YEARS	SUBJECT/NATIONALITIES	LEVEL OF EDUCATION
F	Min. Educ.	1976–1978	French and foreign teachers	
B	Brussels	1979–1981	Belgian teachers	
D	Landau	1981–1982	Further training Italian teachers	
F	Min. Educ.	1982–	French and foreign teachers	

Development of educational material

IT	Istituto della Encicl. Ital.	1980–	For Italian pupils in French-speaking countries	Primary education
GR	Min. Educ.	1982–	For Greek pupils in the Federal Republic of Germany	Primary education
D	Berlin	1982–	For Turkish pupils in the Federal Republic of Germany	Secondary education (10 to 16)
UK	Coventry	1981–1983	For children of Irish migrant workers in Britain	Primary education
{ F	Paris	1983–	Music and singing didactics –	Pre-primary and primary
{ UK	London	1984–	EC and emigration countries	education (3 to 9)

Dissemination of information and educational material

UK	London LMP, LINC*	1980–	Ethnic minorities in the United Kingdom	Primary and secondary education

Comparative evaluation of pilot schemes

D	ALFA*	1976–1979 1979–1982	Reception methods – Teaching of the language and culture of origin – Intercultural education	
F	CREDIF* LARESSO*	1979–1982	Reception methods – Teaching of the language and culture of origin – Intercultural education	

*	LMP	Linguistic Minorities Project
	LINC	Language Information Network Coordination
	ALFA	Ausbildung von Lehrern für Ausländerkinder (Universität Essen)
	CREDIF	Centre de Recherche et d'Etude pour la Diffusion du Français (Ecole Normale Supérieur de Saint-Cloud)
	LARESSO	Laboratoire de Recherche en Sciences Sociales

Appendix C
Published materials produced by the Mother Tongue Project

Text-free materials for any language
Picture Cards
Our Neighbours
Outline Story Book

All published by Philip and Tacey Ltd., Northway, Andover, Hants.

Bengali and Greek materials
Bengali Primary Readers 1 and 2
Bengali Workbooks 1 and 2
Greek Workbook

Set (A) 5 *Story Readers in Bengali*
Set (B) 5 *Story Readers in Bengali*
Set (C) 7 *Story Readers in English*
Set (D) 7 *Story Readers in English*
Set (E) 6 *Story Readers in Greek*
Set (F) 4 *Story Readers in Greek*

Teaching Bengali as a Mother Tongue in Britain
Teaching Greek as a Mother Tongue in Britain

All published by SCDC Publications, London W11.

Materials for teachers in multilingual primary classrooms
Supporting Children's Bilingualism (published by Longman Resources
    Unit,).
All Our Languages (published by Edward Arnold Ltd., London).
Children's Language Project Activity Cards (published by Philip and
    Tacey Ltd.).

Handbooks for teachers of community languages
'Look – No Words' by Deborah Manley (to be published by Longman
   Resources Unit).
'Working with Many Languages' by Paula Tansley, Hasina Nowaz and
   Maria Roussou (to be published by Longman Resources Unit).

Other publications/journal articles
The Mother Tongue Project – papers presented to the EC Colloquium,
   March 1984.
'Mother Tongue Teaching in Britain: a Schools Council Enquiry' by Paula
   Tansley and Alma Craft in *Journal of Multilingual and Multicultural
   Development*, **5**, 5, 1984.
'Supporting Community Languages in the Primary School – the work of
   the SCMTP' in NUT *Primary Education Review*, 18, Autumn 1983.
'Schools Council Mother Tongue Project' in *Multicultural Teaching*, **1**, 3,
   Summer 1983.
'Lessons from the Mother Tongue Project' in *Greater Manchester Primary
   Education*, **2**, 3.
'Mother Tongue Teaching in Britain and the United States; some current
   developments' by David Houlton and Edith W. King in *Journal of
   Multilingual and Multicultural Development*, **16**, 1, 1985.
Greek outside Greece (1984) edited by M. Roussou. York University
   Printing Room: NCMTT.
'Working with many languages' by Paula Tansley in *Multicultural
   Teaching*, **13**, 3, 1985.

Appendix D
Testing materials developed and used by the Project

As part of the evaluation strategy which appears in the original Project brief, it was envisaged that the 'effect of mother tongue teaching' would be monitored in two ways:

(a) to ascertain whether the use of Greek and Bengali materials in mainstream and supplementary classrooms improves the oracy and literacy of pupils in their mother tongue.

(b) to ascertain whether mother tongue teaching has any effect on competence in other subjects (especially the basic skills).

It was envisaged that (a) would be carried out using non-standard tests in Greek and Bengali and (b) would be carried out using standardized tests in English and arithmetic. If possible pre- and post-testing with comparative controls was to be used.

In the event, for a range of practical and theoretical reasons, a more restricted programme was actually implemented. A sample of children in the mainstream Bengali and Greek trial classes was tested in their mother tongue and English, but it was not possible to arrange for comparative control groups. The children's oracy, reading and writing skills in both their mother tongue and English were assessed on two occasions, at the start of the trial year and at the end. Information and discussion of the findings is presented in Chapter 5.

The testing materials[1] used to assess the children were as follows:

---

[1] A small working party composed of some members of the Project's Advisory Group was set up to give advice on the development of the testing materials. Special thanks are due to: Silvaine Wiles, Hilary Hester, Alma Craft, Elizabeth Hunter Grundin. Main responsibility for the tests lies, however, with the evaluator, Paula Tansley.

1.   *Oracy tests*

A specially designed test was developed as no suitable tests were available. It was based on an everyday classroom activity for young children – storytelling – and aimed to give maximum support to the child in the test situation so as to encourage spontaneous language.

All the children were tested in their mother tongue by their mother tongue teacher and in English by their mainstream teacher both at the beginning and end of the trial year.

Altogether four stories were used: two for assessing spoken competence in English (one for 5 – 8 year-olds, one for 9 – 11 year-olds); and two for assessing competence in the child's mother tongue (one for 5 – 8 year-olds, one for 9 – 11 year-olds).

For 5 – 8 year-olds a backdrop plus figurines were provided with the story to stimulate response and for 9 – 11 year-olds a backdrop and sequence cards were also provided.

The stories were:

1.   *The Tiger at the Market*[2], for assessing 5 – 8 year-olds in English.
2.   *The Treasure Hunt,* for assessing 9 – 11 year-olds in English.
3.   *The Escaped Parrot,* for assessing 5 – 8 year-olds in their mother tongue (Bengali or Greek).
4.   *Sparkie the Robot,* for assessing 9 – 11 year-olds in their mother tongue (Bengali or Greek).

Each child was retested at the end of the trial year using the same stories.

Briefly, the tester (either the child's mother tongue teacher or mainstream teacher) tells the child the appropriate story using the 'props' supplied. The child is then required to retell the story using the 'props' if preferred. The child is then asked four simple questions to provide an opportunity for those children who do not respond to the story to show their oral competence in another situation, and for those who can to demonstrate extended oral competence. The child is then assessed using a simple assessment schedule.

2.   *Reading tests*

Initially it was intended that cloze procedure tests in both English and

---

[2] Adapted from a story devised by the Bilingual Under Fives Project which was based at CUES.

[3] Part of the Hunter-Grundin Literacy Profiles, obtainable from: The Test Agency, Cournswood House, North Dean, High Wycombe, Bucks HP14 4NW.

Further information about these tests can be obtained from the Information Section, SCDC, Newcombe House, 45 Notting Hill Gate, London W11 3JB.

Bengali/Greek would be used to test reading. However, many of the children were not able to tackle the tests and so, in addition, reading checklists were drawn up.

The cloze procedure reading tests used by the project consisted of:

– *Reading for Meaning* Tests[3] (levels 1–4) for testing proficiency in English.

– 4 specially written close procedure tests (2 in Greek and 2 in Bengali) for testing reading proficiency in the mother tongue.

3. *Writing tests*

A writing checklist was derived to assess children's written competence. The same checklist was used to assess children's competence in English and in their mother tongue.

Glossary

bilingual	used in this book to describe all children whose first language is not English and who are at some stage along the English language learning continuum.
ceiling effects	applies to tests which are too easy for the target pupils. Consequently most scores bunch at the top end and there is little opportunity for (*a*) distinctions to be made between individual pupils (*b*)progress from one testing time to another to be shown.
community language	the language spoken by or associated with a particular ethnic minority community. It includes 'mother tongue' but in addition provides access to speech communities and cultures across the world.
community mother tongue schools	schools organized and run by members or organizations from the ethnic minority communities for various purposes including language maintenance, cultural support, religious teaching, etc., sometimes called 'community schools' or 'voluntary schools'.
dialect	natural variation in grammar and vocabulary that exists between local forms of the same language in different regions or spoken by different groups.
immersion programmes	in immersion programmes children from the linguistic majority of a country (with a high

status mother-tongue) choose to be educated through the medium of a foreign language.

integrated model where the mother tongue teacher works alongside the mainstream teacher in the same teaching area, often following similar work from their mainstream classroom for mother tongue teaching.

language awareness the recognition that pupils' language needs extend beyond the traditional emphasis on teaching English, and furthermore that their language experiences should be acknowledged and capitalized upon as part of an overall strategy for language development in a multicultural context.

mother tongue a loose term generally applied to the language spoken by a child whose first language is not English. Used 'because it remains most widely used and understood' [Swann Report] but inaccurate in several respects – many children of immigrant origin have actually been born here and speak English as their first and dominant language; for some language groups, e.g. the Italians, the 'mother tongue' may be a dialect but the preferred language of literacy will be the standard language; other groups such as Moslem Panjabi speakers may opt to learn another language (Urdu) as the traditional language of literacy; or parents may prefer children to learn a language which has religious significance for them rather than, or in addition to, the language spoken at home.

mother tongue teaching/teachers usually refers to the teachers/teaching of the 'mother tongue' (see above) either as a support while the child is learning English, or as a subject on the curriculum.

submersion programmes in submersion programmes, children from a linguistic minority of a country with a low status mother tongue are educated through the language of the linguistic majority. There is no element of choice and the teachers are normally unilingual.

transitional model   mother tongue teaching and/or support is provided with the aim of stimulating children's transition from their mother tongue to English.

withdrawal model   where the mother tongue teacher withdraws children from their mainstream classroom for mother tongue teaching.

References

ACKLAND, R. (1985). *Investigating Talk in Cumbrian Classrooms.* York: Longman.

BAKER, C. (1984). 'Two Models for Curriculum Development in Minority Languages'. In: WILLIAMS, P. (Ed) *Special Education in Minority Communities.* Oxford: OUP.

BIRMINGHAM MULTICULTURAL RESOURCE UNIT (1983). *Approaches to Education for a Multicultural Society.* Birmingham: Multicultural Resource Unit.

BROADBENT, J. *et al.* (1983). *Community Languages at 16+.* Harlow: Longman for Schools Council.

ᵡ BROOK, M.R.M. (1980). 'The "Mother Tongue" Issue in Britain: cultural diversity or control?', *British Journal of Sociology of Education,* **1,** 3.

BULLOCK REPORT. GREAT BRITAIN., DEPARTMENT OF EDUCATION AND SCIENCE (1975). *A Language for Life.* London: HMSO.

CAMPBELL PLATT, K. (1976). 'Distribution of Linguistic Minorities in Britain'. In: *Bilingualism and British Education: the dimensions of diversity.* CILT Reports and Papers 14. London: CILT.

COLLINS, R. (1984). 'Commercial Publishing and Community Languages', **III,** 1.

COMMISSION FOR RACIAL EQUALITY (1979). *Ethnic Minorities in Britain: statistical background.* London: CRE.

COMMISSION FOR RACIAL EQUALITY (1981). *Summary of the Main Issues of the Regional Consultations with Mother Tongue Classes.* London: CRE.

COMMISSION FOR RACIAL EQUALITY (1982). *Ethnic Minority Community Languages: A Statement.* London: CRE.

COMMISSION OF THE EUROPEAN COMMUNITIES (1984). *On the implementation of Directive 77/486/EEC on the Education of the*

Children of Migrant Workers. Report from the Commission to the Council. Brussels: EC (Com (84) 54 final).

COUNCIL OF THE EUROPEAN ECONOMIC COMMUNITY (1977). *On the Education of the Children of Migrant Workers:* Council Directive of 25th July 1977. Brussels: EEC (77/486/EEC).

CRAFT, M. and ATKINS, M. (1983). *Training Teachers of Ethnic Minority Community Languages.* A report for the Swann Committee. University of Nottingham School of Education.

CRAFT, M. and CRAFT, A. (1982). 'Multicultural Education'. In: COHEN, L., THOMAS, J. and MANION, L. (Eds) *Educational Research and Development in Britain 1970–1980.* Windsor: NFER-NELSON.

CRAIG and COX (1983). *The Transition Project. An Approach to Language Development in the Middle Years.* Nottingham: The Language Centre.

CUMMINS. J. (1979–80). 'The Language and Cultural Issue in the Education of Minority Language Children', *Interchange 10.*

DAVIS, F.B. (1967). *Philippine language-teaching Experiments.* Quezon City, Philippines: Alemar Phoenix.

DIXON, B. (1977). *Catching Them Young. Sex, Race and Class in Children's Books.* London: Pluto Press.

EVANS, E. (1976). 'Bilingual Education in Wales'. In: *Bilingualism and British Education: the dimensions of diversity.* CILT Reports and Papers 14. London: CILT.

FITZPATRICK, B. (1984). 'Educational justification for the inclusion of minority group language provision in state schools'. In: REID, E. (Ed) *Minority Community Languages in School.* NCLE Papers and Reports 4. London: CILT.

GHUMAN, P.A. (1980). 'Punjabi Parents and English Education', *Educational Studies,* **22,** 2.

GHUMAN, P.A. and GALLOP, R. (1981). 'Educational Attitudes of Bengali Families in Cardiff', *J. Multicult. & Multiling. Devel.* **2,** 2.

GOLDMAN, R.J. (1967). *Research and the Teaching of Immigrant Children.* London: National Committee for Commonwealth Immigrants.

GORMAN, T.P. (Ed) (1977). *Language and Literacy: Current Issues and Research.* Tehran: International Institute for Adult Literacy Methods.

GREAT BRITAIN. DEPARTMENT OF EDUCATION AND SCIENCE (1977). *Education in Schools. A Consultative Document.* CMND 6769. London: HMSO.

GREAT BRITAIN. DEPARTMENT OF EDUCATION AND SCIENCE/WELSH OFFICE (1981a). *The School Curriculum.* London: HMSO.

GREAT BRITAIN. DEPARTMENT OF EDUCATION AND

SCIENCE/WELSH OFFICE JOINT CIRCULAR NO. 5/81 (DES) /NO.36/81 (Welsh Office) (1981b). *Directive of the Council of the European Community on the education of the children of migrant workers.* London/Cardiff.

GREAT BRITAIN. DEPARTMENT OF EDUCATION AND SCIENCE (1982). *Memorandum on Compliance with Directive 77/486/EC on the education of the children of migrant workers.* DES, Elizabeth House, York Road, London.

GREAT BRITAIN. DEPARTMENT OF EDUCATION AND SCIENCE/WELSH OFFICE (1983). *Foreign Languages in the School Curriculum.* A Consultative Paper. DES, Elizabeth House, York Road, London.

GREAT BRITAIN. DEPARTMENT OF EDUCATION AND SCIENCE (1984). *Mother Tongue Teaching in School and Community.* London: HMSO.

GREAT BRITAIN. HOUSE OF COMMONS HOME AFFAIRS COMMITTEE (1985). A Second Report. *The Chinese Community in Britain, Home Affairs Committee Vol. 1.* London: HMSO.

HOULTON, D. and WILLEY, R. (1983). *Supporting Children's Bilingualism.* Harlow: Longman for Schools Council.

HOULTON, D. (1985). *All Our Languages. A Handbook for the Multilingual Classroom.* London: Edward Arnold.

ILEA CENTRE FOR URBAN EDUCATIONAL STUDIES (1975–80). *Language for Learning.* London: ILEA Learning Materials Service or Heinemann Educational Books.

INGHAM, J. (1984). 'The Tiger and the Woodpecker', *English in Education,* **18**, 1, 14–19.

INNER LONDON EDUCATION AUTHORITY (ILEA) (1983a). *1983 Language Census.* Available from County Hall, London.

INNER LONDON EDUCATION AUTHORITY (ILEA). (1983b). *Race, Sex and Class 2. Multiethnic Education in Schools.* London: ILEA.

Issues in Race and Education (1982) No.35. 11 Carleton Gardens, Brecknock Road, London N19 5AQ.

JEFFCOATE, R. (1981). 'Evaluating the Multicultural Curriculum: students' perspectives', *Journal of Curriculum Studies,* **13**, 1.

JOSEPH, SIR KEITH (1984). Speech to EC Mother Tongue Colloquium. March 1984 London. Unpublished.

KERR. A.N. (1978). *Mother Tongue Teaching in Nottingham and Stockholm.* University of Nottingham.

KLEIN, G. (1984). *Resources for multicultural education.* Second edition. York: Longman for Schools Council.

KOCHMAN, T. (1981). 'Classroom modalities; black and white communicative styles in the classroom'. In: MERCER, N. (Ed)

Language in the School and Community. London: Edward Arnold.
LAMBERT, W.E. (1977). 'The effects of bilingualism on the individual: cognitive and sociocultural consequences.' In: HORNBY, P.A. (Ed) *Bilingualism: Psychological, social and educational implications.* New York: Academic Press.
LEWIS, E. GLYN. (1981). *Bilingualism and Bilingual Education.* Oxford: Pergamon Press.
LINGUISTIC MINORITIES PROJECT (1983). *Linguistic Minorities in England.* A Report for the Department of Education and Science. London: ULIE and Heinemann Educational Books.
LINGUISTIC MINORITIES PROJECT (1984a) The Mother Tongue Teaching Directory Survey of the Linguistic Minorities Project. Working Paper No.6. Available from Information Officer, London University Institute of Education.
LINGUISTIC MINORITIES PROJECT (1984b). 'Bilingualism and Mother Tongue Teaching in England'. In: CRAFT, M. (Ed) *Education and Cultural Pluralism.* Lewes: Falmer Press.
LINGUISTIC MINORITIES PROJECT (1985). *The Other Languages of England.* London: Routledge and Kegan Paul.
LITTLE, A. and WILLEY, R. (1981). *Multi-Ethnic Education: The Way Forward.* Schools Council Pamphlet 18. London: Schools Council.
LITTLE, A. and WILLEY, R. (1983). *Studies in the Multi-ethnic Curriculum.* London: Schools Council.
MACDONALD, B. and WALKER, R. (1976). *Changing the Curriculum.* Shepton Mallet: Open Books.
MACKAY, D. and THOMPSON, B. (1971). *Breakthrough to Literacy.* Harlow: Longman for Schools Council.
MACNAMARA, J. (1966). *Bilingualism and primary education: a study of Irish experience.* Edinburgh: University Press.
MERCER, N. and MERCER, L. (1979). 'Variation in Attitudes to Mother Tongue and Culture', *Educational Studies,* **5,** 2.
MITCHELL, R. (1978). *Bilingual Education of Minority Language Groups in the English-speaking World: social research evidence.* Department of Education, University of Stirling (Seminar Papers 4).
MOTHER TONGUE AND ENGLISH TEACHING PROJECT (M.O.T.E.T.) (1981). *Summary of the Report; Vols. I and II.* University of Bradford.
NATIONAL COUNCIL FOR MOTHER TONGUE TEACHING (NCMTT) (1983). *Community Languages: The Supply and Training of Teachers.* York University Printing Room: NCMTT.
NATIONAL COUNCIL FOR MOTHER TONGUE TEACHING (NCMTT) (1985). Spring Newsletter/NCMTT.
NATIONAL UNION OF TEACHERS (1982). *Linguistic Diversity and Mother Tongue Teaching.* Policy Statement. London: NUT.

PEAL, E. and LAMBERT, W.E. (1962). 'The relation of bilingualism to intelligence', *Psychological monographs*, **76**, 1–23.

PERREN, G.E. (1976). 'Bilingualism and British Education'. In: CILT Reports and Papers 14 *Bilingualism and British Education: the dimensions of diversity*. London: CILT.

PERREN, G.E. (1979). 'Languages and minority groups'. In: NATIONAL CONGRESS ON LANGUAGES IN EDUCATION (1979) *The Mother Tongue and Other Languages in Education*. NCLE Papers and Reports 2. London: CILT.

PLOWDEN REPORT. GREAT BRITAIN. DEPARTMENT OF EDUCATION AND SCIENCE. CENTRAL ADVISORY COUNCIL FOR EDUCATION (ENGLAND) (1967). *Children and their Primary Schools*. London: HMSO.

POLLING, O. (1984). 'Towards a rationale'. In: REID, E. (Ed) NCLE Papers and Reports *Minority Community Languages in School*. London: CILT.

PRICE, E. (1984). *Bilingual Education in Wales 5–11*. London: Evans/Methuen Educational.

PRICE, G. (1984). *The Languages of Britain*. London: Edward Arnold.

RADO, M. (1977). 'The Multilingual Project: A Model of Bilingual Education', *R.E.L.C. Journal*, **8**, 1.

RAMPTON COMMITTEE. GREAT BRITAIN. DEPARTMENT OF EDUCATION AND SCIENCE (1979). *Education of Children from Ethnic Minority Groups*. Later became the SWANN COMMITTEE which produced the report (1985) *Education for All*. London: HMSO.

RATHBONE, M. and GRAHAM, N. (1983). *Bilingual Nursery Assistants: their use and training*. London: Schools Council.

REID, E. (Ed) (1984). *Minority Community Languages in Schools*. NCLE Papers and Reports 4. London: CILT.

ROSE, E.J.B. *et al.* (1969). *Colour and Citizenship*. Oxford: OUP.

ROSEN, H. and BURGESS, T. (1980). *Languages and Dialects of London School Children: an investigation*. London: Ward Lock Educational.

ROUSSOU, M. (Ed) (1984). *Greek Outside Greece*. York University Printing Room: NCMTT.

RUNNYMEDE TRUST (1980). *Britain's Black Population*. London: Heinemann.

SAIFULLAH KHAN, V. (1976). 'Provision by minorities for language maintenance'. In: CILT Reports and Papers 14: *Bilingualism and British Education: the dimensions of diversity*. London: CILT.

SAIFULLAH KHAN, V. (1980). 'The mother tongue of linguistic minorities in multicultural England', *J. Multiling. & Multicult. Devel.*, **1**, 1, 71–88.

SCHOOLS COUNCIL (1967). *English for the Children of Immigrants*.

Working Paper 13. London: Schools Council.
SCHOOLS COUNCIL (1973). *Multiracial Education: need and innovation.* Working Paper 50. London: Evans Methuen Educational.
SCHOOLS COUNCIL (1981). Multiethnic Education: the way forward. London: Schools Council.
SCHOOLS COUNCIL (1983–84). Examinations from a Multicultural Perspective: FALLOWS, L. (1983) *English at 16+;* FILE, N. (1983) *History at 16+;* WOOD, A. (1984) *Religious Studies at 16+;* LEAVY, A. (1984) *Art and Design at 16+;* BROADBENT, J. *et al.* (1983) *Community Languages at 16+;* MUKHAPADHYAY, A. (1984). *Social Sciences at 16+;* OLIVER, S. (1984) *Home Economics at 16+;* VANCE, M. (in press) *Biology at 16+.*
SHARP, D. (1976). 'Bilingualism in the Schools of Wales'. In: CILT Reports and Papers 14 *Bilingualism and British Education: the dimensions of diversity.* London: CILT.
SIMONS, H. (1980). EEC Sponsored Pilot Project 'Mother Tongue and Culture' in Bedfordshire, Second External Evaluation Report. September 1978–September 1979. Cambridge Institute of Education.
SKUTNABB-KANGAS, T. and TOUKOMAA, P. (1976). *Teaching migrant children mother tongue and learning the language of the host country in the context of the socio-cultural situation of the migrant family.* Research Report 15 prepared for UNESCO, Department of Sociology and Social Psychology, University of Tampere, Finland.
SKUTNABB-KANGAS, T. (1981). 'Guest Worker or Immigrant – Different ways of reproducing an underclass', *J. Multiling. & Multicult. Devel.,* **2,** 2.
SMITH, G. (1985). *Language, Ethnicity, Employment, Education and Research: The Struggle of Sylheti-speaking People in London.* CLE/LMP Working Paper 13. University of London Institute of Education.
SMYTHE, P. (1985). *Talking and Learning in Small Groups.* York: Longman.
SWAIN, M. and CUMMINS, J. (1979). 'Bilingualism, Cognitive functioning and education', survey article in *Language Teaching and Linguistics:* Abstracts, **12,** 1.
SWANN COMMITTEE. GREAT BRITAIN. DEPARTMENT OF EDUCATION AND SCIENCE. (1985). *Education for All.* London: HMSO.
TANSLEY, P. and CRAFT, A. (1984). 'Mother Tongue Teaching and Support: A Schools Council Enquiry', *J. Multiling. & Multicult. Devel.,* **5,** 5, 366–84.
TAYLOR, M.J. with HEGARTY, S. (1985). *The Best of Both Worlds . . .?* Windsor: NFER-NELSON.
THE CHILDREN'S LANGUAGE PROJECT (1984). (By J. Bingham,

X. Couillaud, D. Houlton and R. Thomson.) Andover: Philip and Tacey Ltd.

THE WORLD IN A CITY (1982) (Materials in 8 languages: Bengali, Chinese, Greek, Gujarati, Panjabi, Spanish, Turkish, Urdu). London: ILEA Learning Materials Service. Distributed by the Commission for Racial Equality, London.

TOMLINSON, S. (1984). 'Home, School and Community'. In: CRAFT, M. (Ed) *Education and Cultural Pluralism*. Lewes: Falmer Press.

TOSI, A. (1979). 'Mother-tongue teaching for the children of migrants', *Language Teaching and Linguistic Abstracts,* **16,** 2, 3–31.

TOSI, A. (1984). 'Mother Tongue Development in the context of second language learning: a model of different teaching approaches'. In: VERMA, G.K. (Ed) *Papers on Biliteracy and Bilingualism.* NCMTT.

TITONE, R. (1978). 'Psychological Aspects of Multilingual Education', *International Review of Education,* **24,** 3.

TOWNSEND, H.E.R. (1971). *Immigrant Pupils in England: the LEA response.* Windsor: NFER.

TOWNSEND, H.E.R. and BRITTAN, E. (1972). *Organization in Multiracial Schools.* Windsor: NFER.

TRUDGILL, P. (1975). *Accent, Dialect and the School.* London: Edward Arnold.

TSOW, M. (1983). 'Analysis of responses to a national survey on mother tongue teaching in local education authorities 1980–82', *Educational Research,* **25,** 3.

URE, J.C. (1981). 'Mother-tongue education and minority languages: a question of values and costs. *J. Multiling. & Multicult. Devel.,* **2,** 4, 303–8.

VERMA, G.K. (1981). A Feasibility Study of 'Books and Minorities'. Mimeograph. School of Research in Education, Bradford University.

WILDING, J. (1981). *Ethnic Minority Languages in the Classroom?* Leicester Council for Community Relations.

WRIGHT, J. (1982). 'Bilingualism in Education', *Issues in Race and Education,* 11 Carleton Gardens, Brecknock Road, London N19 5AQ.

Index